Water Resources: Process and Management

Second Edition

Victoria Bishop

Lutterworth Upper School and Community College

Robert Prosser

Centre for Urban and Regional Studies, University of Birmingham

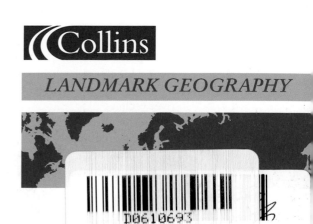

Collins

LANDMARK GEOGRAPHY

Contents

8 Seeking sustainability for UK water resources

9 Water quality and pollution

Appendices

References

Glossary

Index

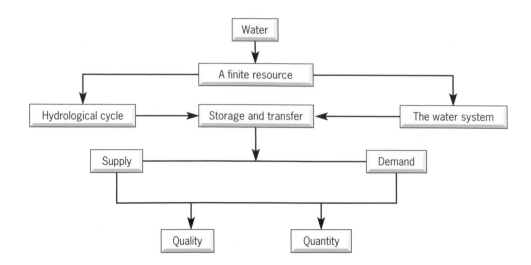

1 Water: a global resource

1.1 A resource for life

'Water is the foundation of life on earth: without it there would be no plants, no animals, no living things' (Bellamy and Quayle, 1986). This opening statement sums up the importance of the central theme of this book: water is a fundamental resource for all life. Without adequate water supplies, human societies and economies are threatened; ecosystems become stressed (Fig. 1.2). Water is also a *finite resource*, and of the huge global volume, less than 8 per cent is readily accessible (Fig 1.1) The rest is stored in saline oceans, or deep below the land surface, or in the polar ice caps. Thus, organisms other than oceanic species compete for the little that is accessible.

As human populations and expectations grow, water is becoming an increasingly *scarce resource*: in many regions of the world, demand continues to increase more rapidly than supply (Fig. 1.4). This reality has led Kofi Annan, Secretary-General of the United Nations, to suggest: 'In the twentieth century, wars were about land; in the twenty-first century, many wars will be about water' (Fig. 1.3). Yet conflict can occur at all scales from international disputes to local tensions, as this example from India illustrates.

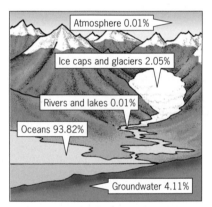

Figure 1.1 Distribution of the world's water

'Just a two-hour drive from Delhi, in Sadiqnagar village, Rehmani, a 60 year old woman, speaks of the daily fights over water. The village in Haryana state in northern India is among the thousands classified as 'problem' villages with inadequate access to clean drinking water. Rehmani, like other women in Sadiqnagar, gets up at the crack of dawn and walks for over an hour to the nearest village with a well. But often there is a huge crowd already, and fights break out many a time, she says. Her pitchers get broken in the clashes and she comes home empty handed.' (from *Water in India*, Chattergee, P).

Yet countries vary enormously in their water availability (Table 1.1). For instance, Canada, a huge, sparsely populated country with significant precipitation over much of its surface, has almost 110 000 m^3 (cubic metres) per person per year. At the other extreme, Egypt has 40 m^3 per person per year. Some countries have water supplies that permanently exceed demand; some have permanent deficits. Others, including the UK (see Chapter 8), shift between surplus and deficit water balances. Water demand and usage vary too with level of economic development. Thus, MEDCs consume more water per capita than LEDCs, especially for non-agricultural uses (Table 1.2).

Table 1.1 Regional variations in water usage, 1997 (*Source*: Development and Cooperation, April 1997)

	Water used per person m^3/y		
	Total	Agricultural	Non-agric.
High-income countries	1167	455	712
Middle-income countries	453	313	140
Low-income countries	386	351	35

Time and water run out for China

CHINA IS STRUGGLING to cope with a catastrophic drought that has turned the Yellow River into a trickle, dried up deep wells and turned vast areas of farmland into arid waste.

Much of the urban drought is caused by reckless overuse as China's new consumer society demands more water. Two-thirds of China's cities, including Beijing, face severe water shortages.

'Beijingers do not appreciate their precious resource,' said the Beijing Youth Daily in a survey of the city's water crisis. The three most wasteful outlets, it concluded, are the 'bottled water industry, on-street car-washes and luxury bathing and beauty salons'.

The northern province of Hebei, which surrounds Beijing, has been worst hit. About 12 000 square miles of farmland will bear no summer crops and planting has been delayed on

another 2000 square miles.

China is finally having to reckon with the hidden cost of massive HEP schemes which have interfered with the natural flow of its great rivers, allowing more water to be diverted and lost by evaporation.

The Yellow River has been worst hit, with no more than a trickle of water flowing in its bed from Henan to Shangdong province on the coast. Authorities at the Xiaolangdi HEP plant are now opening their sluices to let the water run freely and save the farmers' fields downstream.

No solution has yet been found to the well-known paradox that southern China has a surplus of water and has been hit by increasingly severe floods. But long-discussed plans for a south–north water transfer are being revived.

'By the year 2010,' said Wang Xucheng, the water

conservancy minister, 'city-dwellers in Beijing are likely to be drinking Yangtze river water.'

The new economic reforms of the 1980s, which allowed peasants to shift to profitable cash crops, have also led to

overuse as boreholes are drilled ever deeper.

Only about 40% is used effectively in dry areas. Some farmers continued to irrigate crops which had no chance of ripening before the water ran dry.

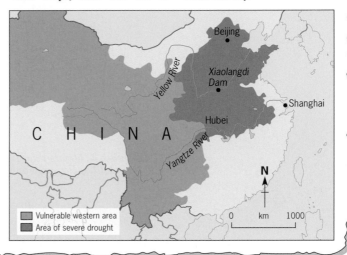

Figure 1.2 Water resource pressures in China
(**Source**: *The Guardian*, 8 June 2000)

Table 1.2 Internal renewable freshwater resources of selected countries

Country	Total (km^3/y)	Per person (000 m^3/y)
United Kingdom	120	2.14
Norway	405	97.10
Cameroon	208	18.84
Egypt	2	0.04
Canada	2901	109.51
Mexico	357	4.11
Brazil	5190	35.21
Peru	40	1.84
Laos	270	59.51
Pakistan	298	2.72
Australia	343	20.78
New Zealand	397	115.57

Note: These figures are for internal resources which are renewable. Many countries rely on sources outside their boundaries, e.g. Egypt.

Figure 1.3 Examples of international tensions and conflicts over water resources (**Source**: *Accountancy*, December 1995)

THE WORLD'S HOT RIVERS – FROM ASIA TO CENTRAL AMERICA

Mekong: Increasing industrialisation means potential rows are brewing between Laos, Vietnam and Thailand.

Ganges: Some 300 million Indian farmers depend on the river, but felling in the Himalayan foothills is disrupting the flow and Bangladesh suffers every year from increasingly disastrous floods caused by the deforestation.

Indus: Pakistan is dependent on the river, two of whose main tributaries are used by India to water the Punjab grain basket.

Jordan: Arguably the world's most valued and disputed river, its source is in Israeli-occupied southern Lebanon and the (nominally) Syrian Golan Heights. From here it flows south to the Dead Sea, via Jordan. On its way, Israel taps 83% of the available water, via the occupied West Bank. Its use is strongly disputed by Jordanians, Palestinians and Israelis. Although the Palestinian–Israeli peace negotiators have announced that a deal on eventual ownership has been postponed until 1997, this is likely to be an almost intractable problem.

Tigris-Euphrates: Rising in Turkey, these two rivers flow south-east through Syria and Iraq to form the 'cradle of civilisation' – the fertile crescent where pre-historic man is believed to have first turned to agriculture. Turkey's recent grandiose GAP irrigation and hydro-electric schemes, have diverted much of the river's volume. Syria and Iraq are deeply concerned by this, although the comparatively water-rich Turkey appears prepared to give way in return for help with Kurdish rebels.

Nile: The Nile flows through ten countries. It provides 97% of Egypt's water. Only Egypt and Sudan have an agreement over use of the river, but water projects upstream in Sudan, Kenya, Rwanda, Burundi, Uganda, Tanzania and Zaire could all threaten Egypt's survival.

Kufrah aquifer: Libya's 'Great Man-Made River' which exploits the southern Kufrah aquifer for use in the arid north, is causing alarm in Cairo. The Egyptians fear that as the water table drops, the Nile could leak westwards, probably through subterranean aquifers, but possibly overland. In this case Egypt has contingency plans to seize a portion of southern Libya until an earth-moving project can be completed to stop further leaks.

Danube: Slovakia's combined irrigation and hydro-electric scheme at Gabcikovo-Nagymaros on the Danube has incensed Hungary and caused concern elsewhere downstream along one of Europe's great rivers. Hungary has appealed to the International Court of Justice.

Rio Grande: The slightest hint of a dry spell provokes tension between US and Mexican farmers over the water flow in this, the major source of water for most of the arid southern US states and for much of northern Mexico.

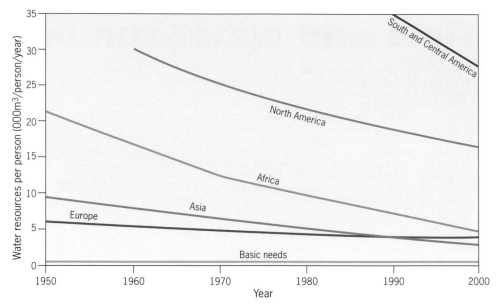

**Figure 1.4 Annual renewable water resources per person, 1950–2000
(*Source*: Development and Cooperation, April 1997)**

Globally, approximately 75 per cent of water use is for agriculture. In terms of the value of crop production, 80 per cent of Pakistan's food, 70 per cent of China's food and over 50 per cent of India's food is grown on irrigated land. Many countries, especially LEDCs, have based their development policies on increasing agricultural production. For instance, the annual renewable fresh water supply in India is 1869 km^3, approximately 4 per cent of the world supply. The per capita annual availability of water is 2200 m^3, compared with a world average of 8500 m^3. India uses 83 per cent of its available water for agricultural purposes, and since Independence in 1947, the government has concentrated on increasing irrigated land. In 1951 there were 8.6 million hectares; by 2000 the estimate was 34 million hectares. However, because of the overall growth in population and especially the urban growth, non-agricultural demand is growing so rapidly that government forecasts suggest that by the year 2020, water supplies to agriculture will have to be reduced by up to 20 per cent.

Fundamental questions arising from the issues of scarcity, competition and conflict, recur throughout the book:
• How much water is there? (Quantity)
• Where and when? (Distribution and frequency)
• How much is needed? (Demand–supply relationships)
• Whose is it? (Ownership)

1.2 Water and the global system

To ensure that humans and other species will survive and thrive in the future, we need to understand how water works in the global environment. We can develop this understanding through the framework of the **hydrological cycle** (Fig. 1.5). Water moves through this cycle in all its three forms – liquid, solid, gas. This book explores those components of the global hydrological cycle tinted pale green on Fig 1.5: the journey of fresh water from its arrival as precipitation, i.e. rain, snow, hail, until its departure back into the atmosphere or into the oceans. This journey may last a few minutes or thousands of years. This constant, variable-speed cycling means that although water is a finite resource, it is also a *renewable resource*. As examples in this book illustrate, this is a key element in *sustainable water resource management*.

1 Use the information in Figures 1.1, 1.3 and 1.4 to support the claim that human demands for water are increasing faster than the available supply.

2 On an outline map of the world, analyse the information in Figure 1.3.
a Draw and name the rivers listed.
b Locate and name the countries involved.
c Add relevant informational labels.
Ongoing project: You may find it useful to update your map from events and issues reported in the media and from further reading.

Figure 1.5 The global hydrological system. At the global scale, the hydrological cycle is a closed system: all the water circulates through the stores; the output from one store becomes an input to the next, and so on. A drainage basin, however, functions as an open system: water enters as an input from the atmosphere, and leaves the basin as an output to the ocean, or to the atmosphere, continuing on through the hydrological cycle.

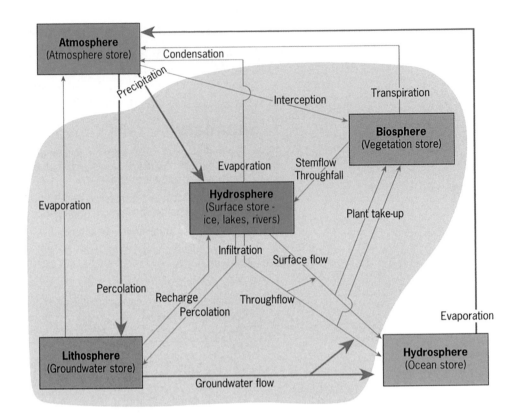

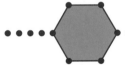

Figure 1.6 The basic system

A systems approach

As Figure 1.5 shows, the set of *pathways* and *stores* which make up the hydrological cycle behaves as a *system*. A system has a form or structure consisting of one or more interacting stores and pathways within an identifiable boundary. It also has a function, consisting of inputs, throughputs and outputs of energy and matter (Fig. 1.6). In the hydrosphere, systems and cycles occur at a wide variety of scales. At the macro-scale, the global hydrological system functions as a *closed system*. Smaller-scale systems such as drainage basins are *open systems*, that is, energy and matter move into and out of the individual systems. For instance, a drainage basin, e.g. the Severn basin, has a boundary (the watershed), and a series of stores linked by pathways along which energy, water and material move (see Chapter 2). However, there are inputs and outputs of water, sediment and energy to and from the basin system, i.e. it is 'open'.

All environmental systems, including rivers and **drainage basins**, possess the ability to adjust and change. For example, if the rainfall input increases, a river may respond by enlarging its channel to cope with the extra water. The channel as a store and a pathway increases its capacity. Processes that work to sustain or restore balance in the way a system works are known as **negative feedback**. However, if inputs of energy and/or material change too severely or too suddenly, the system may be overwhelmed. Then **positive feedback,** or the 'runaway mechanism of progressive change' takes over. When the system settles down once more, it may have a quite different form. For example, a catastrophic flood may result in a river taking a new course. Human activities can cause such fundamental change, e.g. building and operating a **dam** will permanently alter a river's flow **regime** downstream (see the cover photograph).

1.3 Water as a transfer system

Water and sediment in motion signal the presence of energy, i.e. the ability to do work. Moving water plays an important role as the agent of erosion, transportation and deposition of **sediment**. We are constantly reminded of the awesome power, i.e. available energy, of rivers to create and destroy (Fig. 1.7). River channels are the main transfer pathways for water and sediment. It is vital therefore, that we understand how channels work and what their capabilities are: how much water they can hold and transfer; how much energy is available; how much sediment can be moved (see Chapters 3 and 4). These understandings are becoming ever more important as human activities and settlements expand across river basins, especially floodplains (Fig 1.7). Thus, a fundamental goal of water resource management techniques is to control the movement and storage of water and sediment (see Chapters 5 and 6). This is achieved by modifying the stores and pathways of the drainage basin, e.g. building a dam to create a reservoir store; channelising a river to improve flow efficiency, and so on. For such management techniques to be effective, we need reliable data on river and energy regimes, and sediment supply (see Chapter 4).

Floods bring death and destruction to Chinese villages

ENTIRE VILLAGES are being swept away by floods in China as the situation along the swollen Yangtze river reaches a critical stage, Beijing has reveled. Hundreds of thousands of peasants are huddling for safety on the top of crumbling river banks.

The disaster area is a critical choke-point in the central Yangtze valley where the river makes a huge bend through low-lying country near the town of Yueyang to turn east towards Wuhan.

Details of a disaster not far away, in Li county, a week ago are only now coming to light. More than 30 people died, 60 are missing, 46 000 houses were destroyed and 80 000 people are living in shanties on the top of dikes.

Latest figures show a total of 1.9 million civilians struggling to contain the floods in five Chinese provinces along the middle and lower reaches of the Yangtze.

Three flood peaks have swept down the Yangtze in the past month, reaching heights only just below the disaster year of 1954. Millions of people are manning the weakened defences as a fourth peak is reported to be forming in the river's upper reaches.

By the end of last week, the floods had killed 1145 people in six provinces of central and southern China.

Figure 1.7 Flooding in Chinese villages (*Source*: *The Guardian*, 5 August 1998)

1.4 Water quality

Water quality is becoming as important an issue as water quantity in many regions, as human activities intensify and expectations rise, e.g. the increased nitrate concentrations in rivers as a result of the intensification of agriculture to increase productivity. In LEDCs a key issue is the provision of safe drinking water; MEDCs such as the UK have universal, highly regulated, water supply systems, yet sales of bottled water are expanding rapidly as people become dissatisfied with the quality of water from their taps! Issues explored in this book focus around the causes, character, levels, locations, impacts of and remedies for water pollution (see Chapter 9).

There are two important points to remember: first, because the hydrological cycle works as a transfer and storage system, the effects of pollution may be felt at considerable distances from the source of the pollution (Fig. 1.8). Second, pollution affects not only surface waters, but also groundwater, an increasingly important source of supply for human use (Fig. 1.9 and Chapter 7).

?

3 Make a list of the main differences between MEDCs and LEDCs in terms of access to and use of water.

Cyanide from mine threatens Guyana river

Phil Davison, Latin America Correspondent

Cyanide-saturated waste from Guyana's biggest gold mine was gushing into the former British colony's major river yesterday, threatening loggers, native Indians, wildlife and fish along the way. Those who live along the jungled banks of the Essequibo river rely on it for their drinking water and it is renowned for its fishing.

The accident could also close down South America's second biggest gold mine for up to year, a potential economic disaster for a small nation which gets a quarter of its revenue from the mine.

Cyanide is used to extract gold from ore. Afterwards, the highly poisonous residue had been stored in a 'reservoir' at the Omai gold mine, 100 miles south-west of the capital, Georgetown, ever since the mine began in January 1993.

There were around three million cubic metres of cyanide-tainted waste in the reservoir when the dam separating it from the Omai river cracked early on Sunday.

The waste gushed down the river and on into the Essequibo, the country's biggest, which runs to the Atlantic.

Canadian mining engineers sent by the Quebec-based Canadian company, Cambior – which owns most of the mine in partnership with the American firm Golden Star Resources of Denver – were trying to build a new dam on the Omai river yesterday to stem the flow. By midnight on Monday, an estimated 1.25 million cubic metres of waste – almost half the total in the reservoir – had poured out.

Figure 1.8 Water can contaminate a long way from the source of the pollution. The impacts may be environmental, social and economic (*Source*: The *Independent,* 23 August 1995)

Irrigation creates world water crisis

MORE THAN A BILLION people lack access to clean water, despite years of intense efforts by aid agencies to avert droughts and pollution.

The World Health Organisation has revealed that tens of thousands of children die every day of thirst or diseases triggered by infected water. Alarmingly, the report – Water for health: taking charge – shows that attempts to improve irrigation and extraction have worsened the problems and increased suffering.

In Bangladesh, deep wells were drilled to provide alternative sources to contaminated surface waters but these supplies have been found to be poisoned with arsenic. Those who drank such water are now doomed to die, say doctors.

In Egypt and Ghana, man-made lakes have been infected with worms that spread bilharzia. The disease, also known as schistosomiasis, can cause seizures, paralysis and liver, lung and bladder damage.

In other countries, smaller dam projects have created bodies of water in which mosquitoes thrive. In Ethiopia, this has led to a seven-fold increase in malaria cases.

'There is, a mismatch between those supplying water and those trying to ensure the health of people living near such schemes,' said Dr Jamie Bartram, co-ordinator of the WHO's water, sanitation and health pro-gramme. 'Often there is an improvement in average living conditions when a new dam or irrigation scheme is opened, but that is confined to the people living downstream. Those living beside these projects often have their lives made much worse.'

The WHO report says global warming exacerbates the situation. 'The greenhouse effect is already bringing more extreme weather and that means more droughts and more outbreaks of serious flooding.'

With flooding, drinking supplies get contaminated with sewage and people can no longer consume unpolluted water. Epidemics of disease, such as cholera, break out.

Water's critical importance is spelled out in the current issue of Scientific American by Peter Gleick, a leading expert on the subject. He says Earth can now sustain its six billion inhabitants only by exploiting artificial irrigation systems, which nourish 40 per cent of agriculture, and HEP plants generating 20 per cent of its electricity. However, these projects often jeopardise the lives of those they are meant to help.

Figure 1.9 Water quality: a global issue (*Source: The Observer,* 25 February 2001)

4 Study Figure 1.5. For each of the three environmental stores, lithosphere, hydrosphere and biosphere, suggest two ways in which human activities might affect the way the store works.

5 Use examples given in this chapter to illustrate the key understandings introduced in Section 1.3.

6 From Table 1.2:
a List the characteristics of the freshwater resources shown.
b Select two countries showing different characteristics. Suggest reasons to explain their features.

Summary

- Water is a finite, renewable and increasingly scarce resource.
- There are wide variations in availability of and access to water across the world.
- The hydrological cycle is the circulation of water in any of its forms – liquid, solid, gas – through the major stores of the global system: atmosphere, lithosphere, hydrosphere and biosphere.
- A drainage basin is a transfer system with a form of stores and pathways, and a function consisting of inputs, throughputs, processes and outputs.
- A drainage basin functions as an open system.
- Water, sediment and energy move through and are stored within the drainage basin system.
- Feedback is the term used for the processes which create adjustments to a system.
- Human activities are having increasing impacts upon the form and function of hydrological systems.

2 Drainage basin processes

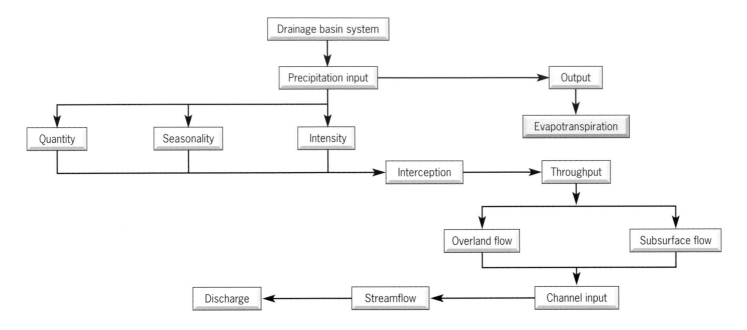

2.1 The drainage basin system

What is a drainage basin?

The **drainage basin** is the **catchment area** for water that drains into and flows down a single river channel, entering eventually into a sea or lake. It is the basic unit for studying hydrological processes. The drainage basin is a system as defined in Figure 2.1: inputs, stores and outputs, working within a definable boundary. This allows us to explore the inputs and outputs of the **hydrological cycle** in a manageable way. The water enters the system as **precipitation** and leaves as **streamflow** (measured in cubic metres per second, m^3/s, often called cumecs) or as **evaporation** or **transpiration**.

These hydrological processes do not operate in isolation. They are linked with geomorphological processes such as weathering and mass movement. Thus, the inputs, throughputs and outputs from the drainage basin system include **sediment** as well as streamflow. The whole system can be explained in terms of the relationships between water, sediment and available energy.

The system structure

Figure 2.1 shows the drainage basin system as a black box. Here, we can see the inputs and outputs are identified, but the contents of the box are not revealed. In this chapter we shall study the main processes at work within this drainage basin box.

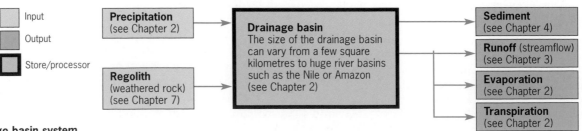

Figure 2.1 The drainage basin system

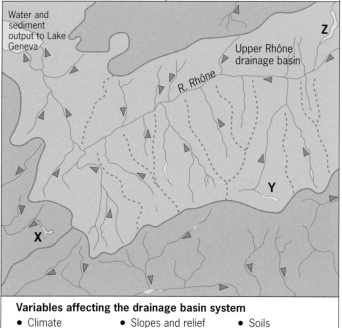

Legend:
- ——— Main basin watershed
- - - - - Minor watersheds
- ◢ Rivers showing direction of flow

1. All rivers input water and sediment to the main Rhône channel.
2. Not all tributaries or minor watersheds are shown.
3. A number of tributaries are glacier-fed. The glaciers show bluish to white in the upper catchments, e.g. X, Y and Z.

Water and sediment output to Lake Geneva

R. Rhône

Upper Rhône drainage basin

Z

Y

X

Variables affecting the drainage basin system
- Climate
- Rock type
- Geological structure
- Slopes and relief
- Mass movement processes
- Vegetation
- Soils
- Time
- Channel and valley form

Figure 2.2 The upper R. Rhône drainage basin, Valais, Switzerland, in partly completed diagrammatic form

Figure 2.3 Landsat image of the upper R. Rhône drainage basin. Notice that the coverage is not identical. Look carefully to identify the boundaries

The component parts of the drainage basin are illustrated in diagrammatic form in Figure 2.2. The boundary of a drainage basin is the **watershed.** Within this rim of high relief, water and sediment move to and through the main river channel. The watershed forms the boundary between drainage basins. For example, in the western USA, the Rocky Mountains are a major watershed between the Colorado drainage basin to the west and the Mississippi drainage basin to the east. Within each drainage basin there are minor watersheds separating the catchments of the basin's tributary streams, i.e. sub-systems.

Each drainage basin is unique, with its distinctive size, shape and internal layout. The principal variables influencing the form and functioning of a drainage basin are listed on Figure 2.2. These variables affect how the hydrological and geomorphological processes will work within the basin, e.g. how much sediment will arrive in a river, where and when.

Streamflow
The usual way we observe the result of the inputs and processes – what is going on in a drainage basin – is as streamflow or **discharge.** We might expect streamflow to be determined mainly by the size of the drainage basin: the bigger the basin, the larger the streamflow. Figure 2.4 shows that this is too simple an assumption. For the 14 major drainage basins in England and Wales (Fig. 2.5), there is only a weak correlation between basin area and mean annual discharge. This means that there must be other factors which influence the amount of streamflow leaving the system. To find out what these factors are, and so to explain how rivers behave, we need to identify these factors and understand how they work.

1 Place tracing paper over Figure 2.2.
a Draw the main Rhône basin watershed.
b Mark as many minor watersheds as you can identify.
c Use arrows to show the location and direction of tributaries flowing into the Rhône.
d Mark the glaciers.

2 Study Figure 2.4.
a Name two rivers which show a close fit to the regression line on the scattergraph.
b Name two rivers which do not show a close fit to the regression line on the scattergraph.

3 On Figure 2.5 four clusters of drainage basins have been identified. Fit the following descriptions to each of the four groups.
a A small drainage basin area and a higher than average discharge.
b Medium-sized drainage basins with a larger than average discharge.
c Small drainage basin areas with a less than average discharge.
d A large drainage basin with a below average discharge.

4 The Spearman rank coefficient of correlation (r_s) for the two sets of data has been calculated as 0.72. Use Appendix 1 to interpret the significance of the correlation.

5 Evaluate the validity of the two techniques (scattergraph and Spearman rank) as ways of showing the relationship between drainage basin area and discharge.

6 Using Figure 2.4, suggest reasons for the level of correlation between drainage basin area and discharge for the 14 drainage basins in England and Wales.

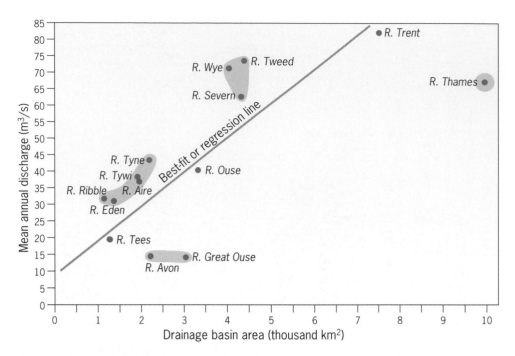

Figure 2.4 The relationship between drainage basin area and mean annual discharge for the 14 major drainage basins in England and Wales

Figure 2.5 The 14 major drainage basins in England and Wales

Hydrological processes

In Figure 2.6 we can see the processes and stores within the drainage basin black box. The drainage basin consists of a series of stores linked by flows and processes which allow water to move through the system. As we have moved down in scale, each of the stores within the drainage basin is shown as a black box. Throughout the book we will open up each of these boxes by investigating the nature of the processes operating within the drainage basin system. Figure 2.7 introduces you to the key terms you will meet in this investigation. You should refer to this diagram and Figure 2.6 throughout.

Figure 2.6 Hydrological processes and stores in the drainage basin system (*After*: Ward and Robinson, 1990)

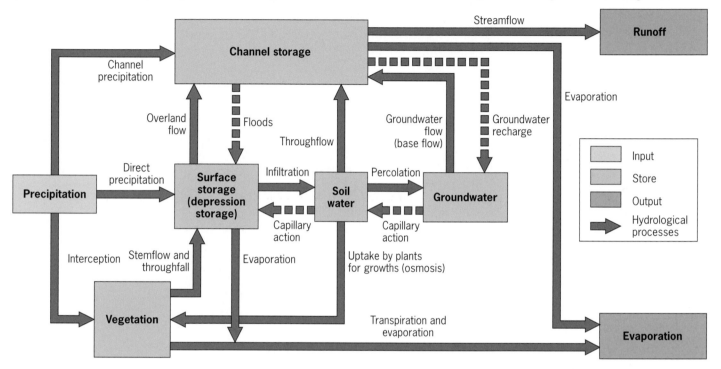

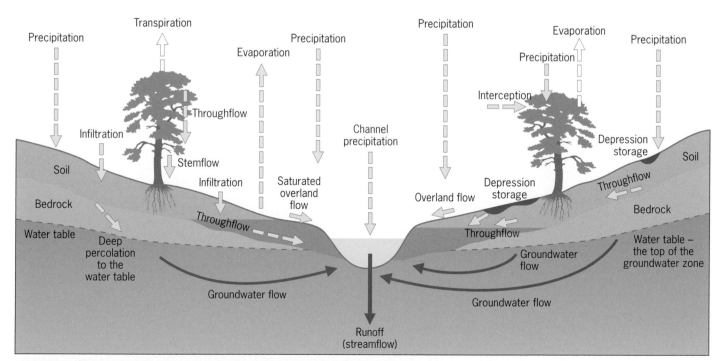

Figure 2.7 Diagrammatic representation of drainage basin hydrological processes

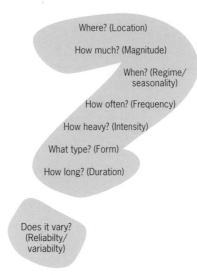

Where? (Location)

How much? (Magnitude)

When? (Regime/seasonality)

How often? (Frequency)

How heavy? (Intensity)

What type? (Form)

How long? (Duration)

Does it vary? (Reliabilty/variabilty)

Figure 2.8 The precipitation input to the drainage basin system

Figure 2.9 Average annual world precipitation (*Source: Collins-Longman World Atlas*, 1992)

2.2 Drainage basin processes: above the surface

Precipitation

The precipitation input is an important factor affecting how rivers behave. Depending upon the size of the drainage basin, precipitation totals will influence the input (the potential amount of water which can enter a system) and the output (the eventual streamflow). The basic understanding is that precipitation varies over space and time at all scales. So, in a study of any river or drainage basin, we need to ask some key questions (Fig. 2.8). It is important also that we separate water delivery to a river into two stages: first, the precipitation as it falls, and second, what happens to it when it arrives at the surface. As only around one per cent of precipitation arrives as channel precipitation, i.e. falls directly on to the river surface, the journey of this second stage is crucial.

Where and how much? (Location and magnitude)

Figure 2.9 summarises precipitation at the global scale. The highest inputs to drainage basins are recorded in equatorial regions. This is because the constantly warm atmosphere and the convergence of the Trade Winds at the Inter-Tropical Convergence Zone (ITCZ) combine to generate high-energy storms which produce heavy rains. The lowest precipitation totals are recorded in two contrasting zones: high-latitude polar regions where cold air has a limited ability to hold and, therefore, to release water, and sub-tropical regions where descending air from the sub-tropical high pressure cells creates hot deserts.

The pattern of precipitation is also influenced by the size and distribution of land masses and oceans. Continental interiors, which are far from moist air mass sources, tend to receive low precipitation totals. This phenomenon is known as continentality. Relief and prevailing winds add further complications to the patterns. For instance, along much of the west coast of North America,

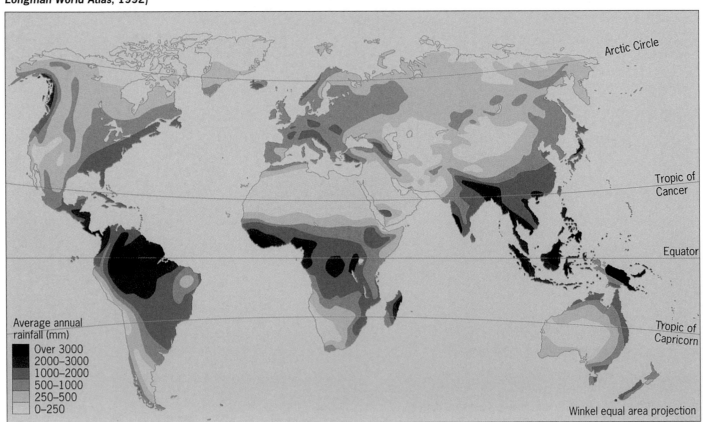

Arctic Circle

Tropic of Cancer

Equator

Tropic of Capricorn

Average annual rainfall (mm)

Over 3000
2000–3000
1000–2000
500–1000
250–500
0–250

Winkel equal area projection

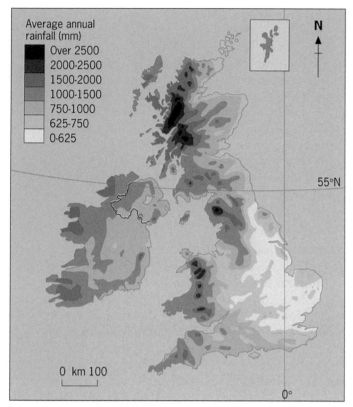

Figure 2.10 Average annual British Isles precipitation (*Source*: Collins-Longman World Atlas, 1992)

prevailing onshore winds from the Pacific Ocean bring heavy precipitation totals to the coastal mountains. In the lee of the mountains, however, there is a marked rainshadow effect and reduced precipitation totals. We can see a similar pattern at a smaller scale across the British Isles (Fig. 2.10). The effects of relief and prevailing winds are clear, with areas of high precipitation (over 2500 mm) in the north and west, and lower totals (less than 600 mm) in the east and south.

We should, however, understand that average precipitation totals, such as those shown on Figures 2.9 and 2.10, are only of limited use. For instance, the British Isles are said to have 'reliable' rainfall, yet long-term records indicate significant fluctuations (Fig. 2.11). More recently, there has been the so-called 'Great Drought' of 1988–92 (see Chapter 8). In all localities, precipitation totals vary from year to year. Hydrologists cannot predict floods nor advise people on land use, unless they have detailed data for each drainage basin showing how precipitation varies over time and space. Figures 2.12 and 2.13 illustrate these variations over a small area and in a short time. Other examples throughout this book demonstrate this essential feature of precipitation inputs.

Figure 2.11 Average annual rainfall for England and Wales, 1720–1990

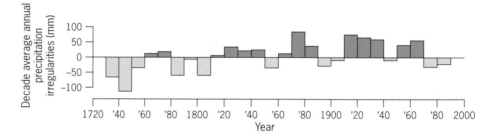

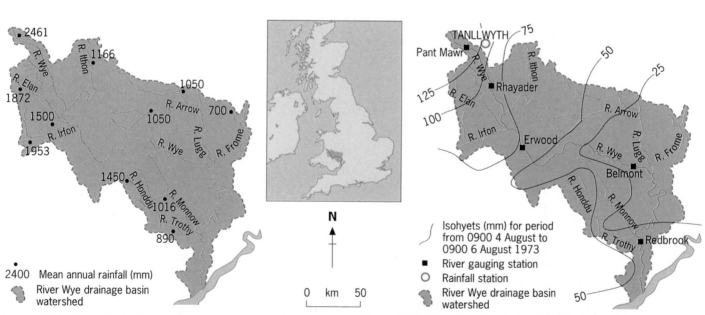

Figure 2.12 River Wye basin: mean annual precipitation (*Source*: Hilton, 1985)

Figure 2.13 River Wye basin: precipitation from one storm event, 5–6 August 1973 (*Source*: Clowes and Comfort, 1987)

Figure 2.14 **The River Amazon, near Manaus. A 'tide mark` or 'trash line' can be seen running along this tropical rainforest. The upper limit of the brownish colouring marks the high water level of July. This photograph was taken in September, when the water had fallen by 6 m. By December the water levels will have dropped a further 8 or 9 m**

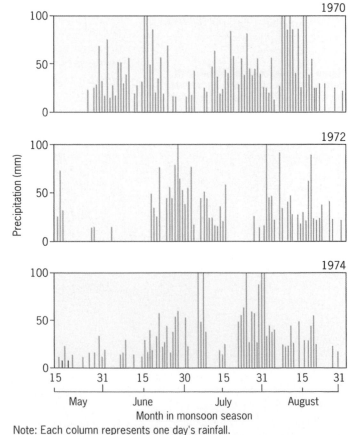

7 From Figures 2.12 and 2.13, estimate the proportion of mean annual precipitation tht fell at (a) Pant Mawr and (b) Rhayader during the storm of 5–6 August 1973.

8 In the Mangalore region most streams are dry at the beginning of May. Compare and contrast the likely flow regimes for the monsoon seasons shown on Figure 2.16.

When and how often? (Regime/seasonality and frequency)

Most regions have some seasonality in their precipitation which is reflected in their river **regimes** (Chapter 4). Even equatorial drainage basins such as the Amazon show marked seasonal discharge fluctuations (Fig. 2.14). Extreme seasonality occurs in monsoon climates, with a single wet season and a sequence of often rainless months (Fig. 2.15). Yet timing and frequency of rainfall vary considerably in such climates too, as Figure 2.16 shows.

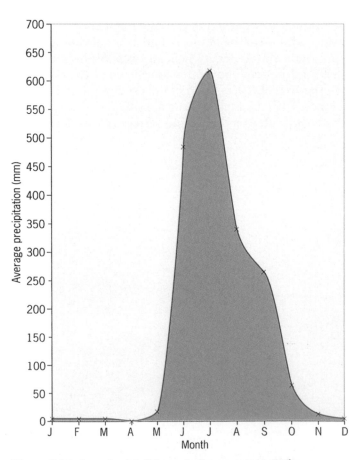

Figure 2.15 **Annual rainfall for an Indian monsoon station**

Note: Each column represents one day's rainfall.

Figure 2.16 **Mangalore, India: rainfall totals, 1970–74**

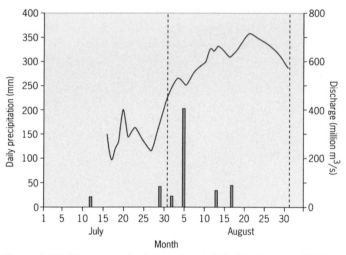

Figure 2.17 Khartoum, Sudan: daily rainfall, July–August, 1988 and discharge of the R. Nile (*Source: Weather*, Feb. 1989)

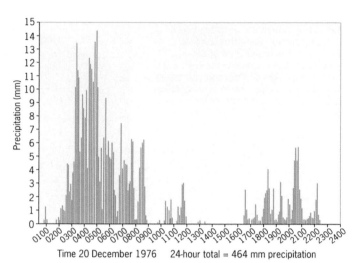

Figure 2.18 Babinda, Australia: daily rainfall, 20 December 1976. Each column represents a 6-minute period during the passage of a tropical storm.

?

9 Describe and explain how Child's Glacier in Figure 2.20 acts as a store and input source for the Copper River. Consider how this influence varies seasonally and how this affects the river regime.

10 From Fig. 2.19, name three drainage basins within these areas receiving more than 4 mm/h during the passage of the frontal system. Use an atlas to help you.

Figure 2.19 Composite rainfall map from a network of five radars, showing the distribution of rain associated with a frontal system crossing Wales and England. (*Source*: Ward and Robinson, 1990)

In arid environments there may be no seasonal regularity, but simply occasional and irregular storms, which may generate short-lived streamflows (Fig. 2.17). At the briefest time scales, rain may arrive in a series of pulses within a single storm (Fig. 2.18).

How heavy? (Intensity)

Rainfall intensity is measured in millimetres per hour (mm/h). It has a significant effect on the route water takes through the drainage basin system, and hence upon river flow. The intensity of steady drizzle is about 0.5 mm/hr, and for moderate rainfall 3 mm/h. Compare this with the intensities generated by tropical storms, which can yield more than 1 mm of rain a minute (Fig. 2.18)! Convectional rainfall occurs typically as short, intense downpours. So, regions having frequent convection storms will experience high rainfall intensities. In the British Isles much of the precipitation occurs as a result of frontal processes. Even in such large-scale weather systems, rainfall intensity can vary considerably as the frontal system moves across a region (Fig. 2.19).

Figure 2.20 The Copper River and Child's Glacier, Alaska: ice as a water store

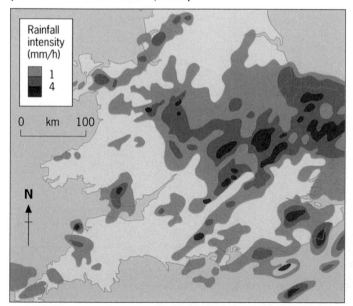

Figure 2.21 The interception capacity of tropical rainforest: even after five hours of heavy rainfall, the stream is still not in full spate. Daintree Rainforest National Park, Queensland, Australia

What type? (Form)

Water can enter the drainage basin as rain, snow, sleet or hail. If snow lies on the ground for days, weeks or months, there will be a delayed delivery of the water input to the stream system. In this way, snow acts as a temporary store of water in the drainage basin. The timing and speed of the snowmelt will determine the nature of the water input and thus affect the seasonal flood risk or the timing of water availability for irrigation. Snow and ice are important water sources (Fig. 2.20), including several of the world's major rivers, e.g. the Rhône in France (Fig. 2.3) and the Colorado in the USA. The 1983 floods along the Colorado were caused in part by a sudden late snowmelt in the mountains.

Interception

The second stage of the precipitation input to a drainage basin system begins once the water has arrived at the land surface.

The amount of incoming precipitation which reaches the ground surface directly depends not only upon its type, volume, intensity and timing, but also upon the surface cover. This may be artificial cover, such as roads and buildings (see Chapter 3), but is mainly natural or cultivated vegetation. The interruption in the arrival of precipitation at the surface is known as *interception*. This is important in determining when and how water moves through the drainage basin system (Fig. 2.21). Some intercepted water will evaporate off vegetation and return to the atmosphere store. This is **interception loss**. Water also moves through vegetation cover to the ground surface (Fig. 2.22), where it may infiltrate into the soil or run over the ground surface as overland flow (see section 2.3).

• Some of the water is held on the plant leaves and is then evaporated back into the atmosphere. This is called the interception loss. Precipitation is lost very quickly from the drainage basin system by this method and is therefore an important consideration for hydrologists.
• Some water falls through spaces in the vegetation directly to the ground, or drips off leaves and twigs to the ground surface. This process is called throughfall.
• Water which trickles along twigs, branches and down the main stem or trunk to the ground surface is called stemflow.
• All the water that is intercepted by the vegetation is stored temporarily. The amount which eventually moves on through the drainage basin, and when it does so, depends upon the storage capacity of the vegetation and the balance between interception loss, throughfall and stemflow.

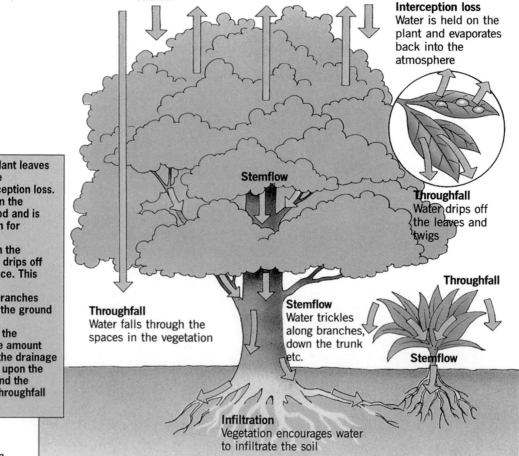

Figure 2.22 Vegetation interception

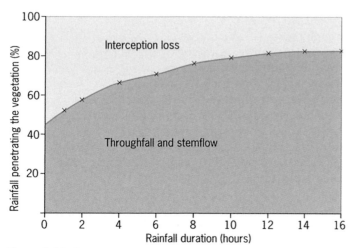

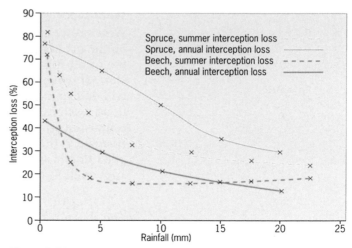

Figure 2.23 The relationship between the amount of rainfall reaching the forest floor (mixed deciduous forest in Poland), interception loss and rainfall duration (*Source*: Ward and Robinson, 1990)

Figure 2.24 Interception losses from spruce and beech forests (*Source*: Ward and Robinson, 1990)

11 Use the information of Figure 2.22 to support the following statements:

a A drainage basin which receives frequent rainfall will lose more water by interception than one where rainfall events occur occasionally.

b Interception loss from intense rainfall will be smaller than from rain falling as slow drizzle.

12 Study Figure 2.24.

a Compare the annual interception loss from spruce and beech forests with less than 5 mm of rainfall.

b How do the two forest types compare in terms of interception loss when rainfall amounts reach 20 mm?

c Account for the differences you have described in parts a and b.

13 Explain why interception loss is high with both types of forest as rainfall begins.

14 Give reasons why interception loss declines rapidly in both types of forest with rainfall amounts less than 5 mm in the summer.

15 Essay: Compare and contrast the ways in which coniferous and deciduous trees control the precipitation interception storage and throughput processes. Use Figures 2.22, 2.23 and 2.24 as the basis for your answer.

The amount of water intercepted is influenced by the characteristics of, first, the precipitation, and second, the vegetation. Significant features of the precipitation are its duration, frequency and type. For instance, interception loss is usually greatest at the beginning of a rainstorm, since the leaves and stems are dry. Each vegetation type has a storage capacity. So, as the leaves become wetter, the water will begin to drip to the ground or run off as stemflow. The longer the duration of the rainfall, the less important interception loss becomes as the vegetation stores fill (Fig. 2.23). As a result, the frequency of the rainfall will be important, because it is in the early stages of each rainfall event that interception loss is greatest. Research suggests that interception loss from snow is very small, because most eventually falls off the vegetation to the ground surface.

Vegetation cover

The type of vegetation cover will determine the interception characteristics. For example, research on grasslands across California suggests that the annual interception loss is between 8 per cent and 13 per cent. Forests give much higher total annual interception losses: 25–35 per cent for coniferous forests and 15–25 per cent for deciduous woodlands. This difference between coniferous and deciduous forests is due to the seasonal leaf cover of deciduous trees. In winter, interception losses from deciduous trees may be as low as 4–7 per cent.

Figure 2.24 shows the contrasts between interception losses from spruce (coniferous) and beech (deciduous) forests. Notice that there are seasonal as well as annual differences, even though both types are in full leaf in the summer. The higher figures for spruce even in summer are due to the water droplets clinging to the individual needles, and the open texture of the needle system which allows air circulation and evaporation. This maintains the interception. In contrast, the larger beech leaves allow water droplets to merge and then to drip to the ground. Also, the denser leaf cover means that there is less air circulating and so evaporation is reduced.

Forest and woodland areas usually have a layered structure, e.g. the canopy, shrub and ground vegetation layers. Thus, some of the throughfall may descend by several stages to the ground surface. This is called *secondary interception*. This may be low during light rainfall, because most of the rain will be intercepted by the main canopy. However, during longer, heavier storms, secondary interception becomes increasingly important as the vegetation stores progressively fill up (see forest layers in Figure 2.22).

Evaporation The process where water (liquid) is changed into water vapour (gas)

Transpiration The process where water is drawn upwards through living plants and evaporated as it emerges from the stomata

16 Study Figure 2.26.
a Compare PET in the UK:
• from north to south
• between coastal areas and inland areas
• between upland areas and lowland areas.
b Suggest reasons for any differences you have identified.

17 Study Figures 2.26 and 2.27. How do the AET rates in the UK compare with the potential values?

18 Explain how Figures 2.26 and 2.27 support the hypothesis that a higher proportion of incoming precipitation is likely to remain in the drainage basin system and reach the stream channels in the north and west of the UK.

Evaporation and transpiration

Some of the precipitation input does not become streamflow. Instead, it is lost from the system by the process of **evaporation**. This evaporated part of the precipitation input is returned directly to the atmosphere (Fig. 1.5). In terms of the total amount of water returned, evaporation from oceans and seas is by far the most important. Within drainage basins, evaporation occurs from intercepted water on vegetation surfaces, from bare soil, from artificial surfaces, and from water surfaces such as rivers and lakes.

Equally important in many environments is **transpiration**. Although this water has reached and penetrated the ground surface, it has been taken up by plants and so has not moved on through the drainage basin. For transpiration to occur there must be a supply of moisture from the soil. Many plants adapt their structures or annual rhythms of leaf fall to reduce transpiration rates when soil water may not be available, e.g. the stomata of some desert plants are sunken; the leaves of some plants drop off in the dry season.

In all but unvegetated deserts and snow or ice fields, the surface will consist of a mixture of bare ground and vegetation. Thus, evaporation and transpiration are usually at work together as **evapotranspiration** (Fig. 2.25). Several factors influence how much water leaves a drainage basin by evapotranspiration.

Potential evapotranspiration

Hydrologists are less interested in the water loss from individual plants than the total evapotranspiration losses from areas with the same vegetation and surface characteristics. As a result they use the concept of **potential evapotranspiration (PET)**. This is the water loss that would occur from an area if there was a constant supply of water to the surface and the transpiring vegetation (Fig. 2.25). Thus PET is the maximum possible water loss for a particular environment. This loss is dependent upon atmospheric factors such as solar energy, precipitation, cloud cover and wind. In many regions, such as semi-arid environments, soil moisture supply is not constant, and actual evapotranspiration (AET) is less than PET. Even in moist environments such as the British Isles, the PET–AET relationship is complex (Figs 2.26 and 2.27).

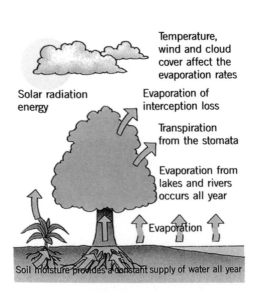

Figure 2.25 The concept of potential evapotranspiration

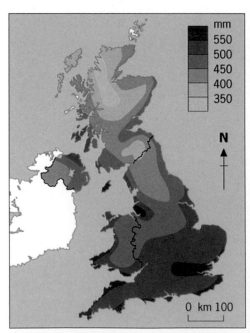

Figure 2.26 Spatial distribution over the UK of mean annual potential evapotranspiration (*Source*: Ward and Robinson, 1981)

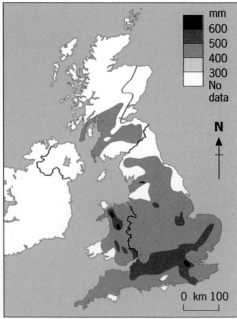

Figure 2.27 Spatial distribution over the UK of mean annual actual evapotranspiration (*Source*: Ward and Robinson, 1981)

Temperature

The main energy source for evaporation is solar radiation. As this varies across the earth, so will the potential for such loss. Higher temperatures allow more evaporation than cooler conditions. Consequently, evaporation rates will vary in different parts of the world (Fig. 2.28), at different times of the year, and at different times of the day. Remember too that vegetation type is a variable that influences evaporation (Fig. 2.29).

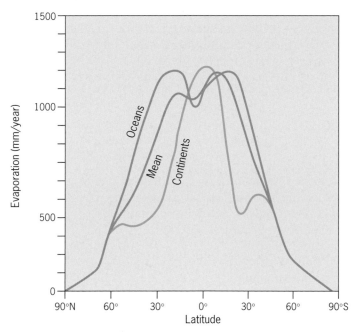

Figure 2.28 Annual change in evaporation with latitude (*Source*: Barry and Chorley, 1985)

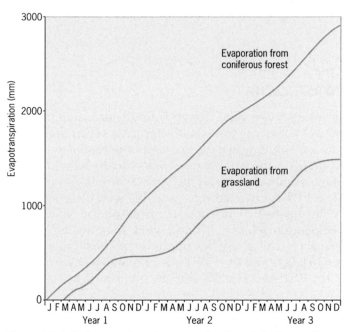

Figure 2.29 Estimates of total evaporation from fully forested and grassed areas in upland mid-Wales over a three-year period (*Source*: Oliver, 1988)

Relative humidity

Relative humidity is the amount of water vapour in the atmosphere expressed as a percentage of the total amount the air could hold at that temperature. As air temperature increases, so air can hold more moisture per unit volume, i.e. warm air can hold more moisture than cold air. At any given temperature, air becomes **saturated** when its relative humidity reaches 100 per cent (dew point). It can hold no more moisture at that temperature. So, when relative humidities are high, e.g. above 70 per cent, the air feels 'damp', and little evaporation will occur. With low relative humidities, the air at that temperature has the capacity to absorb more moisture.

Wind

Air immediately in contact with the water body, land or vegetated surface is first to become saturated. Air movement mixes this saturated layer with the drier layers of air above, allowing further evaporation and saturation. Thus, at any given temperature, evaporation is greater in windy, turbulent conditions than in calm air. We could call this the 'hair-dryer effect'.

Albedo

The albedo is the proportion of incoming solar radiation which is reflected by the earth's surface. The albedo varies for different types of vegetation cover or soil type. The amount of solar radiation not reflected, but absorbed by the vegetation and other surfaces, will influence the amount of energy available for evaporation. Grassland absorbs 70–80 per cent of solar energy and forests,

19 Study Figure 2.29. Suggest reasons why there is a seasonal variation in evaporation for grassland but not for coniferous forest.

20a Explain why cold air may record high relative humidities even though the amount of water vapour present (absolute humidity) is low.
b Suggest what effect this can have upon the working of the hydrological cycle in cold environments.

90 per cent. However, snow, with a high albedo, absorbs only 20 per cent. Darker soils have a lower albedo than lighter-coloured soils and retain more solar energy for evaporation and heating of the atmosphere.

Soil texture and depth
The size and number of the spaces within the soil, i.e. its **porosity,** affect how soil water is held, and how much there will be. Evaporation tends to be high from coarse-textured soils, with their large spaces between the particles. **Capillary action** through the open pore spaces brings the moisture to the surface. Finer soils, such as silts and clays, have numerous, but tiny, spaces and allow low rates of evaporation. Capillary action is more restricted in such soils.

2.3 Drainage basin processes: at and below the surface

Infiltration
Infiltration is the process whereby water enters the soil surface. Hydrologists usually study this water movement by measuring the **infiltration rate** and **infiltration capacity** of the water. The infiltration capacity is the maximum rate at which a particular soil under specific conditions can absorb precipitation. That is, how much water can pass through a given unit of soil in a certain time, measured in cubic millimetres per hour. The infiltration rate refers to how much water is passing through in a certain time.

At any given time, infiltration at a particular site (Fig 2.30) depends upon a complex set of variables. For example, after a rainstorm, look at the school or college grounds: why is it that water is lying on the surface in some places, and yet disappears quickly from other areas? Rainfall intensities and surface/soil characteristics are crucial variables (Table 2.1).

Infiltration is a key process in the drainage basin, because precipitation which arrives at the surface but does not infiltrate is likely to run off quickly into the streams and rivers as **overland flow**. The infiltration capacity decreases rapidly over time during a storm (Fig. 2.31). This is because the air spaces (pores) in the soil become progressively filled with water (see Chapter 7). As the infiltration capacity of the soil falls, further precipitation will be unable to infiltrate (Fig. 2.31).

Figure 2.30 Factors affecting the amount of infiltration

1 Intensity of precipitation
Rainfall of great intensity, i.e. downpour, is less likely to infiltrate than low intensity rainfall, e.g. drizzle.

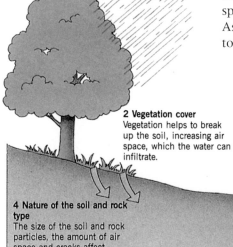

2 Vegetation cover
Vegetation helps to break up the soil, increasing air space, which the water can infiltrate.

4 Nature of the soil and rock type
The size of the soil and rock particles, the amount of air space and cracks affect infiltration. A sandy soil has larger particles and more air spaces than a clay soil. This encourages infiltration.

3 Angle of slope
Water will run off a steeper slope more easily than a gentle slope. The quicker the water runs off, the less likely it is to infiltrate.

Rainfall which does not infiltrate runs over the ground surface as overland flow. The soil might be washed away, causing erosion.

water table

5 Depth of the water table
If the water table is near to the surface, the soil will become quickly saturated and less infiltration will occur.

6 Time
If rainfall occurs over a long period of time, infiltration will decrease as the soil store fills up, i.e. high antecedent moisture conditions.

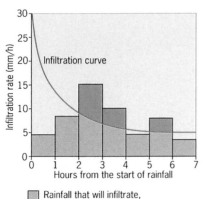

Rainfall that will infiltrate, i.e. below the infiltration capacity per hour

Rainfall that will form depression storage and overland flow, i.e. above the infiltration capacity per hour

Figure 2.31 An infiltration curve imposed on a rainfall histogram to show the rainfall in excess of infiltration capacity
(*After*: Weyman and Wilson, 1975)

Table 2.1 Infiltration capacity for different soils in relation to typical UK rainfall statistics
(*Source*: Burt, 1987)

Soil type and use	Infiltration capacity (mm/h)	Rainfall type (mm/h)			
		Drizzle (0.5)	Moderate rain (2.5)	Heavy rain (10)	Violent rainstorm (50)
Old pasture	60	Yes	Yes		
Moderately grazed pasture	20	Yes	Yes		
Heavily grazed pasture	5	Yes	Yes		
Bare soil after compaction by rainbeat: Clays	2	Yes	No		
Silts	5	Yes	Yes		
Sands	7.5	Yes	Yes		
Freshly ploughed soil	100	Yes	Yes		
Woodland soil	150	Yes	Yes		
Dry clay soil under grass	20	Yes	Yes		
Moist clay soil under grass	10	Yes	Yes		
Wet clay soil under grass	0.5	Yes	Yes		

How quickly the soil store fills up depends not only on rainfall intensity and the infiltration capacity, but also on the weather conditions over the previous days and weeks. It is particularly important to know the antecedent rainfall, i.e. rainfall in the days preceding the rainfall event we are studying. If there has been significant rainfall, then the soil store may already be partially full, and so overland flow will occur quickly at the arrival of further precipitation.

Throughflow

Water which does infiltrate the soil will move vertically downwards at first. Then movement swings progressively downslope due to the effects of gravity, and the decrease in infiltration capacity of the soil with increasing depth. As Figure 2.32 shows, soils become more compacted with depth: they have fewer spaces and cracks in the lower horizons of the profile. Also, horizons in the soil profile vary in their infiltration capacity. This downslope movement of soil water is called **throughflow.**

Unless the soil contains many spaces, root systems and animal burrows, throughflow is a slow process. Research suggests that movement ranges between 0. 01 mm and 1 mm per minute. Eventually, however, the water arrives at the slope base or slope foot.

Percolation

Some water will continue downwards to the **water table** by the process of deep **percolation.** At the water table it becomes part of the **groundwater store.** (This is considered fully in Chapter 7.)

21 On a copy of Table 2.1 complete the last two columns to show whether or not precipitation will infiltrate into the land uses and soil types shown.

22 Write a paragraph describing and explaining how the type of soil, land use and the nature of the precipitation affect infiltration.

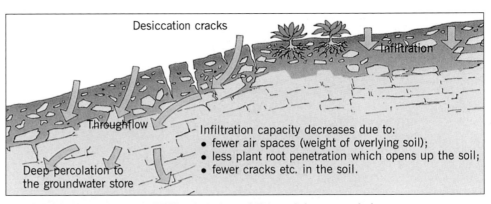

Desiccation cracks

Infiltration

Throughflow

Infiltration capacity decreases due to:
• fewer air spaces (weight of overlying soil);
• less plant root penetration which opens up the soil;
• fewer cracks etc. in the soil.

Deep percolation to the groundwater store

Figure 2.32 The processes of infiltration, throughflow and deep percolation

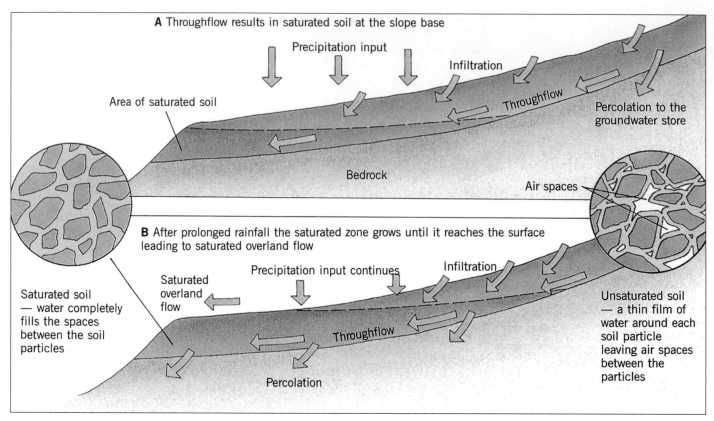

Figure 2.33 Processes leading to saturated overland flow

Overland flow
Water which cannot infiltrate collects on the ground surface in any hollows and depressions as **depression storage**. If these hollows become full, then the water may flow over the ground surface in trickles, rivulets and even thin sheets as overland flow. Vegetation-covered surfaces have a high infiltration capacity (Table 2.1) and, consequently, overland flow is relatively rare under natural conditions. It is most likely to occur if the ground surface is frozen in winter, or has dried leaving a surface crust, or if there is an unusually violent rainstorm. Human activities which result in soil compaction, e.g. the passage of farm machinery, or trampling by animals, can increase overland flow.

Soils at the slope foot readily become saturated due to the downslope movement by throughflow. This prevents further infiltration and results in the process of saturated overland flow following a rainfall event (Fig. 2.33). Saturated overland flow becomes increasingly important with a long rainstorm, or during a series of wet days. It is more common under natural conditions than overland flow, due to the precipitation input exceeding the infiltration capacity. The occurrence of saturated overland flow is a key process in the delivery of water quickly to river channels and has an important effect upon the nature of the storm hydrograph (see Chapter 3).

2.4 Overview

This chapter has followed the journey of water into and through the drainage basin system as far as the slopes surrounding the stream channels. We have taken each process separately, but the important understanding is that all are closely interlinked. Some processes take the water out of the system, e.g. evapotranspiration. Others, such as infiltration, lead the water into the basin. Figure 2.34 summarises how precipitation and runoff in the drainage basin stores and flows vary during a rainstorm.

?

24 Study Figure 2.34.
a Read off the percentage of rainfall in each store or process at:
• the beginning of the storm
• midway through the storm
• at the end of the storm.
b Explain any differences in the percentage of rainfall entering the water stores or moving by different processes over the duration of the storm event.

25 Essay: Discuss the value of a systems approach to understanding the hydrological processes operating in a drainage basin.

A second important understanding is how variable the inputs and processes are, both within individual basins and between different basins. Each basin is unique in the way it works, and may change over time. Yet all work by the same variables and principles. These understandings provide an essential foundation for our investigation of stream channels as transfer systems for water and sediment (Chapter 4). They are a basis too, for the study of drainage basin management (Chapters 6 and 8).

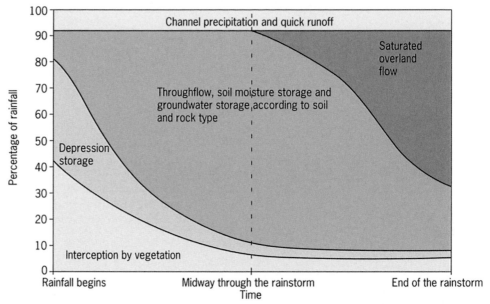

Figure 2.34 **Components of the rainfall–runoff process as they vary in proportion during a rainstorm**

Summary

- A drainage basin is the catchment area within which water collects and drains into a main river channel.
- The drainage basin works as an open system and is the basic unit for the study of hydrological processes.
- The precipitation input variable, and the processes at work in the basin, combine to determine streamflow.
- Aspects of precipitation which influence the drainage basin system are magnitude, regime, location, frequency, duration, intensity, reliability and form.
- When precipitation arrives, it may fall directly on to the river or lake surfaces, or on to soil or the ground, or it may be intercepted by the vegetation cover, and so reach the surface indirectly.
- Some precipitation is lost to the drainage basin by evaporation and transpiration; the rest is delivered at varying speeds, by several surface and subsurface routes, to stream channels.
- The balance between infiltration, subsurface movement and overland flow is influenced by the nature of the precipitation, the character of the soil and the antecedent conditions.

3 Streamflow and human influences

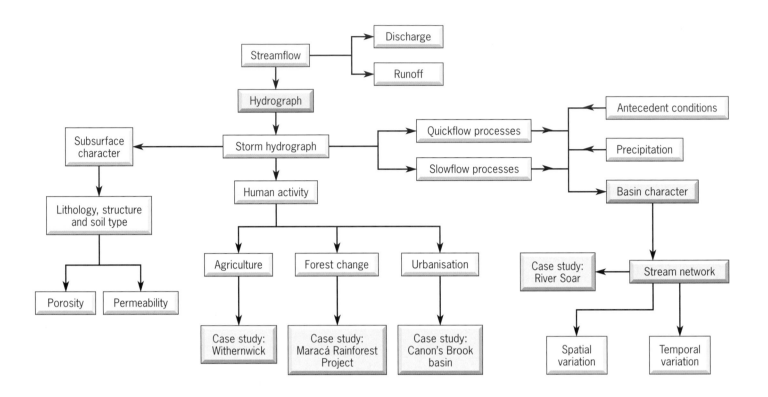

3.1 Introduction

From Chapter 2 we have learned how water enters and is stored in the **drainage basin** system. In this chapter we shall investigate the effects these stores and processes have upon **streamflow.** We shall use the **hydrograph** for this investigation, as it is the basic technique for recording and predicting fluctuations in the channel flow.

As there are few regions of the world where human activity has no influence on hydrological processes, later sections of the chapter introduce the impacts of these activities on streamflow and hydrographs. People influence the ways that drainage basin systems work both intentionally, e.g. by flood control schemes, irrigation projects, energy generation, and unintentionally, e.g. deforestation, urbanisation. The changes affect the processes in the basin and the streamflow, and are recorded in the changing hydrographs.

3.2 Streamflow in the river channel

Streamflow is generated by the outputs from the stores in the drainage basin system (Fig. 3.1). As Figure 3.2 illustrates, it occurs when the stores fill up, or when they have sufficient water to release it steadily. The stores release water at different rates and at different times. Also, the processes which deliver the water to the river channel operate at different speeds. At times of extreme conditions, water inputs may not enter a store, but move directly to the stream by **overland flow.** As a result, streamflow fluctuates constantly.

Figure 3.1 Water in a stream channel is delivered by overland flow, release from subsurface stores, plus a small proportion from direct precipitation

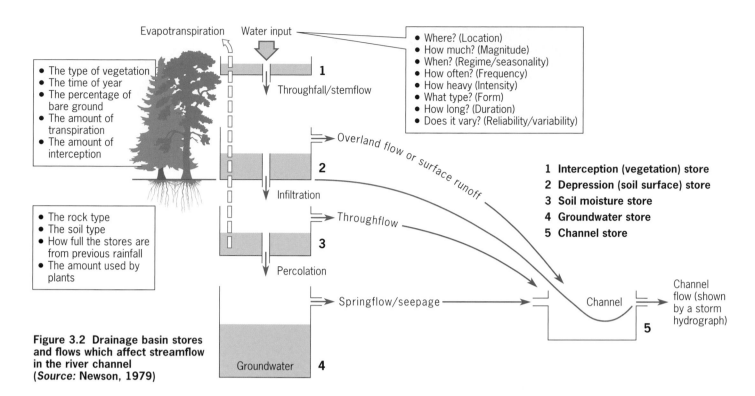

Evapotranspiration   Water input

- Where? (Location)
- How much? (Magnitude)
- When? (Regime/seasonality)
- How often? (Frequency)
- How heavy (Intensity)
- What type? (Form)
- How long? (Duration)
- Does it vary? (Reliability/variability)

- The type of vegetation
- The time of year
- The percentage of bare ground
- The amount of transpiration
- The amount of interception

Throughfall/stemflow

Overland flow or surface runoff

1

2

Infiltration

1 **Interception (vegetation) store**
2 **Depression (soil surface) store**
3 **Soil moisture store**
4 **Groundwater store**
5 **Channel store**

- The rock type
- The soil type
- How full the stores are from previous rainfall
- The amount used by plants

Throughflow

3

Percolation

Springflow/seepage

Channel

Channel flow (shown by a storm hydrograph)

5

Figure 3.2 Drainage basin stores and flows which affect streamflow in the river channel (*Source*: Newson, 1979)

Groundwater   **4**

Figure 3.3 A gauging station

We measure this varying streamflow in two ways:

1 Discharge (Q) is the volume of water passing a specific gauging station per unit of time (Fig. 3.3). Discharge is expressed as cubic metres of water per second (m³/s), often abbreviated to cumecs.

2 Runoff is the volume of water passing a **gauging station**, represented as the thickness of water spread over the drainage basin area above the gauging station. Runoff is expressed as millimetres per month or year. Measuring runoff allows us to compare the amount of water discharged by a river system with the **precipitation** inputs over the drainage basin.

Recording channel flow – the hydrograph
A hydrograph is a continuous record of fluctuating streamflow. Time is plotted along the x-axis. Discharge, in m³/s, is plotted on the y-axis. Figure 3.4 is a typical example. It tells us, for instance, that during 1989, at the Craigiehall gauging station, the River Almond's mean daily discharge ranged from less than 1 m³/s to over 90 m³/s.

Figure 3.4 River Almond, Craigiehall (a catchment area of 369 km²): daily flow hydrograph, 1989 (*Source*: Institute of Hydrology, 1989)

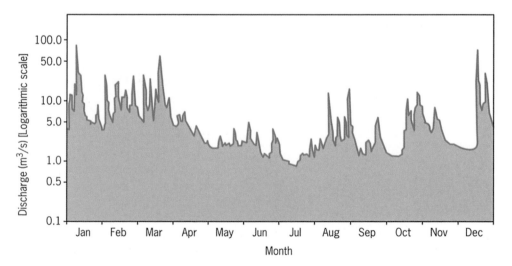

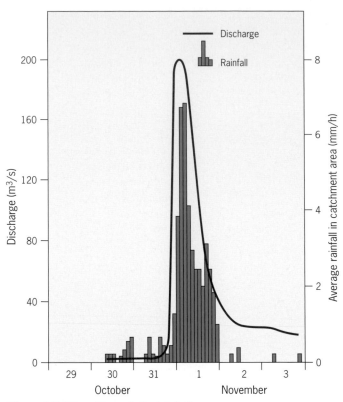

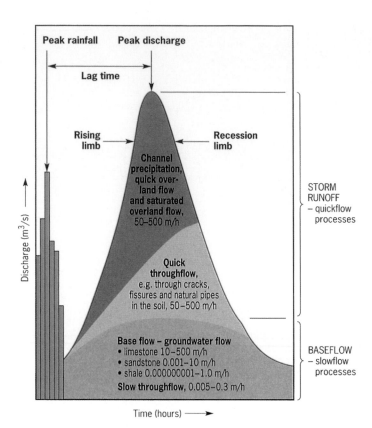

Figure 3.5 River Almond, Craigiehall: storm hydrograph, 29 October 1977 (*Source:* Institute of Hydrology, 1977)

Right: **Figure 3.6 The storm hydrograph: terminology and processes**

1a Make a copy of Figure 3.5 and annotate it with the following terms:
• peak rainfall, • peak discharge,
• rising limb, • recession limb,
• slag time, • storm runoff,
• base flow.
b Give precise figures to illustrate the times and amount of discharge at each stage.

2 Explain how saturated overland flow can cause the peak of the storm hydrograph, even though it does not operate as a process until the middle of the storm.

3 Figure 3.6 shows the observed range of rates of movement of water by the various processes. Describe the factors which will affect the actual rate of these processes at a particular place or time.

The storm hydrograph

A **storm hydrograph** records the discharge pattern of a river at a specific gauging station, following a single rainstorm event. In order to show the relationship between the precipitation input and the discharge of the water past the gauging station, most storm hydrographs include the rainfall graph (Fig. 3.5). This relationship is important to the hydrologist because it determines the speed and scale of the rise in discharge, and therefore the likelihood of flooding.

Figure 3.6 takes a closer look at a storm hydrograph and how it helps our analysis of streamflow. During dry spells, a permanent stream maintains a low discharge known as its **base flow**, sustained by **slowflow processes**. Following a rainfall event, streamflow rises by storm runoff, supplied by **quickflow processes**. The hydrograph plots this increased input along the rising limb. Eventually, discharge peaks; an important piece of information is the lag time between the rainfall maximum and this peak. As the water inputs to the channel decrease, the hydrograph records this along its recession or falling limb.

3.3 Understanding streamflow patterns and hydrographs

A hydrograph only *describes* what happened to streamflow. We need to be able to interpret the graph in order to *explain* what happened. In turn, this will help us to predict and forecast what might happen. Such forecasting is difficult because the inputs, stores and processes in a drainage basin change constantly over time and space.

Stores and flows
The antecedent moisture conditions will influence how a drainage basin responds to a rainfall event (see Section 2.3). Thus, the same storm may

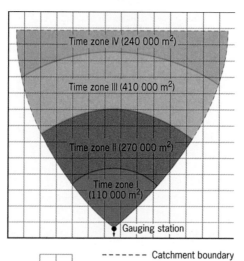

Figure 3.7 The River Severn floods near Worcester, in October 2000

cause a different discharge response and hydrograph pattern at different seasons. In the British Isles in summer, drainage basin stores are unlikely to be full, and **evapotranspiration** will be relatively high. In winter, water stores tend to be nearer to capacity and evapotranspiration rates are lower. As a result, the same storm in January is likely to have a greater and quicker effect on streamflow than it would in July. The storm hydrograph for the January event would be higher and steeper than the July pattern. In the shorter timescale, the same storm will have a different impact on streamflow and the hydrograph if it follows several wet days than if it ends a dry spell. In January 1994, much of Britain experienced serious flooding (see Fig. 6.1). Hydrographs showed steep rising limbs, high peaks and short lag times. (We call such steep, high patterns 'flashy' hydrographs.) Hydrologists identified three conditions which caused the hydrograph patterns and the floods:

1 Rainfall was prolonged.
2 The water stores in the drainage basins were already full.
3 Evapotranspiration ouputs were low.

The same combination triggered the disastrous floods at the end of October 2000 (Fig. 3.7). Drainage basin stores were near to capacity from prolonged rains and widespread floods earlier in the month when a series of depressions delivered further heavy rainstorms.

Rainfall intensity

If we look again at Figure 3.2 it is clear that steady rainfall, even over several days, will allow the various water stores to fill up gradually and efficiently. This controls the speed and volume of runoff to the stream channels. This will be reflected in a broad, flat hydrograph. If, however, the precipitation input is intense and exceeds the soil **infiltration** and vegetation **interception** capacities, quickflow processes, e.g. overland flow, dominate, even when the basin stores are not full. Discharges rise suddenly and flooding is likely – a situation identified by a 'flashy' hydrograph.

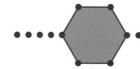

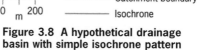

Figure 3.8 A hypothetical drainage basin with simple isochrone pattern (ignoring contour effect)

Simulating a drainage basin hydrograph

Constructing the model

In order to show clearly the way in which a hydrograph is generated, we need to simplify reality. We will therefore make three assumptions:

1 The drainage basin is a smooth surface without surface depressions and with no permanent stream.
2 The basin is completely impermeable, so all rainfall immediately runs off as overland flow.
3 The overland flow moves at a constant velocity of 0. 1 m/s, i.e. there is no variation with discharge.

A hypothetical drainage basin is shown in Figure 3.8. Let us say that a rainstorm of 4.5 mm lasts four hours (Fig. 3.9). If overland flow moves at the rate of 0.1 m/s, the one-hour isochrone (line of equal time of travel to the gauging station) will be 360 m from the gauging point (0. 1 m × 3 600 s).

In this exercise we are assuming that water will flow on a flat surface and we are not taking into account drainage basin relief. We can draw isochrones for two and three hours from the gauging station. The area within each isochrone contains the water which will reach the gauging station in hourly intervals:

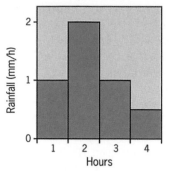

Figure 3.9 A hypothetical four-hour rainstorm

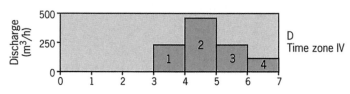

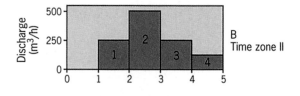

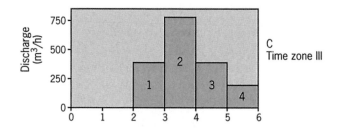

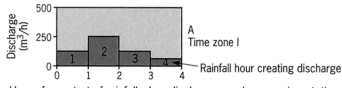

Hours from start of rainfall when discharge reaches gauging station

Figure 3.10 The hydrographs created by each time zone according to the time the water arrives at the gauging point

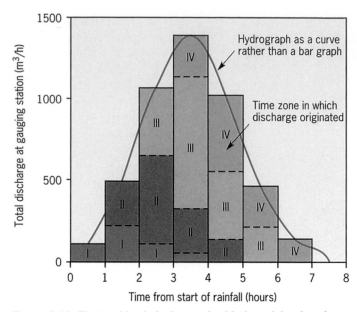

Figure 3.11 The total basin hydrograph with the origin of each discharge unit shown

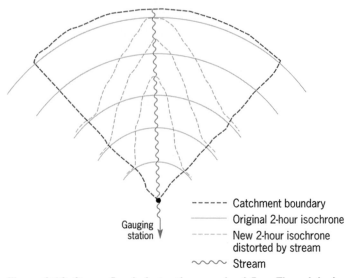

Figure 3.12 Streamflow is faster than overland flow. The original arc-shaped overland flow isochrones are distorted with the introduction of streamflow

- time zone I, 0–1 hours after the start of the rainfall
- time zone II, 1–2 hours after the start of the rainfall
- time zone III, 2–3 hours after the start of the rainfall
- time zone IV, 3–4 hours after the start of the rainfall.

We can calculate the area of each time zone and thus the amount of rainfall which runs off from each time zone. For example, for time zone II:

- hour 0–1: 0.001 m rain × 270 000 m² = 270 m³
- hour 1–2: 0.002 m rain × 270 000 m² = 540 m³
- hour 2–3: 0. 001 m rain × 270 000 m² = 270 m³
- hour 3–4: 0.0005 m rain × 270 000 m² = 135 m³.

We can graph this information and repeat the calculation for each time zone (Fig. 3.10).

Analysing the model hydrograph

The runoff from each successive time zone starts to arrive one hour later than runoff from the preceding zone and finishes one hour later. Thus, water from

4 Describe and explain:
a the structure of the model hydrograph shown on Figure 3.11.
b the isochrone distortion on Figure 3.12.

time zone I starts to arrive at zero hours and finishes at four hours; water from time zone II starts to arrive at one hour and finishes at five hours; water from time zone III starts to arrive at two hours and finishes at six hours, etc. The total volume of water arriving at the gauging station for each hour is added to give a final basin hydrograph (Fig. 3.11).

In this simulation the hydrograph is shown both as a bar graph and a line graph. However, hydrographs are usually only curved line graphs, because time intervals are shorter when the line graphs are produced.

The effect of streamflow

In the above simulation we assumed that overland flow ran evenly across the drainage basin at a constant speed. This simplification helps us to understand the lag effect caused by location within a drainage basin. In reality, however, much of the water arriving at a gauging station is delivered via stream channels. Streamflow transfers water more quickly than overland flow. The result is the distortion of the isochrones and time zones, as shown in Fig. 3.12.

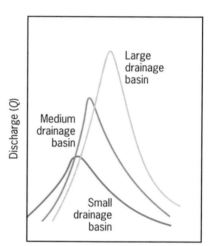

Figure 3.13 The effect of increasing basin size on the hydrograph (*Source:* **Gregory and Walling, 1973**)

3.4 The effect of drainage basin character on the hydrograph

Basin size

The volume of runoff, the discharge (Q) and the lag time tend to increase with the size of the drainage basin, as the model of Figure 3.13 illustrates. This model may be applied to humid environments such as the British Isles. However, in arid and semi-arid regions, such as the Sahel of Africa, runoff and discharge volume may decrease downstream, i.e. as basin size above a gauging station increases. This is due to high evaporation rates, loss by seepage of water into the channel bed, and the absence of inputs from tributaries.

Basin shape

The shape of a drainage basin will affect the pattern of the time zones and therefore the shape of the storm hydrograph (Fig. 3.14). An elongated basin will take longer to achieve a throughput of water from a rainstorm than a short, broad basin. The most efficient shape is one in which the **watershed** is circular and all the water disappears down a hole in the middle – rather like a circular washbasin!

5 Construct a three-hydrograph model (see Fig. 3.13) for a gauging station in a:
a small
b medium
c large drainage basin in a semi-arid environment. Use the same axes as in Figure 3.13. Describe and explain the patterns of the graphs you have drawn.

6 Describe and explain the relationship between the basin shape and hydrograph pattern for the three examples of Figure 3.14.

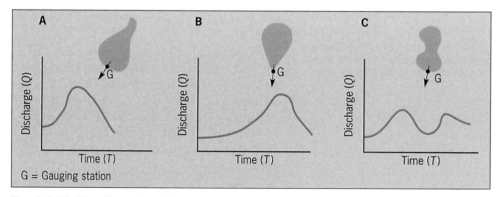

Figure 3.14 The effect of basin shape on the hydrograph
a In a triangular-shaped basin with the apex in the upper catchment, the largest area is in the early time zones. This causes an early peak of the hydrograph.
b In a triangular-shaped basin with the apex near to the gauging station, there will be a delayed peak because the largest time zone is furthest from the gauging station.
c A basin with a small area in the middle time zones, increasing near to and far from the gauging station will produce a double peak.
(*Source:* **Gregory and Walling, 1973**)

We use two methods to measure drainage basin shape: **basin circularity** and **basin elongation** (Fig. 3.15). Remember that both assume that rainfall is evenly distributed across the drainage basin. In reality this is rarely the case.

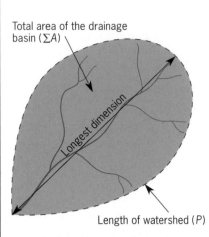

Total area of the drainage basin (ΣA)

Longest dimension

Length of watershed (P)

Figure 3.15 Basin circularity and basin elongation are ways of describing objectively the shape of a drainage basin. Comparisons can then be made between drainage basins.

Basin circularity

We use basin circularity to compare the area of the drainage basin to the area of a circle of the same circumference.

If $P = \pi D$, then $D = \dfrac{P}{\pi}$ and $A_0 = \pi \left(\dfrac{D}{2} \right)^2$

Basin circularity $= \dfrac{\Sigma A}{A_0}$ where:

P = the length of the perimeter of the basin, i.e. the watershed
D = the diameter of a circle equivalent in circumference to P
A_0 = area of the circle, of diameter D
ΣA = the total area of the drainage basin
The nearer the answer is to 1, the more circular the drainage basin shape.

Basin elongation

Basin elongation compares the longest dimension of the basin to the diameter of a circle of the same area as the basin.

$\Sigma A = \pi r^2$, therefore: $r = \sqrt{\dfrac{\Sigma A}{\pi}}$

Basin elongation $= \dfrac{Dl}{d}$ where:

ΣA = the total basin area
Dl = the longest dimension
d = the diameter, i.e. 2π.

Stream network characteristics

Stream networks

The pattern of streams within a drainage basin influences the transfer of water and consequently the shape of the hydrograph, i.e. the stream response to rainfall events. Two key variables are involved:

• *Stream density* = The total length of the drainage channels, divided by the drainage basin area. For example, using the calculation, the R. Wallington (Fig. 3.17) has a drainage density of 1.22 km of channel length/km^2.

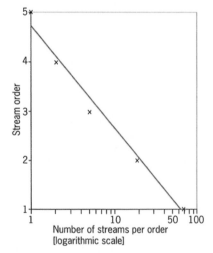

Figure 3.16 River Wallington: number of streams against stream order. The number of streams of each order plotted against stream order on logarithmic graph paper shows a clear negative relationship.

Calculating stream density

$Dd = \dfrac{\Sigma L}{\Sigma A}$ where:

Dd = the drainage density in kilometres per square kilometres
ΣL = the sum of the total stream lengths in kilometres
ΣA = the **catchment area** in square kilometres.

• *Stream order* = The way the various stream channels in a drainage basin fit together. The most widely used method for describing this stream arrangement has been devised by A. N. Strahler (1952). As Fig 3.17 shows, this is based on a hierarchical set of stream orders, giving a negative relationship between stream order and number of streams (Fig 3.16). This ratio is called **Horton's law of stream numbers** (see box on bifurcation ratio, p.33). Analysis of the stream order structure in a drainage basin can help in predicting the shape of hydrographs (Fig. 3.18), and hence flood forecasting (see R. Soar case study).

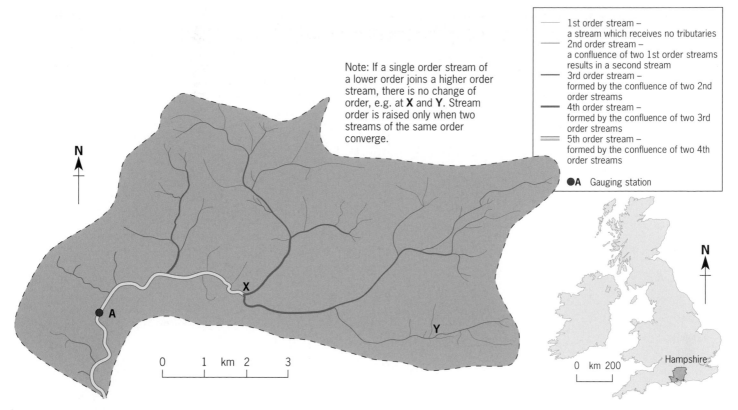

Note: If a single order stream of a lower order joins a higher order stream, there is no change of order, e.g. at **X** and **Y**. Stream order is raised only when two streams of the same order converge.

— 1st order stream –
a stream which receives no tributaries
— 2nd order stream –
a confluence of two 1st order streams results in a second stream
— 3rd order stream –
formed by the confluence of two 2nd order streams
— 4th order stream –
formed by the confluence of two 3rd order streams
═ 5th order stream –
formed by the confluence of two 4th order streams

●A   Gauging station

0   1   km 2   3

N

N

0   km 200

Hampshire

Figure 3.17 The drainage network of the River Wallington, Hampshire, showing stream orders according to Strahler's system

?

7 Describe the R.Wallington drainage basin (Fig. 3.17) in terms of stream density and stream order.

8 Use Figure 3.18 to suggest the relationship between stream order structure and the hydrograph structure in a drainage basin.

9 Which of the two storm hydrographs shown on Figure 3.18 is likely to fit the storm hydrograph for gauging station A in the R. Wallington drainage basin. Give reasons for your choice. (You may choose neither – but should then explain why.)

The bifurcation ratio (R_b)

The rate of change of stream order is shown by the **bifurcation ratio** (R_b) This is calculated using the formula:

$$R_b = \frac{\text{number of streams in order}}{\text{number of streams in the next highest order}}$$

For example, for the R. Wallington (Fig. 3.17) for first and second order streams:

$$R_b = \frac{69 \ (\text{number of streams in order})}{19 \ (\text{number of streams in the next highest order})} = 3.6.$$

If we repeat the calculation for second and third order streams, and third and fourth order streams, we can then find the average bifurcation ratio for the drainage basin. The results for the R. Wallington are shown in Table 3.1. Most bifurcation ratios for natural streams lie between 3 and 5. Lower values indicate a low level of stream development, higher values indicate a high level of stream development.

Table 3.1 River Wallington: network characteristics

Stream order	Number of streams	Bifurcation Index	Total stream length (km)	Mean stream length (km)	Ratio of stream lengths
1	69		26.3	0.38	
		3.6			2.8
2	19		20.5	1.08	
		3.8			1.4
3	5		9.8	1.96	
		2.5			1.7
4	2		6.5	3.25	
		2.0			2.0
5	1		6.5	6.50	
		$R_b = 2.97$	$L = 69.6$		$R_L = 1.97$

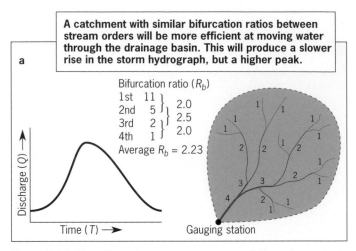

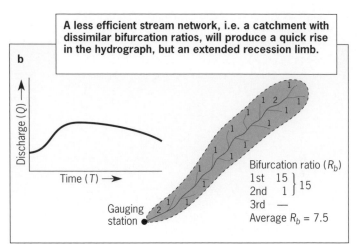

Figure 3.18 The effect of stream arrangement (bifurcation ratios) on the storm hydrograph

3.5 Factors influencing stream networks and the hydrograph

Drainage network measurements allow us to compare drainage basins and to predict how they would respond to precipitation inputs. It is important that we understand the factors which influence these networks. Research by Gregory (1976) in the UK produced two main findings:

- As precipitation increases, so does the drainage density.
- Impermeable drainage basins have higher drainage densities.

High drainage densities transfer precipitation inputs relatively quickly to the main river channels. So, each of these situations is likely to produce steep hydrographs and increase the likelihood of flooding. The evolution of a high-density drainage network is one way a drainage basin responds to the need to deal with the precipitation input. It is a form of **negative feedback**.

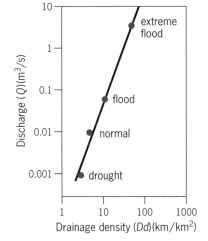

a A drought situation, discharge is $0.00056\,\mathrm{m^3/s}$

b A normal situation, discharge is $0.0084\,\mathrm{m^3/s}$

c A flood situation, discharge is $0.056\,\mathrm{m^3/s}$

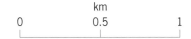

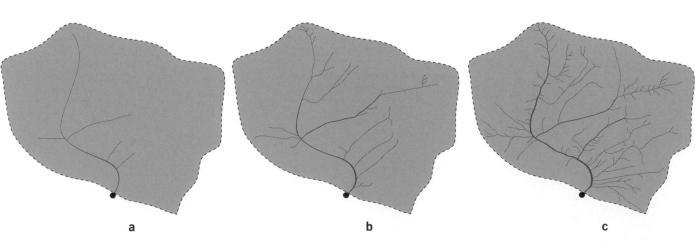

Figure 3.19 Seasonal variation of drainage density and stream network, Swildon stream, Somerset, England (*Source:* White at al 1986)

?

Draw copies of Figures 3.19 a, b, c.

10 Label the three stream networks according to Strahler's system of stream ordering.

11 Calculate the bifurcation ratios for each stream network.

12 For each situation, draw the shape of the storm hydrograph you would expect to see. Add notes to explain the shape of your graphs.

Seasonal variation in drainage density
Precipitation inputs and conditions in the drainage basin water stores vary seasonally, e.g. in the UK rising **groundwater** levels and **saturated** soils during wetter winter months produce increased runoff. The result is noticeable variations in the extent and density of the stream network (Fig. 3.19). Over longer time periods, drainage densities increase as a network evolves across a landscape. The sequence could be similar to that shown on Figure 3.19.

River Soar, Leicestershire, England

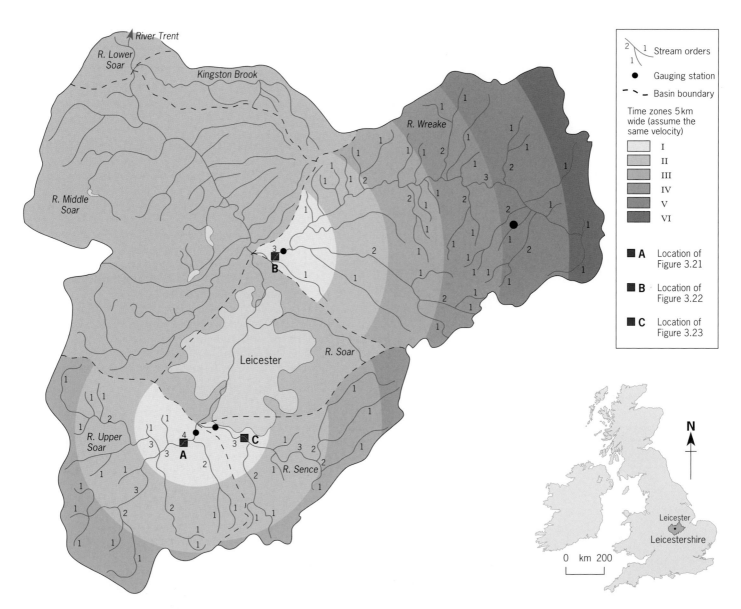

Figure 3.20 The three sub-catchments of the River Soar, Leicestershire, England (*Source:* Severn-Trent Water Authority, 1978)

Table 3.2 Characteristics of the River Soar sub-catchments

Sub-catchment	Area (km²)	Mean annual flow (m³/s)	Basin perimeter (km)	Basin circularity	Basin elongation	Drainage density*
Upper Soar	202	1.44	60.75	0.69	0.87	0.48
Sence	133	1.02	61.56	0.44	1.46	0.44
Wreake	414	2.80	87.8	0.67	1.33	0.52

*These drainage density figures are relatively low since they only include main channels

The Rivers Upper Soar, Wreake and Sence (Fig. 3.21–3.23) have similar rock types – impermeable Keuper Marl, Rhaetic and Lias clays. Their relief height is also similar, although the River Wreake has a larger area of higher relief extending further downstream in the drainage basin. This results in a large number of low-order streams.

Figure 3.21 R. Soar at Narborough, looking upstream Jan. 1994.

Figure 3.22 R. Wreake at Syston, looking upstream Jan. 1994.

Figure 3.23 R. Sence at Kilby Bridge, looking upstream Jan. 1994.

Table 3.3 Stream orders and bifurcation ratios for the River Soar sub-catchments

Stream order	Soar	R_b	Sence	R_b	Wreake	R_b
1	18		8		35	
		3		2.66		3.5
2	6		3		10	
		3		3.0		10.0
3	2		1		1	
		2				
4	1		–		–	
		R_b=2.67		R_b=2.83		R_b=6.75

?

13 What evidence is there in Figures 3.21–3.23 to indicate that the R. Soar basin (Fig. 3.20) has recently experienced heavy rainfall?

14 Use Figure 3.20 and Tables 3.2–3.3. Link statements a–h with each drainage basin. Using a–h, explain how drainage basin characteristics affect the storm hydrograph. As more than one characteristic will apply to each of the three drainage basins, the actual hydrograph may be quite complex (Figs 3.24–3.26).
a The largest drainage basin (the greatest number of time zones) which will produce a higher peak discharge but a longer lag time on the hydrograph.
b An elongated basin relative to its size which results in a longer lag time on the hydrograph.
c A relatively circular basin which will be efficient at moving water through the system, giving a relatively short lag time and a higher peak discharge on the hydrograph.
d A well-developed stream network with similar bifurcation ratios producing a slower rise but a higher peak discharge on the hydrograph.
e A less-developed stream network which has dissimilar bifurcation ratios resulting in a quick rise but a more drawn out hydrograph.
f A higher-order stream giving a lower peak and a longer time lag on the hydrograph.
g A high drainage density which drains the basin efficiently giving a rapid response in the storm hydrograph.
h A small drainage basin giving a short lag time but a smaller peak discharge on the hydrograph.

15 Which basin has the most efficient shape? Explain.

16 How would you expect the time zones of each drainage basin to affect their storm hydrographs? Consider the stream density in each time zone in your answer.

?

17 Essay: Study Figures 3.24 to 3.26 and compare the responses of the three sub-basins to the same storm events. Does the response of the three sub-basins follow the theoretical ideas concerning drainage basin size, shape, drainage density and stream arrangement? Support your answer with precise evidence from the storm hydrographs.

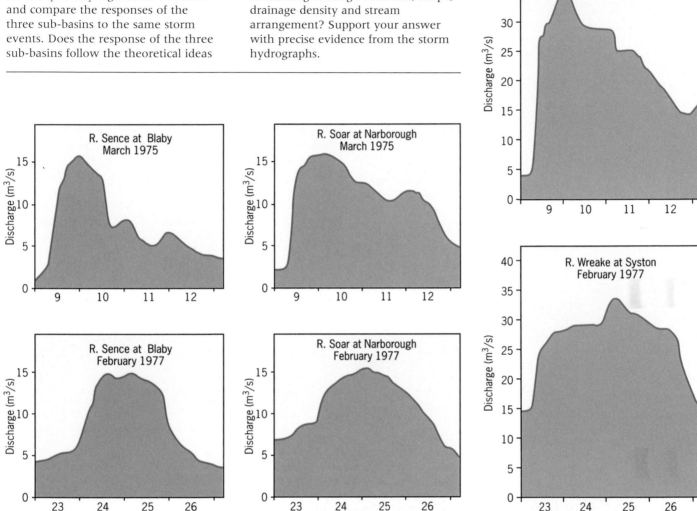

Figure 3.24 Flood hydrographs for the River Sence at Blaby (*Source*: Severn–Trent Water Authority, 1978)

Figure 3.25 Flood hydrographs for the River Soar at Narborough (*Source*: Severn–Trent Water Authority, 1978)

Figure 3.26 Flood hydrographs for the River Wreake at Syston (*Source*: Severn–Trent Water Authority, 1978)

Table 3.4 Porosity of various materials (*Source*: Ward and Robinson, 1990)

Material	Average porosity	Range (%)
Soils	55	50–65
Clay	50.5	42–59
Silt	43.5	37–50
Sand	35	30–40
Gravel	34	29–39
Sand & gravel	27	20–34
Sandstone	18	8–28
Limestone	20	5–35
Shale	8	2–14
Crystalline rock	5	1–10

3.6 The effect of structure and lithology on the hydrograph

As we have learned in Chapter 2, a proportion of the precipitation input passes through the soil store, to **percolate** more deeply into the **groundwater** store. It is the groundwater store which regulates the slow flow supply and base flow of streams. (Chapter 4 looks at river **regimes** and so examines base flow.) The behaviour of this store is influenced by the geological structure, i.e. folding, faulting, tilting of rock formations, and the lithology, i.e. rock type. Together they are an important control upon both the surface stream network and the subsurface transmission of water. In any hydrographs we study, we need to take them into account. (The groundwater store is studied in more detail in Chapter 7.)

18 Study Figures 3.27 and 3.28 carefully, then:

a Describe the streamflow of each for 1986.

b Compare and contrast the two hydrographs.

c Suggest how lithology might explain any differences you identify.

Rocks vary in their **porosity** (Table 3.4) and **permeability,** and so in their ability to hold and transmit water. For instance, crystalline, igneous and metamorphic rocks often have low porosity and permeability. In moist environments, drainage basins underlain by such rocks are likely to have dense drainage networks. They will be dominated by the quickflow processes of soil **throughflow** and overland flow. However, even rocks of low porosity may transmit water efficiently if they are well-jointed and criss-crossed by fissure systems. For example, Carboniferous Limestone is crystalline and has a low porosity, but generally has joint, bedding plane and fissure systems which give it permeability.

The hydrographs of Figures 3.27 and 3.28 are for two catchments within the Thames drainage basin. Both are for the same year, and both catchments experienced similar weather conditions. Note that the Kennet basin is bigger than the Loddon basin. The key difference is in their geological foundation: the Kennet basin is largely permeable, while the Loddon is underlain mostly by impermeable rocks.

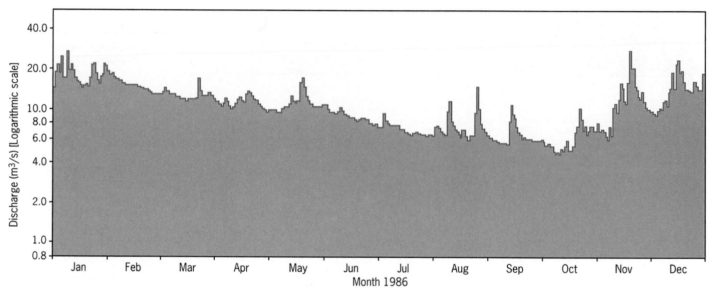

Figure 3.27 Hydrograph of the River Kennet, Theale, 1986 (Catchment area of 103.4 km^2)
(*Source:* **National Water Archive, Institute of Hydrology, 1993**)

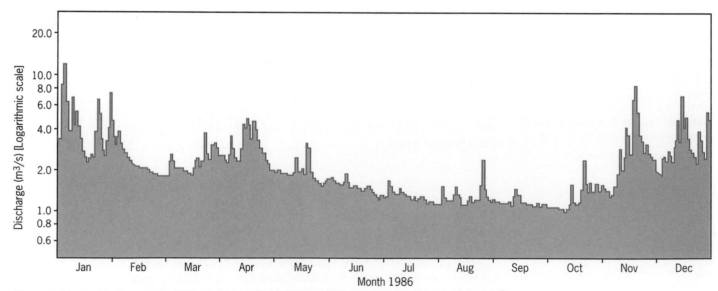

Figure 3.28 Hydrograph of the River Loddon, Sheepbridge, 1986 (Catchment area of 164.5 km^2)
(*Source:* **National Water Archive, Institute of Hydrology, 1993**)

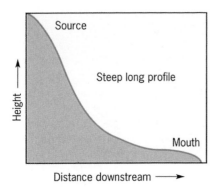

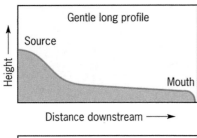

Figure 3.29 The effect of basin relief on the hydrograph: steep long profile

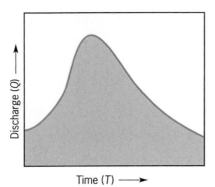

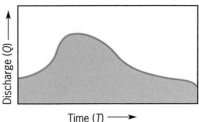

Figure 3.30 The effect of basin relief on the hydrograph: gentle long profile

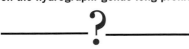

19 The cross-sections and hydrographs of Figures 3.29 and 3.30 use only basic relief as an influential variable. For each type of relief, draw pairs of hydrographs for basins with (a) impermeable or permeable rocks, (b) forest or grass vegetation. Add labels to your hydrographs, describing and explaining the differences from the hydrographs shown on Figures 3.29 and 3.30.

3.7 The effect of basin relief upon the hydrograph

The importance of slopes

A drainage basin with steep slopes is likely to show more quickflow, a shorter lag time and higher peak discharge on the hydrograph than a basin which has gentle slopes and low relief. This is because steeper slopes encourage more overland flow, faster runoff and faster throughflow processes which produce rapid water collection at the slope base and saturated conditions. Basins with strong relief are also likely to give relatively steep stream **long profiles** (Figs 3.29 and 3.30). We must beware, however, as steeper channel gradients do not always mean higher flow velocities.

The importance of soil structure

When considering relief and slopes we must not forget the role of the soil store. Generally, areas of high relief tend to have shallow soils. Except where there is a peat 'blanket', these soils have limited storage and transmission capacities, which encourage overland flow and high drainage densities. Extensive areas of the uplands of northern and western Britain illustrate these characteristics. However, the typical scarp-and-vale topography of lowland England contradicts this general rule: drainage densities are low on the higher relief, thin soils and permeable rocks of the Chalk Downs and the Cotswolds. In contrast, the nearby impermeable clay vales have higher drainage densities.

3.8 The effects of agriculture on hydrological processes

Farming activity may speed up or slow down delivery of surface and subsurface water to the stream. For instance, many soil conservation measures are designed to reduce runoff and soil erosion which accompany overland flow. Popular strategies are hill-slope terracing (Fig. 3.31), or planting of permanent grassland on vulnerable soils. These techniques will reduce quickflow. In contrast, the purpose of land drainage is to accelerate the transfer of water to the stream channel.

In general, the more intensive the farming, the greater the modification of the natural processes. When high technology is added to intensive farming, the hydrological regime is likely to be changed fundamentally, e.g. large-scale water basin transfers for irrigation in arid regions.

Intensive farming

Intensive farming practices change the way water is stored and its movement through the soil horizons. Firstly, changes in vegetation cover will affect interception, surface runoff, infiltration and percolation. Secondly, ploughing, the application of fertiliser, and the impact of equipment and animals all alter the soil texture and so the storage and infiltration capacities. The timing of activities can be important. For example, in the former USSR, ploughing fields in the autumn rather than the spring reduced runoff in the forest zone by 1.5–2 times. In the forest-steppe zone the reduction was 2–4 times, and in the steppe zone, 4–8 times. In each zone there was also an increase in recharge of the groundwater store.

Land drainage

The primary aim of most land drainage schemes is to lower the **water table** and so prevent waterlogging. This is done by a combination of cutting deeper ditches and laying pipes beneath the field surfaces. The improved drainage permits the intensification of farming practices, e.g. a change from grazing to arable cropping (see Withernwick case study, p. 41).

Figure 3.31 Rice terraces, Bali

?

20 Suggest reasons for the impacts of changing the ploughing patterns in the former USSR.

21a Make a sketch of the rice terraces in Figure 3.31.
b How do the terraces modify hydrological processes? Add these as annotations to your sketch.

22 You live beside a river downstream from a large farm. The owner of this farm wants to put in a field drainage scheme. Most of the farm soils are heavy clays. Write a letter to the farmer, stating what effect the scheme will have upon your property, and whether or not you support the proposal.
b Would your opinion be the same if the soils on the farm were light sand? If not, say why.

The Institute of Hydrology in the UK has carried out research into the impacts of field drainage and stream channel improvement, and makes these key conclusions:
• The drainage of heavy clay soils which, when undrained, are prone to prolonged surface saturation, generally results in a lowering of large and medium peaks on the storm hydrograph of neighbouring streams. This is because their natural response is 'flashy', resulting from limited soil water storage capacity. When these soils are drained, however, surface saturation and therefore quickflow surface runoff is largely eliminated.
• On more permeable soils, which are less prone to surface saturation, the usual effect of drainage is to improve the speed of subsurface discharges. This tends to increase hydrograph peak flows in nearby streams.
• Stream base flows are higher from drained rather than undrained lands, mainly as a result of an increase in channel depth.
• At the river catchment scale, main channel improvements lead to larger peak flows downstream, due to higher channel velocities and a reduction in overbank flooding and storage.
• The combined effect of field drainage and main channel improvement is to increase streamflow peaks and dry weather base flows.
• At the drainage basin scale, artificial drainage produces a significant shortening of hydrograph lag times.

Withernwick, Holderness, England

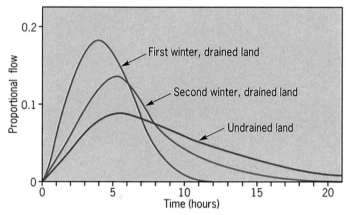

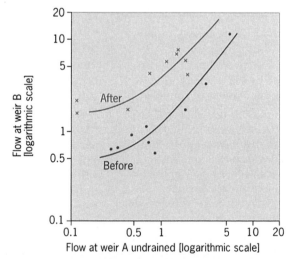

Figure 3.33 Withernwick: field drainage site (*Source:* Robinson, 1990)

The field drainage scheme

Withernwick lies on the flat, intensively farmed Holderness plains (Fig. 3.33). The local soils consist of clay loams increasing in density and massive structure with depth. Between 1974 and 1975, hydrologists studied four fields on Westland Farm before and after a field drainage scheme was completed on 81 per cent of the area.

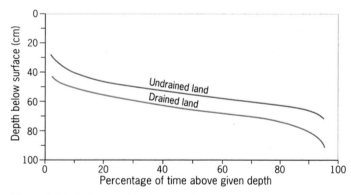

Figure 3.34 Comparison of one-hour unit hydrographs, before and after drainage. Delivery of rainwater to the drainage ditches was accelerated by the field drainage network (*Source:* Robinson, 1990)

Figure 3.32 Soil water levels in drained and undrained land at Withernwick. The mean water table levels fell by approximately 10–15 cm after drainage (*Source:* Robinson, 1990)

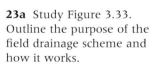

?

23a Study Figure 3.33. Outline the purpose of the field drainage scheme and how it works.
b Suggest what the effects might be on the water flow through fields 1 to 4, if similar drainage improvements were applied to fields X and Y.

24 Using Figures 3.32 to 3.35, describe and explain the effects of field drainage upon streamflow.

Figure 3.35 Base flows, i.e. stream discharge during dry weather, at Withernwick as the percentage of the study area artificially drained was increased from 25 to 56 per cent (*Source:* Robinson, 1990)

3.9 The impacts of changing forest cover

Afforestation

Afforestation of watersheds is a popular technique used to slow down runoff and control erosion. The aim is to even out stream discharge and 'flatten' the hydrographs, making them less 'flashy'. The increased **transpiration** losses also divert some of the precipitation inputs. Trees are thirsty organisms, and their removal frequently results in rising water tables and wetter soils, e.g. the extensive peat cover of the Scottish Highlands is the result of Medieval forest clearance causing waterlogging. A more recent example comes from southern Australia where the natural eucalyptus woodland has been cleared for cattle and sheep grazing. Water tables have risen and soil salinity has become a serious problem. As a result reforestation schemes are under way, whose purpose is to 'suck up' water and so lower the water tables once more.

Deforestation

Deforestation has become a high-profile global issue. One aspect of the impacts is the acceleration of runoff and erosion, leading to an increased likelihood of flooding. A well-known example is the claim that deforestation in the Himalayas, the headwater catchments for the River Ganges, is increasing flood frequency and intensity in Bangladesh. In Europe, forest clearance for ski developments in the Alps is blamed for increased flood damage in farmland and settlements downstream. Figures 3.36 and 3.37 summarise the impacts of deforestation on the routes water takes through the **hydrological cycle** and hence the input to streamflow.

26 Study Figures 3.36 and 3.37. Describe and explain the changes in runoff, infiltration and evapotranspiration on:
• flat ground
• sloping ground.

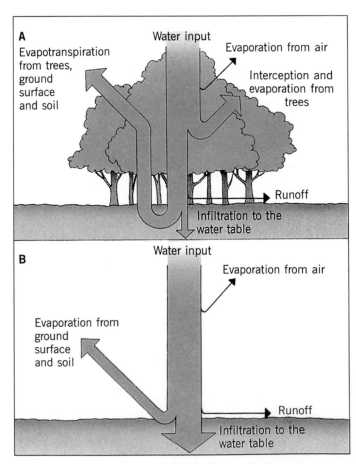

Figure 3.36 The hydrological cycle (a) before and (b) after deforestation on flat ground (*Source:* Tivy and O'Hare, 1981)

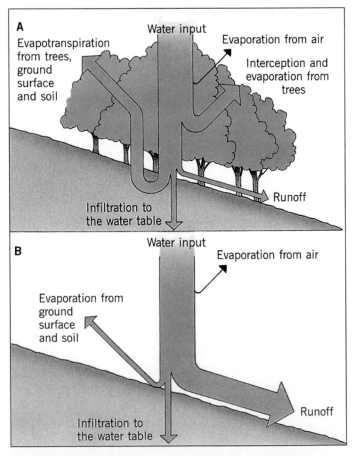

Figure 3.37 The hydrological cycle (a) before and (b) after deforestation on sloping ground (*Source:* Tivy and O'Hare, 1981)

These changes depend on:
• the size of the deforested area
• the slope of the land
• the climatic and meteorological conditions, especially the amount and intensity of the rainfall
• soil texture and organic content
• the nature of the remaining or succeeding vegetation.

Perhaps the most controversial deforestation issues focus on the tropical rainforests. The hydrological cycle interacts with this complex ecosystem in a very special way, and forest clearance can have severe impacts (Fig. 3.38). For example, in the central Amazon basin in Brazil there are growing concerns that deforestation is causing greater extremes of flow (see Maracá case study, p. 44).

Figure 3.38 Hydrological processes in undisturbed tropical rainforest

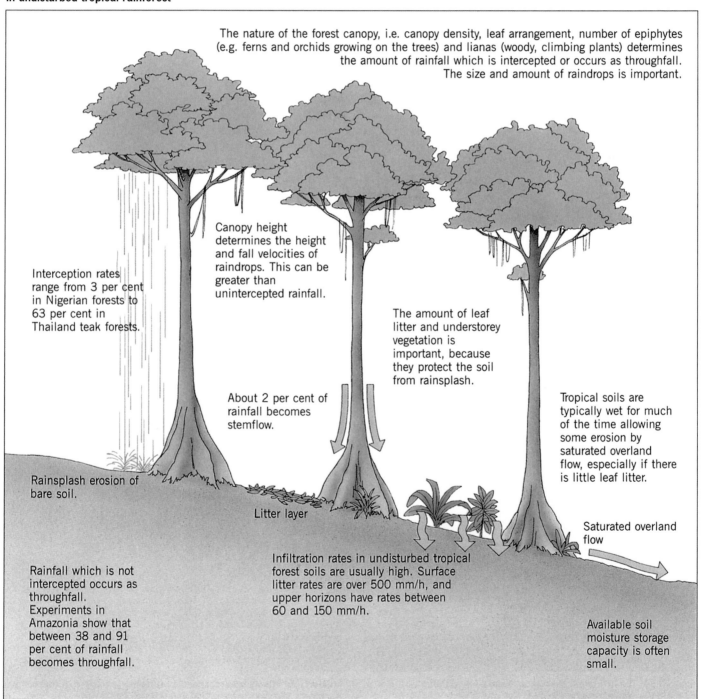

The nature of the forest canopy, i.e. canopy density, leaf arrangement, number of epiphytes (e.g. ferns and orchids growing on the trees) and lianas (woody, climbing plants) determines the amount of rainfall which is intercepted or occurs as throughfall. The size and amount of raindrops is important.

Interception rates range from 3 per cent in Nigerian forests to 63 per cent in Thailand teak forests.

Canopy height determines the height and fall velocities of raindrops. This can be greater than unintercepted rainfall.

The amount of leaf litter and understorey vegetation is important, because they protect the soil from rainsplash.

About 2 per cent of rainfall becomes stemflow.

Tropical soils are typically wet for much of the time allowing some erosion by saturated overland flow, especially if there is little leaf litter.

Rainsplash erosion of bare soil.

Litter layer

Saturated overland flow

Rainfall which is not intercepted occurs as throughfall. Experiments in Amazonia show that between 38 and 91 per cent of rainfall becomes throughfall.

Infiltration rates in undisturbed tropical forest soils are usually high. Surface litter rates are over 500 mm/h, and upper horizons have rates between 60 and 150 mm/h.

Available soil moisture storage capacity is often small.

The Maracá Rainforest Project, Brazil

The Ilha de Maracá in northern Brazil (Fig. 3.39) was studied by the Royal Geographical Society (RGS) in 1987 at the invitation of the Brazilian Environment Secretariat. It provided a rare opportunity to study an area of little-disturbed, moist tropical forest. The RGS established experimental plots to investigate the effects of partial and complete forest clearance on hydrological processes (Figs 3.40, 3.41). The soils of the experimental area are coarse-textured and quartzitic, with a thin layer of surface organic matter. Laterite occurs at about 1000–1200 mm. This is exposed at the surface where erosion has occurred. The forest canopy is 20–25 m high, with a large number of understorey palms, especially near stream channels.

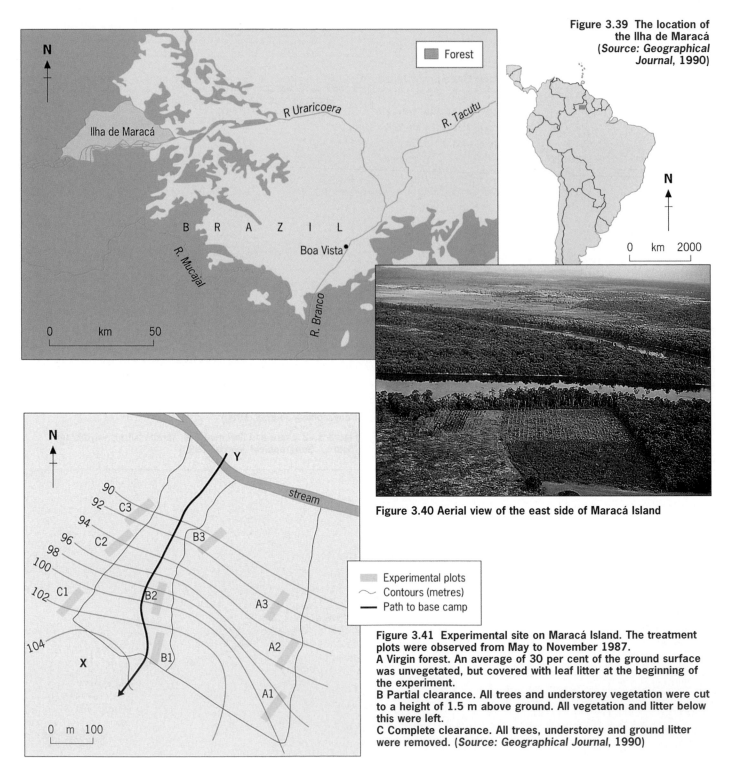

Figure 3.39 The location of the Ilha de Maracá (*Source: Geographical Journal*, 1990)

Forest

Figure 3.40 Aerial view of the east side of Maracá Island

Experimental plots
Contours (metres)
Path to base camp

Figure 3.41 Experimental site on Maracá Island. The treatment plots were observed from May to November 1987.
A Virgin forest. An average of 30 per cent of the ground surface was unvegetated, but covered with leaf litter at the beginning of the experiment.
B Partial clearance. All trees and understorey vegetation were cut to a height of 1.5 m above ground. All vegetation and litter below this were left.
C Complete clearance. All trees, understorey and ground litter were removed. (*Source: Geographical Journal*, 1990)

Throughflow

In the wet season, throughflow on the totally cleared plots was higher than on the partially cleared and uncleared plots (Fig. 3.42). We can partly explain this by the total clearance. However, if this was the only reason, we would expect the totally cleared plots to respond more sensitively to storm events, i.e. show increased throughflow after each rainfall event as water infiltrates the cleared plot, and not respond as in Figure 3.43.

The explanation lies in the linkage of the upper and lower slopes by strong throughflow. Figure 3.44 explains what is happening. Throughflow feeds water to the slope foot (**floodplain**) and keeps moisture high. This offsets the different rates of forest transpiration and excess runoff losses as a result of forest clearance. The cleared plots are like 'windows' in a system dominated by subsurface water movement. The lateritic layer hinders drainage in the wet season, encouraging saturated overland flow.

27 Study Figure 3.41. Draw a cross-section from X to Y.

28 Using Figure 3.43, describe the rate and pattern of throughflow on the three types of plot in response to the dry season rainfall on 15 October.

29a Explain why the three types of plot behave in a similar pattern in the dry season.
b Suggest why the forest plot shows faster soil water movement than the totally cleared plot.

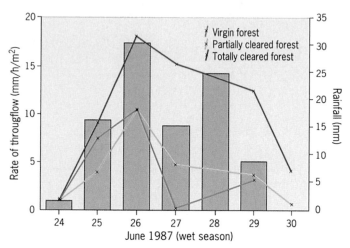

Figure 3.42 Rate of throughflow in the wet season (*Source: Geographical Journal*, 1990)

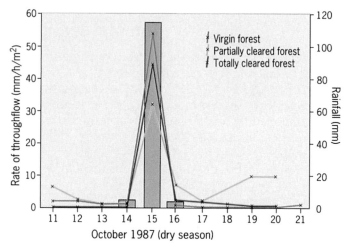

Figure 3.43 Rate of throughflow in the dry season. Soil moisture conditions were monitored using neutron probes. (*Source: Geographical Journal*, 1990)

Figure 3.44 Store and flow model of Maracá hillslope hydrology (*Source: Geographical Journal*, 1990)

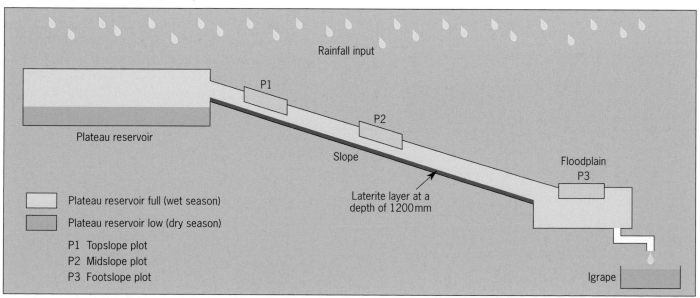

Subsurface processes

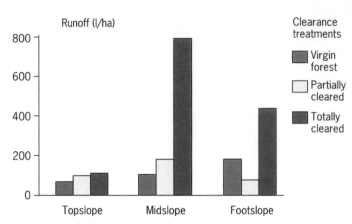

Figure 3.45 Runoff levels for the three plots (*Source: Geographical Journal*, 1990)

?

30a Study Figure 3.42. Compare the responses of the three types of plot to the rainfall inputs in the wet season.
b Why do you think overall soil moisture movement is slower in the wet season than in the dry season?

31 Study Figure 3.43 and 3.44. How does the lateritic layer affect surface and subsurface soil water movement at the study sites?

32 Use Figure 3.45 to compare runoff for the three plots.

33 Draw two annotated diagrams, similar to Figure 3.38, to show the hydrological processes on partially cleared and completely cleared plots.

34 Essay: Evaluate the findings of the work at Ilha de Maracá and their importance for users of tropical forest areas.

3.10 The effects of urbanisation on hydrological processes

Impermeable surfaces

The most obvious change that urbanisation brings to a drainage basin is that it replaces vegetated soils with less permeable surfaces, e.g. tarmac roads (Fig. 3.47). There is less surface storage and less water enters the soil and groundwater stores. The reduced surface water storage and vegetation cover mean lower evapotranspiration outputs. Consequently, the percentage of rainfall that runs off increases.

Figure 3.46 The effects of urbanisation on hydrological processes (*Source:* Hollis, 1988)

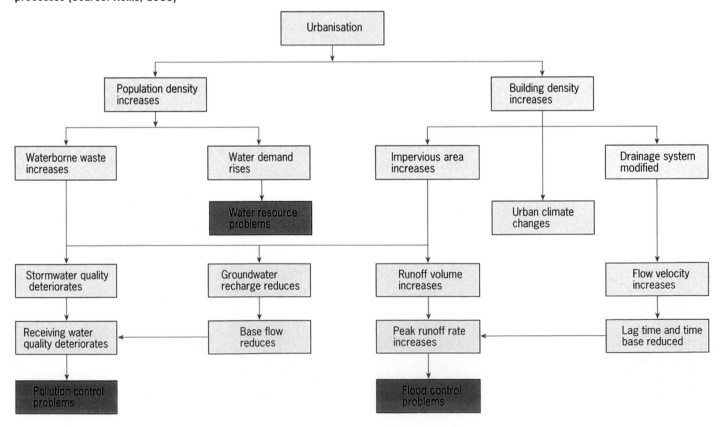

Figure 3.47 In the UK, impermeable surfaces cover 20 per cent of urban areas built after 1945. This rises to 90 per cent in city centres and falls to under 5 per cent in areas of suburban detached housing. Water is moved quickly and efficiently by gutters, drains and sewers. They are designed to be smooth and efficient at transferring water, usually into the nearest river channel

Urban areas are designed to shed water quickly (Fig. 3.47). For example, roads have cambers and gutters to remove surface water and roofs are shaped for rapid shedding of water. However, all surfaces absorb some water and are therefore affected by antecedent moisture conditions. Surfaces have irregularities which store water. Studies in Redbourn, Hertfordshire, show that runoff from roads averages 11.4 per cent and roofs 56.9 per cent. As with all surfaces, runoff will also depend on the amount and intensity of rainfall.

Effects on the storm hydrograph
The urbanised part of a drainage basin responds quickly to a rainfall event. We can identify this in the storm hydrograph which is typically steeper with a shorter lag time (Figs 3.48 and 3.49). The amount of water reaching a river by slow flow processes of throughflow and groundwater flow is reduced. This means that base flow is lower. Water managers have to respond to these changes in the storm hydrograph in order to prevent flooding in the urban area or downstream (see Canon's Brook case study, p. 48).

?

35 Use the processes of quickflow and slowflow to explain the contrasts in storm hydrograph form shown on Figures 3.48 and 3.49.

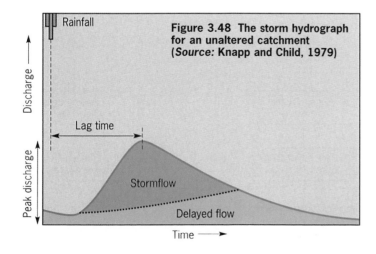

Figure 3.48 The storm hydrograph for an unaltered catchment (*Source:* Knapp and Child, 1979)

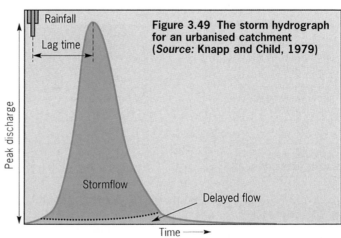

Figure 3.49 The storm hydrograph for an urbanised catchment (*Source:* Knapp and Child, 1979)

The Canon's Brook basin, Harlow, England

Figure 3.50 The Canon's Brook drainage basin is 21.4 km^2 in area, rising from 36.58 to 109.73 m above sea level. The basin is underlain by London Clay with some glacial boulder clay and sand and gravels on the valley floor

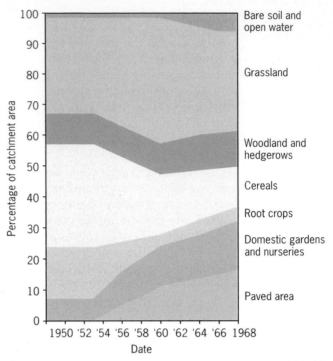

Figure 3.51 The land use of Canon's Brook catchment, 1950–68

Figure 3.52 The changes in the modal, median and quartile flows of the Canon's Brook, water years 1950–68

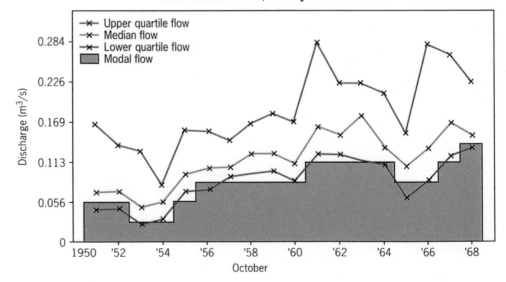

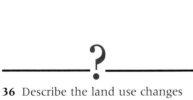

36 Describe the land use changes in the drainage basin shown in Figure 3.51.

37 Study Figure 3.52. Compare the quartile, median and modal flows of the Canon's Brook for 1952, 1960 and 1968.

Building for Harlow New Town began in late 1951 and resulted in the land use changes shown in Figure 3.51. By 1968, 16.6 per cent of the catchment was covered by impermeable surfaces which drained via sewers directly to the Canon's Brook. The changes in the flows of the Brook are shown in Figure 3.52. The rainfall inputs have shown no significant changes and so any changes in streamflow can largely be attributed to the impacts of urbanisation. A 15 per cent paving of the catchment increased runoff by 59.4 mm, i.e. an increase of about 30 per cent above the rural catchment runoff.

Seasonal variations

An interesting finding was in the seasonal variations in the increased runoff (Fig. 3.53). The urbanised catchment produces noticeably higher flows than the simulated rural catchment during the summer months or during relatively dry years. There is also an increased frequency of high flows due to thunderstorms over the developed catchment compared to rural areas.

Urbanisation appears to have little effect on winter flows. The reasons for this are that the urban catchment responds to every rainfall event, because water is quickly shed into the stream. In the rural catchment, summer flows tend to be low as a result of soil moisture storage and higher evapotranspiration losses. Only moderate to heavy rainfall would produce a response in the stream of the simulated rural catchment. Thus, low flows in the summer of 0.028–0.057 m³/s per second for the pre-urban catchment have been replaced by higher flows of 0.100–0.283 m³/s per second in the urbanised catchment. In the winter, the rural catchment's clay soils would be saturated, causing storm rainfall to run off rapidly. This would behave in a similar way to a paved area after building work.

38 Study Figure 3.53.
a In which years is the simulated (rural) flow at its greatest difference from the gauged (urban) flow?
b For the years 1966–68 inclusive, find the amount and time of year with the greatest difference between the simulated rural flow and the gauged urban flow.
c Suggest reasons for the simulated rural flow being greater than the urban flow in late 1965.

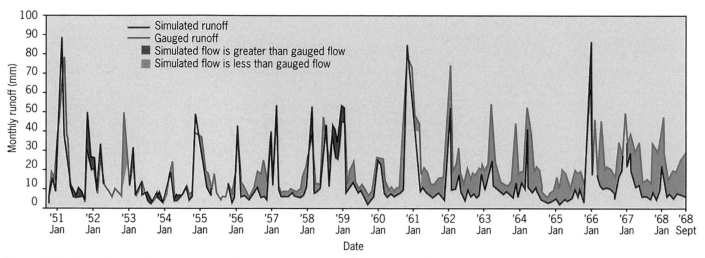

Figure 3.53 Gauged monthly flows from the Canon's Brook, 1950–68, and the simulated flow from a rural version of the catchment

Managing urban hydrological systems

Urban development increases flood frequency by reducing hydrograph lag times and increasing peak discharges. However, since urban water management involves storm drains and sewage systems, their combined effect on flooding is more complex than simply increasing quickflow processes from impermeable surfaces.

River system management includes water storage, **abstractions** and transfer of water for urban supply. Thus, urban areas frequently have inputs of water from outside the drainage basin for public water supply. After use in homes and businesses, it is passed on for treatment in sewage works before being discharged into the urban river. How this management operates has a significant effect upon the discharge and hydrograph downstream. Figure 3.54 sets out four types of management system.

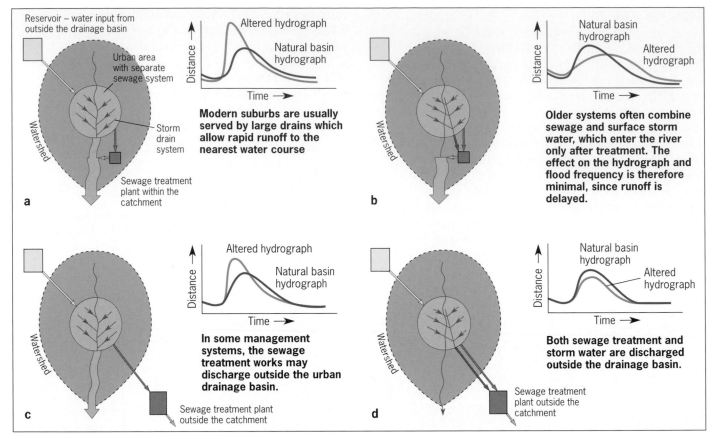

Figure 3.54 Variability of urban hydrological systems in the UK and the implications for changes in flood hydrographs (*Source:* Roberts, 1989)

?

Study Figure 3.54.

39 Construct a table to show the four types of urban hydrological system in the UK under the following headings:

a Type of system (A–D)

b Comments on sewage and storm water management

c Impact on discharge downstream

d Impact on flood hydrograph.

40 For each of the four types of urban water management system, explain the impact on the amount of discharge downstream and on the flood hydrograph.

41 What will be the implication of urban hydrological management on:

a the river that the water is abstracted from?

b the river that the water is discharged into?

42 What factors should be considered when deciding on the water management system in an area of new urban development?

Summary

- The amount of water in a river is expressed as discharge or runoff and consists of two components: base flow and quick (storm) flow.

- Streamflow takes place in response to changes in the status of stores of the drainage basin. Changes in streamflow are shown by hydrographs.

- Rainfall intensity, persistence and periodicity influence the form of the hydrograph.

- Base flow results from slowflow processes, and storm flow from quickflow processes.

- A key quickflow process is saturated overland flow which results from the combined effects of prolonged rainfall inputs and high antecedent soil moisture conditions, high water tables, i.e. water stores are full, and low evapotranspiration outputs.

- Drainage basin characteristics – size, shape, relief, geology, soil, geological structure, stream density and arrangement – have important effects on the nature of the storm hydrographs.

- The porosity and permeability of the soil and rock types in a drainage basin have important impacts on the balance between quickflow and slowflow processes.

- Human activities have major impacts on runoff processes and the nature of the storm hydrograph. The largest effects are produced by agricultural enterprises and changes in land use, e.g. deforestation and urbanisation.

4 Water balance, river regimes and sediment budgets

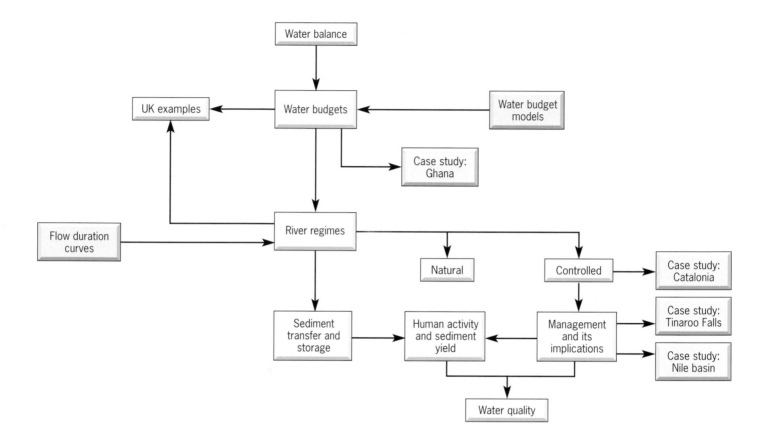

4.1 Introduction

Our study of **hydrographs** in Chapter 3 emphasised that **streamflow** varies constantly – from day to day, from month to month, and from one year to another. None the less, if we examine records over longer periods of time, we find that the main river in any **drainage basin** has, under natural conditions at least, a seasonal rhythm of **discharge**. We call this rhythm the river **regime**. The regime varies in amplitude, but it is always present. It is controlled by the varying availability of water in the drainage basin. This water supply or input is ample in some months, scarce in others. We express this fluctuation in terms of the **water balance** or **budget**.

This chapter examines the relationship between the water balance in a drainage basin and the streamflow regime. This is a particularly important topic, as the rhythms of all life forms, including humans, are influenced by the annual rhythm of water availability.

Figures 4.1 and 4.2 illustrate how water availability varies from season to season within the same environment. Our understanding of the processes affecting the water balance and how to manage water supply effectively is becoming increasingly urgent as global water demands expand. Water resource management modifies the water balance and the river regime. We therefore need to distinguish between natural and controlled balances and regimes.

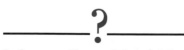

1 Compare Figures 4.1 and 4.2 and describe the implications of seasonal river flow for water availability.

Figure 4.1 The Black Volta River, Ghana, at base flow during the dry season

Figure 4.2 The Black Volta River, Ghana, nearing high flow during the wet season

4.2 The water balance

Streamflow can only occur when the water stores in the drainage basin are capable of releasing water, and when there is direct surface runoff. Thus, in order to understand the pattern of streamflow, or the regime of a river over the year, we need to understand the shifting balance between the three key variables: precipitation; **evapotranspiration**; soil and **groundwater storage**.

This dynamic relationship can be expressed in terms of the water balance equation:

Precipitation (P) = streamflow (Q) + evapotranspiration (E) $\pm$ change in storage (S).

Transposing this in terms of streamflow, it becomes:

$Q = P - E \pm S$.

The water balance concept can be applied at all scales from the global patterns of water deficiency (Fig. 4.3) through comparison between countries (Table 4.1), to individual drainage basins.

Water balance at the drainage basin scale

Within an individual drainage basin we can expect to find a seasonal rhythm in the water balance. This should be reflected in the streamflow regime (Figs 4.1 and 4.2). Remember, the greater the proportion of the precipitation input which is transferred to streams as runoff, the more positive is likely to be the water balance.

2 Use an atlas and Figure 4.3 to relate two arid areas to climate type.

3 Use a map of world population distribution to identify one area in each continent which is likely to have severe water management problems, i.e. both an arid climate and a dense population.

4a On an outline map of Western Europe, present the data in Table 4.1 as located proportional pie graphs. Use the precipitation input for the size of the proportional circles. Use different colours to shade the runoff and evapo-transpiration outputs.
b Describe and explain as fully as you can the variations in the water balance equations over Western Europe.
c Classify the countries of Western Europe into those having a surplus of water, and those with a deficit.

**Table 4.1 The water balance for countries of Western Europe
(*Source*: Marsh and MacRuairi, 1993)**

Country	Precipitation (mm)	Runoff (mm)	Evapotranspiration (mm)
Switzerland	1500	1000	500
Norway	1450	1250	200
Austria	1200	670	530
Great Britain	1090	550	540
Italy	1000	600	400
Portugal	900	220	680
Belgium	850	360	490
France	750	300	450
Germany	750	260	490
Netherlands	750	250	500

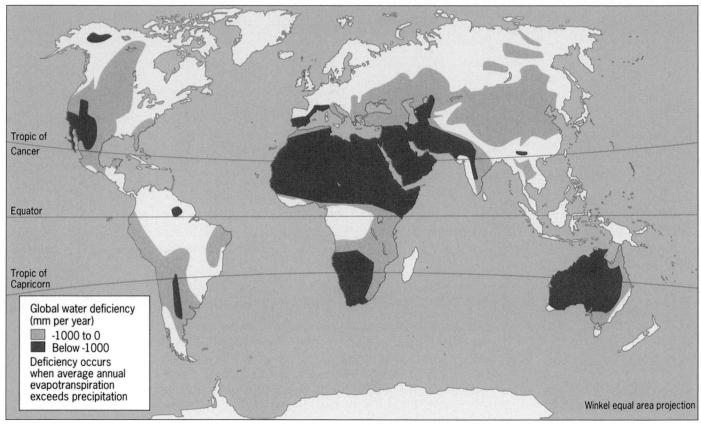

Figure 4.3 Regions of the world with water deficiency under natural conditions (*Source*: Falkenmark, 1977)

The River Thames at Kingston and the River Taw at Umberleigh, Devon, illustrate this seasonal rhythm and the relationship with runoff (Tables 4.2 and 4.3). The fluctuation in water balance is more marked than the seasonal rainfall variation. Thus, in regions with strongly seasonal rainfall we can expect even wider fluctuations in water balance (see Ghana case study, p. 56).

5 Using Tables 4.2 and 4.3, draw line graphs on the same axes to show the percentage of precipitation occurring as runoff for both drainage basins. Show the two lines in different colours and add a title and a key.

6 For the two drainage basins:
a In which month(s) are water losses from the drainage basin highest? Suggest why.
b Suggest how groundwater storage and seepage will affect the runoff figures.

Table 4.2 Rainfall and runoff data for the River Thames at Kingston (*Data source*: National Water Archive, Institute of Hydrology)

Month 1883–1991	Mean precipitation (mm)	Mean runoff (mm)	Mean precipitation as runoff (%)
January	65	37	57
February	49	33	67.3
March	53	31	58.5
April	48	22	45.8
May	54	17	31.5
June	53	13	24.5
July	58	9	15.5
August	63	9	14.3
September	57	9	15.8
October	72	13	18.0
November	72	21	29.2
December	72	30	41.7
Total	716	245	34.2

Location: SE England
Catchment area: 9948 km^2
Maximum altitude: 330 m
Rocks and land use: diverse

Table 4.3 Rainfall and runoff data for the River Taw at Umberleigh
(*Data source*: National Water Archive, Institute of Hydrology)

Month 1953–87	Mean precipitation (mm)	Mean runoff (mm)	Mean precipitation as runoff (%)
January	129	116	89.9
February	84	82	97.6
March	91	67	73.6
April	71	46	64.8
May	73	31	42.5
June	68	17	25.0
July	71	15	21.1
August	87	19	21.8
September	92	24	26.0
October	116	62	53.4
November	130	92	70.8
December	139	119	85.6
Total	1151	690	56.0

Location: SW England
Catchment area: 826.2 km^2
Maximum Altitude: 604 m
Rock and land use: Dartmoor granite and Devonian shales and sandstones/ agriculture
Note: The percentage of precipitation which forms runoff has been calculated using the water balance equation, i.e. $Q = P - E$. It is not possible to calculate short- or long-term groundwater storage with this type of data.

Effects of vegetation on the water balance

We know from Chapter 3 that runoff and, therefore, water balance will be influenced by a number of variables. One important variable is vegetation cover, which affects **interception**, **infiltration**, soil **throughflow** and evapotranspiration.

Table 4.4 Comparison of upper Severn forested area and Wye: the precipitation–runoff difference
(*Source*: Institute of Hydrology)(mm)

Year	Severn forested area Precipitation (P)	Severn forested area Streamflow (Q)	P–Q	Wye P–Q	Forest-Wye Δ (P–Q)
1975	2016	1230	786	413	373
1976	1638	1061	577	378	199
1977	2655	1852	803	413	390
1978	2390	1787	603	341	262
1979	2677	2002	675	367	308
1980	2560	1887	673	300	373
1981	2690	2030	660	350	310
1982	2207	1737	470	325	145
1983	2530	1912	618	399	219
1984	2074	1442	632	320	312
1985	2251	1711	550	258	292
Mean	2336	1695	641	351	290

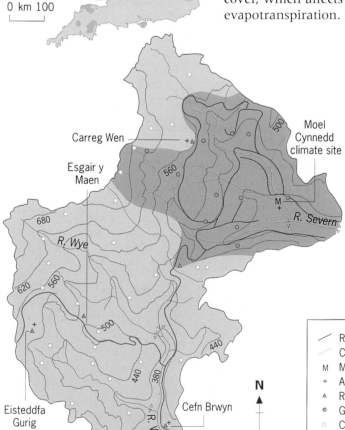

Figure 4.4 The Plynlimon research catchments showing the Rivers Severn and Wye and their tributaries and the main measuring networks
(*Source*: Institute of Hydrology)

?

7 Use your understandings of the way a river drainage basin system works to explain the patterns and relationships revealed by Tables 4.2 and 4.3 and your graphs. Look especially at identifiable seasonal rhythms and the differences between the two basins.

8 Interrogate Table 4.4 to support or reject the hypothesis: 'As both the grassland (upper Wye) and forested (upper Severn) catchments receive similar precipitation totals, the runoff arriving in stream channels will be similar in both catchments.'

For more than 20 years researchers have been comparing two catchments, the upper Wye and Severn on the edges of Plynlimon in upland Wales (Fig. 4.4). One of their objectives has been to discover the effects of afforestation on river regimes and the water balance. Some researchers argue that afforestation improves water storage and produces a steady release of water as soil and groundwater flow to the stream. This reduces seasonality of regime, 'flattens' storm hydrographs, increases lag times and so reduces the likelihood of downstream floods. Other researchers claim that coniferous plantations take up more water than grassland and plagioclimax moorland ecosystems. This moisture is then lost to the drainage basin through transpiration. Thus, although the forest modifies the stream regime and dampens the likelihood of floods, it does not benefit the water balance of the drainage basin.

The upper Wye catchment has a grassland and moorland cover, and the upper Severn catchment has a 62 per cent cover of coniferous forest. Both catchments have a similar mean annual rainfall of around 2400 mm and range in altitude from 370 m to 700 m. The researchers measured 'catchment loss' for the two study areas, i.e. that part of the precipitation input which does not reach the stream. The amount of water moving into the groundwater store was similar for both catchments. So, if vegetation type is an influential factor, then catchment loss should be different in each catchment, i.e. that evapotranspiration is different and is the key variable (Table 4.4).

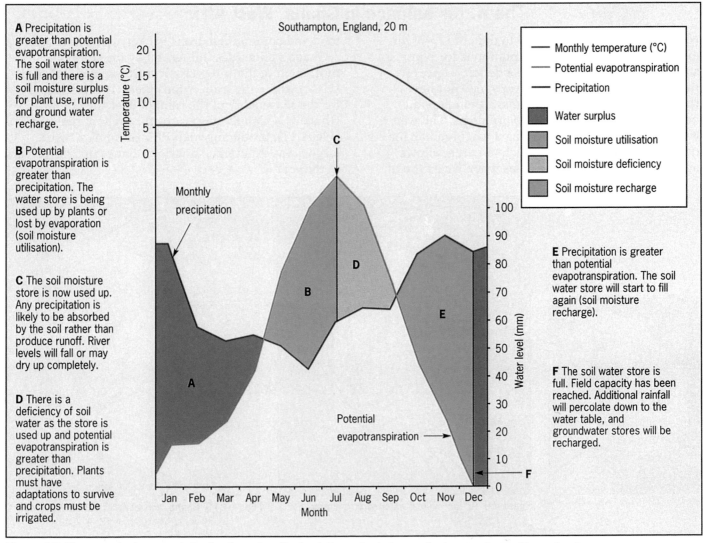

A Precipitation is greater than potential evapotranspiration. The soil water store is full and there is a soil moisture surplus for plant use, runoff and ground water recharge.

B Potential evapotranspiration is greater than precipitation. The water store is being used up by plants or lost by evaporation (soil moisture utilisation).

C The soil moisture store is now used up. Any precipitation is likely to be absorbed by the soil rather than produce runoff. River levels will fall or may dry up completely.

D There is a deficiency of soil water as the store is used up and potential evapotranspiration is greater than precipitation. Plants must have adaptations to survive and crops must be irrigated.

E Precipitation is greater than potential evapotranspiration. The soil water store will start to fill again (soil moisture recharge).

F The soil water store is full. Field capacity has been reached. Additional rainfall will percolate down to the water table, and groundwater stores will be recharged.

Southampton, England, 20 m

— Monthly temperature (°C)
— Potential evapotranspiration
— Precipitation

Water surplus
Soil moisture utilisation
Soil moisture deficiency
Soil moisture recharge

Figure 4.5 The water budget graph for Southampton, England: the water balance of a temperate maritime climate

Study Figures 4.5, 4.6 and 4.7.

9 Describe the yearly pattern of the balance between temperature, precipitation and PET for the three climatic areas.

10 Suggest why the soil moisture surplus is greater for England than Bolivia, even though the precipitation input is smaller.

11 Which area(s) would require irrigation water for crops which continue to grow from year to year (perennial agriculture)?

The research found that the forested catchment loses more water by evapotranspiration. Grassland returns about 16 per cent of the precipitation input to the atmosphere by **evaporation,** almost all as **transpiration** from the vegetation. In the forested catchment, evapotranspiration accounts for 30 per cent. The vital finding is that 25 per cent of all precipitation is lost from the forested area by evaporation of water which has been intercepted by the trees. Only 5 per cent is transpired from the stomata.

Water budget models
A useful way of investigating the water balance of a location over the year is by plotting temperature, precipitation and evapotranspiration rates on to a single graph to show the balance between them. These water budget graphs (Fig. 4.5) look quite complicated at first glance, but remember that they are only line graphs shown together. They can be used to compare climate types (Figs 4.5, 4.6, 4.7) and to identify water resource management issues.

Water budget graphs usually show potential evapotranspiration (PET), i.e. the amount of water which would evaporate if an adequate supply was continuously available to the covering vegetation. Actual evapotranspiration (AET) will be less than this.

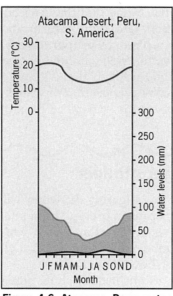

Figure 4.6 Atacama, Peru: water balance of a desert climate

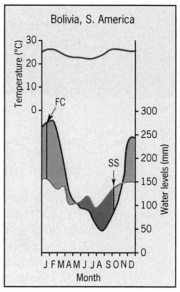

Figure 4.7 Bolivia: water balance of a tropical forest climate

The water balance in Ghana, West Africa

Natural vegetation is adapted to the climate of an area. One purpose of this adaptation is for plants to survive periods of soil moisture deficit. However, many food and commercial crops may not have suitable adaptative mechanisms, although plant breeding tries to minimise the problems. The water balance model, as well as being a useful model for understanding runoff patterns in an area, allows agriculturalists to identify times when irrigation of food and commercial crops is likely to be necessary.

Ghana's climate is influenced by the seasonal movement of the Inter-Tropical Convergence Zone (ITCZ) where the trade winds meet. It is responsible for the seasonality of the rainfall over the country. Ghana has high temperatures throughout the year, producing high PET rates. As a result, large areas experience a water balance deficit for part of the year (Figs 4.8, 4.9, 4.10).

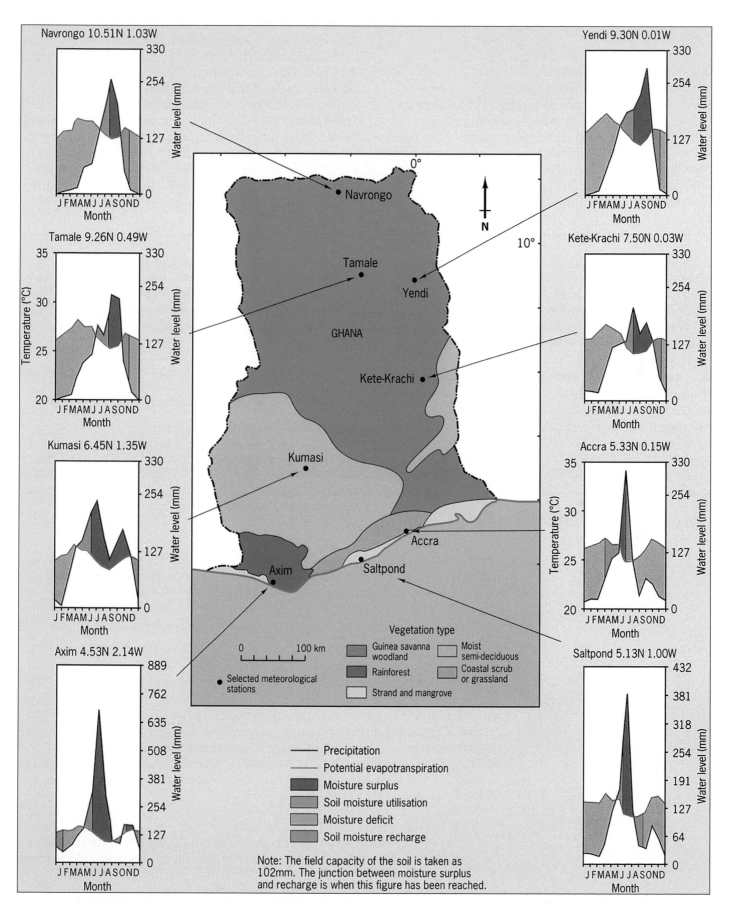

Figure 4.8 Ghana: vegetation and water budgets for selected locations, 1961–70

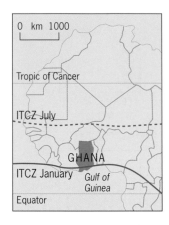

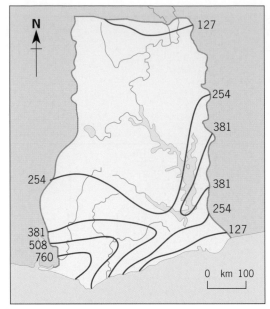

Figure 4.9 Ghana: wet season water surplus in mm

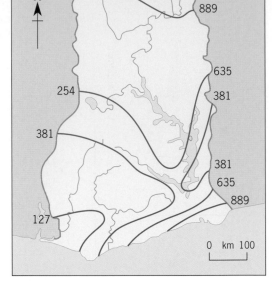

Figure 4.10 Ghana: dry season water deficiency in mm

Soil moisture conditions

PET rates are low in the wet season, but more than double in the dry season. As the PET rises following the wet season, soil moisture is used up rapidly, leading to a desiccated state, particularly in the north and south-east. Any rainfall is quickly evaporated during these drier months. The AET rates will depend upon the amount of water available for evaporation and the transpiration rates of the vegetation type in the area.

In the north and east of Ghana, the savanna dies down as the **soil moisture deficit** increases.

The **field capacity** of the soils in Ghana is taken as 102 mm. Once this amount of water has been absorbed, as **soil moisture recharge**, the soils will have a **soil moisture surplus**. Surface runoff and infiltration to the subsoil and groundwater stores will occur. After the rainy season, soil moisture take-up by plants or evaporation of at least 102 mm will result in a soil moisture deficit. The areas of maximum aridity or water deficiency occur in the north and along the east coast.

12 A wet month in Ghana is defined as when rainfall is 102 mm or more, and is over and above the PET for that same month. Using Figure 4.8, compare the duration of the wet season at: • Axim, • Accra, • Tamale, • Navrongo.

13 For Axim, Accra, Kumasi and Navrongo, give a precise comparison of the water balance. Explain any differences that you find.

14 Relate the vegetation types at Axim, Kumasi and Navrongo to the water budgets of the area (Use Figs 4.8, 4.9, 4.10).

15 Draw the expected river regime graph for a river starting at Yendi. Put time on the x axis and discharge on the y axis. No figures are needed; it is the pattern of flow over the year that you need to show.

16 On an outline map of Ghana, divide the country into three areas:
• areas needing little or no irrigation
• areas needing irrigation for three months of the year or less
• areas needing irrigation for over three months.

4.3 River regimes

The river regime is controlled by fluctuations in the water balance equation and the changing contributions from **quickflow** and **slowflow processes**. Each drainage basin produces its unique streamflow regime, but the rhythms can be grouped into three types according to their flow duration: ephemeral; intermittent; perennial.

Ephemeral streams

Ephemeral streams are found in arid and semi-arid environments with permanent moisture budget deficits (Fig. 4.6). Streamflow occurs irregularly for short episodes, and the stream channel, often poorly defined, is dry for long periods (Fig. 4.11). Precipitation inputs arrive in localised, occasional, sudden downpours. Vegetation cover is sparse and, as a result, rainfall interception is minimal. Thus, when rainfall intensity exceeds the infiltration capacity of the surface materials, quickflow processes, e.g. **overland flow**, deliver water directly to the channel.

The result is a 'flash flood' which flows in a rapid surge downstream (Fig. 4.12). Streamflow may only last a few hours after the rain ceases. Because the water input is short-lived, the discharge declines rapidly downstream as water infiltrates the channel bed to recharge the soil and groundwater stores. For example, in the 150 km^2 of the Walnut Gulch catchment in Arizona, USA, only 15 per cent of the runoff entering the channel actually leaves the drainage basin.

Figure 4.11 Armagosa Valley, California. Sparse vegetation indicates the line of poorly defined channel bed

Figure 4.12 Armagosa River, flash flooding the day after a thunderstorm over the surrounding mountains. Twenty four hours later the stream bed was dry again.

Intermittent streams

Intermittent streams are seasonal streams. They are characteristic of climates with well-defined wet and dry periods and strong seasonal contrasts in the water balance, e.g. monsoon, tropical savanna (Fig. 4.8) and Mediterranean climates. During the wet season there is a water budget surplus, and quickflow and slowflow processes combine to give high flows. When the rains end, quickflow processes cease. As the water balance graphs indicate, slowflow processes from the soil and groundwater stores sustain flows during the early part of the dry season. Eventually, however, this supply ends and the streams dry up. Except during rare 'freak' storms, any rain falling during the dry season is likely to remain in the drainage basin as recharge to the soil and ground-water stores.

In years, or series of years, with above average rainfall, streams flow longer into the dry season and may maintain some discharge all year. In contrast, during dry years flows may be brief. This variability has serious implications for animals and for human communities. For example, most stream networks of Africa's Sahel are intermittent. During the great drought of 1968–73, streamflow shrank in extent and duration. Also, recharge of the soil and groundwater stores was reduced.

A Uniform regime

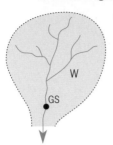

Environmental conditions, including climate, are consistent across the drainage basin (W). The regime, as recorded by the hydrograph at the gauging station (GS), reflects this simple pattern. A uniform regime is typical of small drainage basins.

B Dual regime

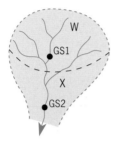

The headwater catchment (W) has different conditions, including precipitation inputs, from the lower basin (X). The regime is determined by the environment at W, and the dominant pattern is given by the hydrograph of gauging station GS1. As the river crosses X, the regime is modified. The hydrograph at GS2 will be a modified version of that at GS1.

C Complex regime

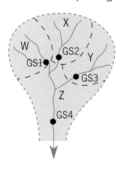

The headwater catchments extend across several environments with different precipitation inputs (W, X and Y). Each of the gauging stations in the upper basin (GS1, 2 and 3) produces a distinct hydrograph. The regime recorded by the hydrograph of GS4 will reflect elements of each of the upper catchment discharge regimes. The complex regime is typical of large drainage basins.

Figure 4.13 A model of regime classification

Perennial streams

Perennial streams are permanent streams. They flow throughout the year, even where there is a period of lower precipitation and moisture deficit. Thus, although quickflow processes may cease, slow flow from the groundwater store is sufficient to sustain **base flow**. For example, major rivers in Britain maintain baseflow discharge even during summer droughts.

In many drainage basins there may be streams of more than one category. In the chalk catchments of southern England, headwater stretches may be intermittent as the **water table** rises and falls. Downstream, the streams become permanent due to the water table level and the groundwater zone which feeds the channel (see Chapter 8).

Simple and complex river regimes

The natural regime of a river is controlled by the environmental conditions of the drainage basin, especially the precipitation inputs. As each drainage basin is unique, so the regime, as recorded by the hydrograph, is unique. Within this diversity two classes of regime have been identified: simple and complex. A generalised model of this classification is set out in Figure 4.13.

Simple regimes

Simple river regimes are divided into distinct periods of high and low flow. Water inputs are delivered from a headwater catchment of a single environmental type. The simplest pattern, called the **uniform regime**, occurs typically in small river basins, such as those draining from Exmoor to the north Devon coast. Even some larger rivers, such as the Volga in the Russian Federation (Fig. 4.14), whose regime is strongly influenced by severe winters followed by snowmelt across the majority of the basin, show these simple rhythms.

Other rivers may be glacier and snowmelt-fed in their headwater catchments, e.g. the River Rhône in France (Fig. 4.14). However, their lower basins may lie in quite different environments, and the regimes are progressively modified towards the river mouths. These are defined as **dual regimes**.

Complex regimes

Large river basins are likely to include headwater catchments with different runoff patterns and stream regimes. Each imposes a distinct discharge rhythm upon the main river. The result is a complex regime which shows the influences of several headwater catchments. Furthermore, there is progressive change as a river crosses its lower basin. The Nile and Mississippi both have complex regimes.

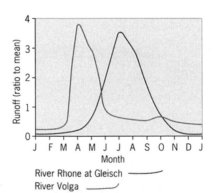

Figure 4.14 Simple regime of the River Volga (plains snowmelt) and River Rhône (glacier melt) (*Source*: Ward and Robinson, 1990)

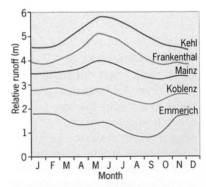

Figure 4.15 The complex regime of the River Rhine, Europe (*Source*: Ward and Robinson, 1990)

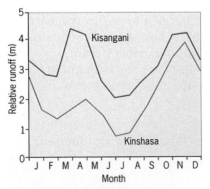

Figure 4.16 The complex regime of the River Zaire, Africa (*Source*: Ward and Robinson, 1990)

Figures 4.17 to 4.20 European river regimes (*Source*: Institute of Hydrology)

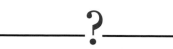

17 Using Figures 4.17 to 4.20, list the river regimes which show: • the most • the least variation from the mean flow. Suggest reasons for your answer in each case.

18 Match the four regime hydrographs in Figures 4.17 to 4.20 to the following descriptions, giving reasons for your answer in each case:

a west coast, temperate oceanic climate

b glacier melt, mountain climate

c Mediterranean climate, river with intermittent flow

d Mediterranean climate with semi-permanent flow.

19 For each of the regimes in Figures 4.17 to 4.20, state whether it is simple, dual or complex.

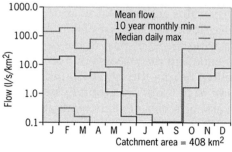

Figure 4.17 R. Vascão, Portugal

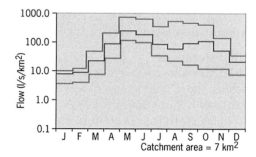

Figure 4.18 R. Roggiasca, Switzerland

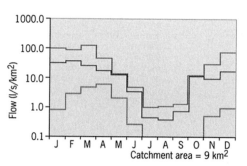

Figure 4.19 R. Valescure, France

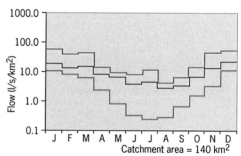

Figure 4.20 R. Wold, Netherlands

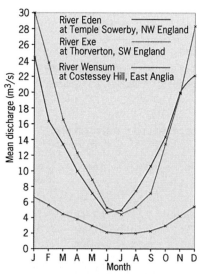

Figure 4.21 Annual discharge regimes for three English rivers: the Eden, Exe and Wensum (*Source*: Goudie, 1990)

In Europe, the Rhine (Fig. 4.15) is fed by glaciers and snowmelt in its upper catchment, to give early summer peak flows. Downstream it receives tributaries which are increasingly influenced by temperate oceanic climates. These produce low flows during the summer, e.g. the River Mosel, France. Thus, by Emmerlich at the Dutch border, the meltwater input from upstream gives the Rhine a secondary summer peak.

In equatorial Africa, the River Zaire (Congo) has a complex regime produced by the distinct climates of the northern and southern hemisphere. The river at Kisangani shows the double peak regime which reflects the equatorial rainfall pattern (Fig. 4.16). However, large parts of its headwater catchments lie in the southern hemisphere, with December rainfall maxima. This complicates the regime downstream at Kinshasa. Although Kinshasa is in the northern hemisphere, the river regime shows the influence of the southern hemisphere tributaries.

4.4 British river regimes

British rivers are small by world and even European standards and, as with all rivers, they show variability of flow (Fig. 4.21). Most have simple regimes. However, some rivers in the north and west of the UK show more complex regimes due to spring snowmelt or reduced summer evapotranspiration. Periods of maximum runoff show a tendency to come later in the year towards the south and east of the UK (Figs 4.22 and 4.23). This is due to the differences in evaporation patterns, but also the nature of the rocks. In the north and west the rocks are mainly older, impermeable metamorphic and igneous rocks which will encourage more quickflow processes. The south and east are dominated by younger, permeable sedimentary rocks which release water slowly into the channel from the groundwater store. Remember that the regimes and patterns shown in Figs 4.21, 4.22 and 4.23 are mean values based on long-term data, and that flow regimes vary from year to year (Table 4.5).

?

20 Figure 4.21 shows the discharge regimes for three rivers in different parts of England.
a Suggest reasons why the Eden and the Exe show a more varied discharge over the year than the Wensum.
b Explain how these river regimes support the work of Ward and Robinson in Figures 4.22 and 4.23.

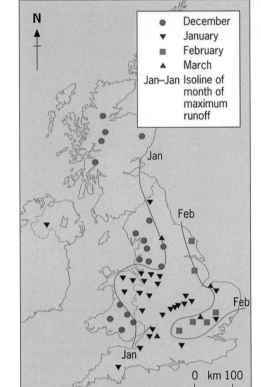

Figure 4.22 The UK: month of maximum runoff (*Source*: Ward and Robinson, 1990)

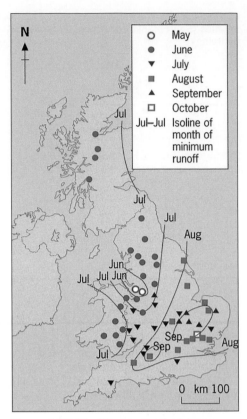

Figure 4.23 The UK: month of minimum runoff (*Source*: Ward and Robinson, 1990)

Table 4.5 River Taw, Umberleigh, England: mean monthly discharge data (m³/s) for 1980–7
(*Data source*: National Water Archive, Institute of Hydrology)

Month	1980	1981	1982	1983	1984	1985	1986	1987	Mean	Min.	Max.	Standard deviation
Jan	28.18	29.83	40.86	48.92	62.10	26.03	42.73	20.00	?	20.00	62.10	13.03
Feb	43.82	16.86	18.54	19.18	36.47	19.95	7.16	19.45	22.68	7.16	43.82	10.95
Mar	27.45	52.14	42.17	14.44	7.45	15.65	15.19	27.28	25.22	7.45	52.14	14.34
Apr	14.49	7.78	6.04	17.89	5.48	25.02	24.08	28.85	16.20	5.46	28.85	?
May	2.42	19.55	2.46	37.00	2.26	3.56	13.28	3.58	10.51	2.26	37.00	11.65
Jun	9.84	9.11	2.72	4.47	1.33	5.99	9.54	5.09	6.01	1.33	9.84	3.02
Jul	8.79	2.75	8.56	1.65	0.79	3.97	3.31	3.59	?	0.79	8.79	2.77
Aug	5.63	2.21	2.59	0.84	0.80	19.13	18.01	1.74	6.37	0.80	19.13	7.19
Sep	11.43	9.80	4.28	3.25	3.59	9.62	7.91	1.81	6.47	1.81	11.43	3.43
Oct	40.53	47.73	24.26	14.98	20.64	9.49	19.15	32.38	26.14	9.49	47.73	?
Nov	28.95	24.21	52.83	11.13	49.39	6.64	54.32	34.17	32.71	6.64	54.32	17.25
Dec	33.35	46.35	55.45	46.91	37.38	36.83	47.04	15.96	?	15.96	55.45	11.26
Year mean	21.17	22.52	21.81	18.48	18.92	15.15	21.91	16.12	19.51	15.15	22.52	2.62

Flow duration curves

A useful way of showing the variation in flow of a river is the **flow duration curve** (Figs 4.24 and 4.25). This shows the percentage of time that a given discharge is exceeded, or the probability of the river having a certain discharge. Flow duration curves which are steeply sloping throughout show highly variable flows due to the importance of quickflow processes, e.g. the Rivers Tees and Tamar. Rivers which have gently sloping curves, e.g. the Rivers Ver and Wharfe, are largely fed by base flow and respond more slowly to rainfall inputs.

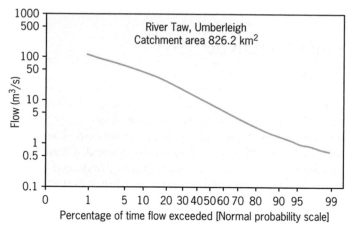

Figure 4.24 Flow duration curve for River Taw, Umberleigh

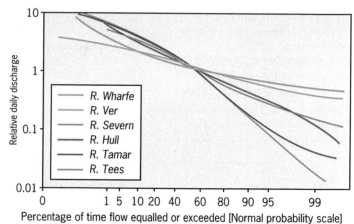

Figure 4.25 Flow duration curves for six British rivers (*Source*: Ward and Robinson, 1990)

?

21 Study Figure 4.24. Notice that the graph has a logarithmic scale on both axes.
a For the River Taw, what is the probability of a discharge of:
• 1.0 m³/s? • 10 m³/s? • 80 m³/s?
b What is the discharge exceeded for:
• 90 per cent of the time? • 20 per cent of the time?

22 Standard deviation is a measure of the dispersal of the discharges for each month around the mean for that month. The larger the standard deviation, the more variable the discharge data for that month. The smaller the standard deviation, the less variation there is around the mean.
a Complete Table 4.5.

b Using your data:
• Draw a hydrograph of river flow to show the characteristic regime. Plot line graphs in different colours on the same axes for mean, minimum and maximum figures for each month.
• Present the standard deviation figures as a bar graph on the same piece of graph paper and with the months on the same scale as your hydrographs.
c Interpret the data as fully as possible. Include flow pattern over the year, months of high and low discharges and months when discharge variation is smallest and greatest from the mean.
d What factors could explain the patterns you have described in **c**?

Water resource problems in Catalonia, Spain

Catalonia in north-east Spain (Fig. 4.26) is a popular holiday destination. It is also a thriving agricultural and industrial region, centring on Barcelona (population two million; 42 per cent of Catalonia's total). Urban and industrial water demands are not specifically seasonal, but agriculture and tourism have strong summer demand peaks. May to September is the period of water budget deficits, minimal runoff and base flow discharges. So, if we are lucky enough to be enjoying a Mediterranean holiday in Catalonia and to relax in a leisurely shower or bath after a long day in the sun, we are consuming a scarce resource.

The Mediterranean climate in this region gives hot, dry summers, with spring and autumn rainfall maxima (Fig. 4.27). The general rhythm of river regimes follows this pattern, with summer minima and floods most likely in early spring. However, the individual drainage basin regimes in Catalonia vary widely (Fig. 4.28). This is a reflection of the climatic differences, influenced by the physical geography of the region. For instance, if we compare the physical and climatic maps (Figs 4.26 and 4.28) we can see that the higher precipitation totals of over 1000 mm. in the north are explained by the presence of the Pyrenees mountains. The Lerida basin in the west lies in the rainshadow of the coast ranges and so has rainfall totals of less than 400 mm.

Equally important in determining the river regimes is the low proportion of the precipitation inputs which becomes runoff. For example, even in the cooler, wetter north, only 38 per cent of the rainfall reaches the river channels. The figures then decline southwards, as evapotranspiration rates increase. Varying amounts of rainfall enter the groundwater store.

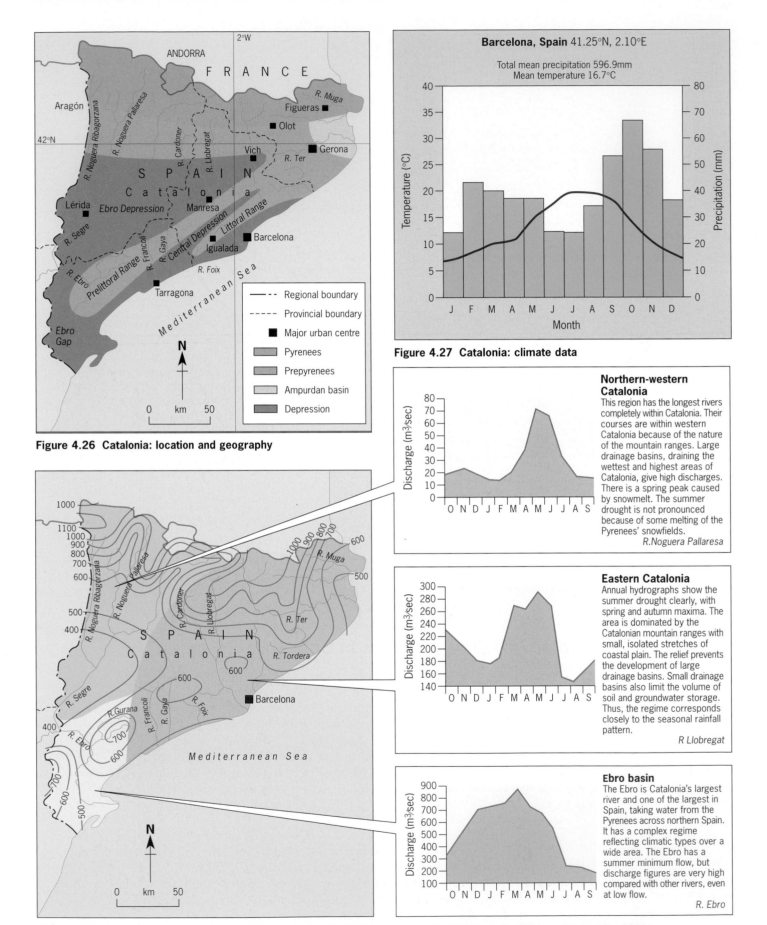

Figure 4.26 Catalonia: location and geography

Barcelona, Spain 41.25°N, 2.10°E

Total mean precipitation 596.9mm
Mean temperature 16.7°C

Figure 4.27 Catalonia: climate data

Northern-western Catalonia
This region has the longest rivers completely within Catalonia. Their courses are within western Catalonia because of the nature of the mountain ranges. Large drainage basins, draining the wettest and highest areas of Catalonia, give high discharges. There is a spring peak caused by snowmelt. The summer drought is not pronounced because of some melting of the Pyrenees' snowfields.

R.Noguera Pallaresa

Eastern Catalonia
Annual hydrographs show the summer drought clearly, with spring and autumn maxima. The area is dominated by the Catalonian mountain ranges with small, isolated stretches of coastal plain. The relief prevents the development of large drainage basins. Small drainage basins also limit the volume of soil and groundwater storage. Thus, the regime corresponds closely to the seasonal rainfall pattern.

R Llobregat

Ebro basin
The Ebro is Catalonia's largest river and one of the largest in Spain, taking water from the Pyrenees across northern Spain. It has a complex regime reflecting climatic types over a wide area. The Ebro has a summer minimum flow, but discharge figures are very high compared with other rivers, even at low flow.

R. Ebro

Figure 4.28 Catalonia: the geography and flow regimes of selected rivers, and rainfall in mm (*Source: Geography*, 1988)

Demand–supply issues

Water availability in Catalonia, therefore, varies spatially. The crucial issue for water resource managers is that the geographical distribution of demand is not well matched with this potential supply (Fig. 4.30). Water for industrial, domestic and agricultural use comes from two main sources: rivers and their reservoirs, and the groundwater stores. Reservoirs are used to store spring and autumn high river flows. A conflict exists in this storage policy. Many reservoirs are primarily for hydro-electric power (HEP) generation which supplies 21 per cent of Catalonia's electricity needs. HEP requires a constant high head of water to drive the turbines. Thus, the reservoirs cannot be drawn down too low during the shortage periods of summer drought (Fig. 4.29).

To overcome the shortfall, several small-scale inter-basin transfer schemes have been built. However, these are inadequate and groundwater stores are increasingly used. Fortunately, the major river valleys in the east contain up to 200 m of Pleistocene sands and gravels. These unconsolidated **sediments** are highly permeable, creating useful **aquifers** (see Chapter 7). Winter recharge of the aquifers becomes available for summer **abstraction**. In addition, the local geology of limestones and sandstones provides useful aquifers which people draw upon for agriculture in particular.

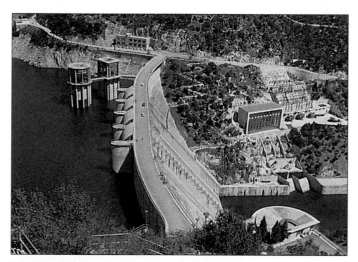

Figure 4.29 HEP generation in Catalonia

?

23 From Figures 4.26 and 4.28, describe the relationship between physical geography, rainfall and river regimes.

24 Use Figure 4.30 to analyse the variations in water demand–supply relationships.

25 Assess the role of surface and groundwater stores in present and future water resources policies for Catalonia.

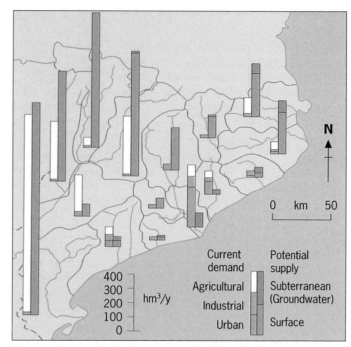

Figure 4.30 Catalonia: the geographical distribution of water demand and potential supply. The region is divided into drainage basins, with a pair of bar graphs for each (*Source: Geography, 1988*)

The regional plan for future supply relies heavily on large-scale water transfer schemes, e.g. the Segre–Tarragona Canal and the Ebro Pirineo Aqueduct, being developed to supply southern Catalonia (Fig. 4.31). Both draw on mountain catchments with relatively high precipitation totals.

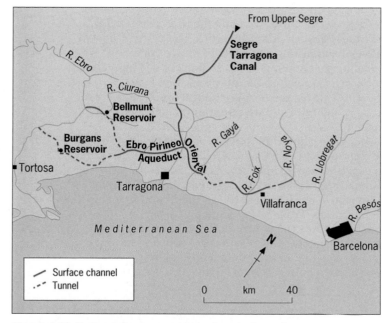

Figure 4.31 Proposed water transfer schemes in southern Catalonia (*Source: Geography, 1988*)

26 Study Table 4.6.
a Which two water regions in England and Wales have the highest and lowest amount of water abstraction?
b Suggest reasons for the amount and type of abstraction.

4.5 River regimes and human activity

Water is abstracted from rivers for domestic consumption, industrial and irrigation purposes (Table 4.6). The reasons for water abstraction will vary according to country and region depending upon climatic conditions, irrigation demands and the level of economic activity, especially urban and industrial development. Continually increasing demands upon a finite resource inevitably create problems (see Catalonia case study p.63).

Abstraction for urban use will alter the regime of a river, because, although much of the water is returned via sewerage systems, the amount and timing of the return may be different to the natural regime. The sources of water may be

Table 4.6 Abstraction from surface water and groundwater by purpose and region in England and Wales, 1990 (megalitres/day) (*Source*: Newson, 1992)

Region	Piped mains water	Agriculture	Industry Electricity generating companies	Industry Other	Abstraction of surface water	Abstraction of groundwater	Total
Anglian	1 928	231	2	295	1 365	1 091	2 456
Northumbria	1 060	1	–	38	1 037	61	1 098
North West	1 883	8	161	734	2 457	330	2 787
Severn-Trent	2 421	77	2 991	451	4 914	1 026	5 940
Southern	1 621	38	–	1 184	1 500	1 343	2 843
South West	630	35	210	28	955	48	1 003
Thames	3 827	26	111	167	2 594	1 537	4 131
Welsh	2 671	18	8 475	310	11 393	81	11 474
Wessex	798	32	–	137	546	421	967
Yorkshire	1 498	39	662	351	2 184	367	2 551
England and Wales	18 336	507	12 612	3 795	28 945	6 305	35 250

remote from and outside the drainage basin of the areas of actual use (see Chapter 7). Yet sewerage systems discharge into the nearest river. The net result is a transfer of water between drainage basins (see Chapter 9). Up to 34 per cent of the flow volume of the River Trent in England during average conditions is provided from sewerage rather than natural sources. Some of this input may have originated in other basins. Because of evapotranspiration losses, a smaller proportion of the water abstracted for agricultural use is returned to the river.

Abstractions of river water have significant impacts on levels of lakes along their courses or at their mouths. The world's largest lake, the Caspian Sea in central Asia, has fallen almost 4 m since 1929. Human usage, especially along the R. Volga, the major supplier to the Caspian, accounts for much of this fall. Also in central Asia, the Aral Sea has endured a dramatic fall and a fourfold increase in **salinity** since water was abstracted from its two main feeder rivers – the Amu Darya and Syr Darya – for massive irrigation schemes in this arid environment (Fig. 4.32). Water is lost from the system by evapotranspiration during irrigation. The reduced return flow from the irrigated soils has a progressively higher salt content. In most years the rivers no longer reach the Aral Sea and the sea is shrinking rapidly (Fig. 4.33). Any water inputs are so saline that the aquatic ecosystem has collapsed, the fish and the once prosperous fishing industry have disappeared (Fig. 4.34).

27 Use Table 4.6 to describe the main purposes of water abstractions and identify any regional variations. How can these be explained?

28 Study Figure 4.37.
a For discharges of 0.116 Ml/d and 1.16 Ml/d, compare the pre- and post-dam occurrences.
b What are the pre-dam and post-dam discharges which were equalled or exceeded for:
• 1 per cent of the time?
• 50 per cent of the time?
• 95 per cent of the time?
c Describe how the dam has changed the flow pattern for low, medium and high flows.

29 Describe the growth of world dam construction shown in Figure 4.35.

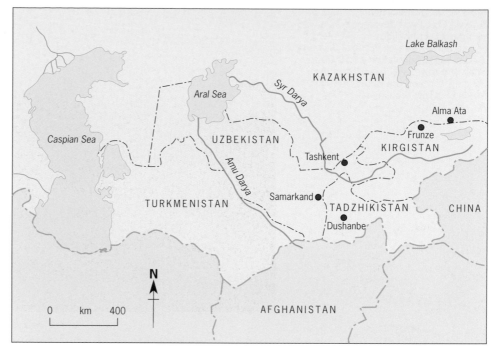

Figure 4.32 Location of the Aral Sea

The impacts of dam construction

The second half of the twentieth century saw a rapid worldwide expansion of **dam** construction, encouraged by growth in water and energy demands and the advance of technology (Fig. 4.35). By 1990 there were approximately 37 000 dams over 15 m in height in the world, with at least a further 1000 under construction. Dams may have a specific purpose, e.g. water storage, HEP, flood control, navigation; or they may be multi-purpose, involving all or some of these.

Building a dam has impacts both above and below the structure. The primary upstream impact is flooding of the valley by the impounded reservoir, which in turn creates a new local base-level. We can analyse the downstream impacts in terms of a hierarchy as the river seeks a new equilibrium:
1st order: Changes to discharge regime and sediment load
2nd order: Adjustments to channel morphology
3rd order: Ecological adaptation.

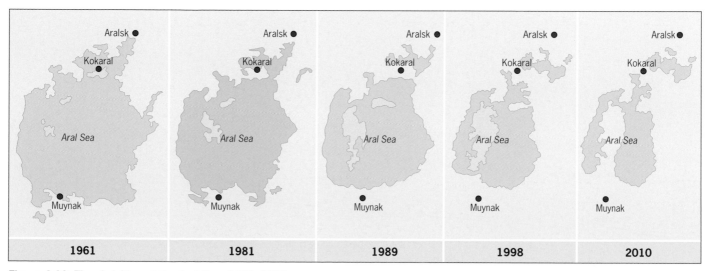

Figure 4.33 The shrinking of the Aral Sea, 1961–2010

Figure 4.34 Derelict fishing boats at Muynak. This town developed as a fishing port and holiday resort along the southern shore of the Aral Sea. In 1970 it had a population of 40 000. Today, the town is 100 km from the receding sea and the population has shrunk to a few thousands.

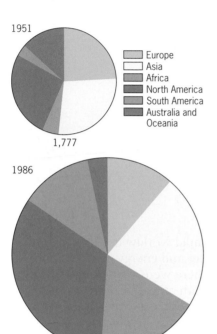

1951

1,777

1986

4,982

Figure 4.35 Growth of reservoirs, by continent, 1951,1986 (*Source*: Newson, 1998)

Changes to discharge and regime are immediate. In general, mean flows decrease. For example, the mean annual flow of the R. Waiau in South Island, New Zealand fell from 560 m³/s to 140 m³/s following the completion of the Manapouri Dam in 1969 (Fig 4.36). Not all controlled rivers suffer such severe impacts, as the flow duration curves for the Cudgegong River, New South Wales, Australia show, following the completion of the Windamere Dam in 1984 (Fig. 4.37). Two common features of controlled rivers are the reduction in high flood discharges and a reduced variability of flow from year-to-year. Thus, as we can see, along the Cudgegong River, flows above 30 million litres/day are less common since the operation of the dam, and flood magnitudes downstream have been reduced by 57 to 72 per cent. However, every dam and reservoir system has its storage capacity and uncontrolled releases do occur in extreme conditions, e.g. the 1983 floods along the R. Colorado, USA were caused by snowmelt flood surges overwhelming the storage capacity of the series of reservoirs along this great river; the scale of the catastrophic 1993

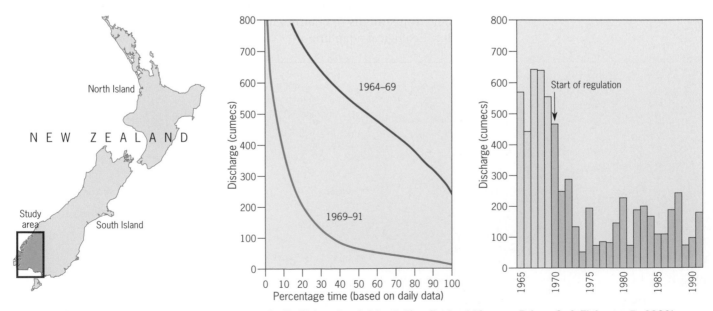

Figure 4.36 The impact of the Manapouri dam on the R. Waiau, South Island, New Zealand (*Source*: Brizga S. & Finlayson B. 2000)

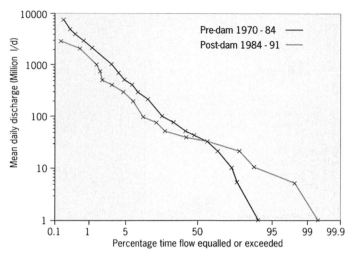

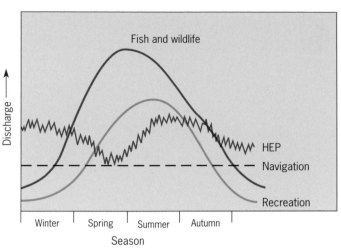

Figure 4.37 Cudgegong River, New South Wales, Australia: flow duration curves downstream of the Windamere Dam (*Source*: Benn and Erskine, 1994)

Figure 4.38 The regime requirements for different uses (Source: Newson, 1992)

30 Suggest which physical and human factors will affect the number of dams built in a region. (Think in terms of the dam site, economic development and the reasons for dam construction.)

Mississippi floods was due in part to uncontrolled releases through dams in the upper basin. Thus, occasional high magnitude floods, i.e. floods with a long recurrence period, are likely (see Tinaroo Falls Dam case study, p. 69).

The rhythm of regulated releases and hence the discharge regime may be determined by the purpose of releases (Fig 4.38). As a result, there may be tensions between the needs of different uses in multi-purpose schemes. For instance, the primary function of the Clwyedog dam and Llyn Clwyedog reservoir along the upper R. Severn in Wales is water storage and so releases to sustain river flows downstream during dry spells are restricted to 1 per cent of the reservoir capacity.

The Tinaroo Falls Dam, Australia

The scheme

The Tinaroo Falls Dam that impounds the R. Barron on the Atherton Tablelands in northern Queensland was completed in 1958 (Fig. 4.39). The catchment climate is tropical, with 85 per cent of the 1400 mm mean annual rainfall arriving in the November to March wet season. The capacity of the L. Tinaroo reservoir is approximately 400 million cubic metres.

The two main purposes of the scheme are to supply irrigation water via a diversion channel system to 140 km² in the Mareeba district, and to release controlled flows required for the Barron Falls HEP plant at Kuranda. In addition, L. Tinaroo has been developed as a major recreational resource (Fig. 4.40).

The impacts

Flow

Mean annual flows at Mareeba (31 km below the dam) have been reduced by 23 per cent, due mainly to the irrigation diversions. However, year-to-year variations in flow have increased since 1960. The data in Table 4.7 help to explain this increase. Over the 1961–1990 period, 37 per cent of total flow remained as

Figure 4.39 The Barron River catchment and Lake Tinaroo (*Source*: Brizga S. & Finlayson B. 2000)

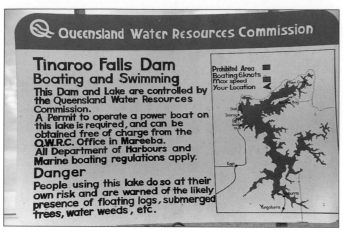

Figure 4.40 Lake Tinaroo has become an important resource for water-based recreation

Fig. 4.41 Unregulated release over the Tinaroo Dam spillway and exit sluices as reservoir capacity is reached following a season of above average rainfall

'unregulated' (Fig. 4.41). In wet years, e.g. the 1970s, this proportion reaches 50 per cent of total flow, while in dry periods, e.g. the 1980s, unregulated flows are much lower. The control system of storage and release has reduced the occurrence of minor floods but has increased the potential for occasional high level floods.

Table 4.7 Mean annual releases (% of total)

Period	Irrigation channel system	Controlled river flow	Unregulated spillway	Total (million m³)
1961–70	22	49	29	244
1971–80	19	29	52	441
1981–90	48	40	25	204

Factors: 1 1970s was a wet decade; 1980s, relatively dry
2 Progressive increase in irrigation demands

31 Describe the changing balance of releases shown in Table 4.7 and suggest reasons for the changes.

32 To what extent does the Tinaroo example illustrate the three-level hierarchy proposed on p. 67 for the impacts of dam construction?

The R. Barron illustrates the effect of geology upon channel dynamics. For the first 20 km below the dam, the river is contained by resistant rock formations and there has been little change in channel form. As the river approaches Mareeba the channel is formed by more erodible materials. This allows some sediment entrainment during high discharge episodes. However, during the increasingly prolonged periods of low flow – and low energy – sand and gravel bars have been deposited. As a result, the mean channel width at Mareeba has been reduced by 27 per cent. The new, narrower channel is becoming stabilised by progressive riparian vegetation encroachment, i.e. ecological adaptation.

33 From Fig. 4.38, how does the ideal regime for various uses vary? Suggest reasons for the variations and identify the areas of possible conflict.

Channel dynamics

Impacts on channel form tend to be strongest in the reaches immediately below a dam, although channel geology may influence the location and character of impact, e.g. the Barron River channel below the dam at Tinaroo Falls. The most common effect is for the river channel to become narrower, the result largely of reduced flow and hence energy levels. This adjustment period may take several decades as the river seeks a new equilibrium between the new discharge regime and channel form. Despite the reduced sediment supply below a dam, sand and gravel banks are slowly built up and subsequently stabilised by vegetation. The longer term ecological adaptation is affected by the quantity, regime and character of the water. For example, mean summer water temperatures of the R. Goulburn in Victoria, Australia fell by 7°C for up to 50 km below the Eildon Dam after its completion in 1955. The colder water wiped out the native fish species but has proved ideal for introduced trout that supports a thriving recreational fishing industry.

34 Use the example of dam/reservoir schemes to illustrate the difficulties encountered in attempting to implement policies of sustainable development. (Remember the dimensions of sustainability: economic; social; environmental; political.)

Figure 4.42 Impacts and ethics of dam construction: an example from Turkey (*Source: The Guardian*, 10 March 2000)

MP put conditions on support for Turkey dam

THE GOVERNMENT'S BACKING of the Ilisu dam project in Turkey was thrown into doubt last night after MPs delivered a stinging report into the affair.

Members of the trade and industry select committee said plans to spend £200m of taxpayers' money on the dam would have to be dropped unless the Turkish government agreed to certain guarantees.

The main stumbling block is trade secretary Stephen Byers' insistence that Turkey consult Syria and Iraq on its proposal to restrict the flow of the river Tigris into their territory. Turkey will not do so according to Olcay Unver, president of the Turkish administration in charge of the project.

MPs conceded that British commercial interests in Turkey and political relations between the two countries would be damaged if Britain did not pledge the £200m.

MPs said yesterday their worst fears were for the Kurdish people whose homes would be drowned and their livelihoods lost. The failure to consult even the mayors of the affected towns was 'lamentable'.

The committee said: 'The principal result of the dam will be the movement of yet more people from the land to overcrowded cities.

The greatest remaining obstacle to granting export credit for the dam is the prospect of a programme of displacing thousands of local residents without proper consultation, compensation and resettlement.'

Issues raised by dam construction

River regulation projects undoubtedly bring benefits, but experience from existing schemes shows that there may be significant negative impacts, often far from the dam site. For instance, in the former USSR, discharges reduced by 50–60 per cent by dams along the Dnestr, Dnepr and Don rivers have increased the accumulation of salts and pollutants in the Black Sea coastal waters. Dams have also blocked the migratory routes of some fish. The Russian commercial sturgeon fisheries of the Black, Azov and Caspian Seas were once amongst the most productive in the world, but have been virtually eliminated by dam construction. (Impacts on sediment movements and landforms are discussed in Chapters 5 and 7).

It has become increasingly clear that impacts and the issues they raise have economic, social and political as well as environmental dimensions (see R. Nile case study, p. 72). As a result, over the past 20 years much more critical assessment has emerged, especially of mega-projects. For example, the Turkish government plan to build the Ilisu Dam in south-east Turkey has raised objections from Syria and Iraq because the dam may threaten downstream flows along the R. Euphrates. There have been strong international objections too, concerning the displacement of communities and the flooding of historic settlements (Fig. 4.42). In China the Three Gorges project under construction on the Yangtse River is the largest in the world. It will provide much-needed electricity for China's growing economy and population, and should protect more than 75 million people living downstream from flooding hazards (Fig. 4.43b). Yet opponents claim that the huge cost, the social disruption and environmental damage will more than outweigh the benefits (Fig. 4.43a).

The gigantic Three Gorges project has inspired awe and opposition ever since it was first proposed 75 years ago. To opponents, it is a symbol of mankind's monstrous interventions in nature, an enterprise that will not only displace people but also devastate wildlife and alter the landscape forever.

Chinese leaders argue just as vehemently that Three Gorges is vital to their country's future – and actually good for the environment as a whole. They say it will prevent the periodic flooding that has claimed 500 000 lives in this century. More important, its production of clean hydro-electric power will reduce China's reliance on coal, the dirtiest of all fossil fuels, which now supplies 75% of the country's energy needs. The burning of coal has cast a pall of pollution over major Chinese cities and helped to make pulmonary disease the nation's leading cause of death.

If China maintains its annual economic growth rate of 11 per cent, the country will need to add 17 000 megawatts of electrical generating capacity each year for the rest of the decade. Within ten years, that would be as much new power as the US generates overall today. If China uses mostly coal to produce that power, the greenhouse effect could be catastrophic.

Many opponents of Three Gorges have no quarrel with the effort to move away from coal towards hydro-power. But they argue that for lower price, numerous smaller dams could produce more power and greater flood-control benefits. They fear that a dam so large on the notoriously muddy Yangtse will lead to dangerous build-ups of silt in some parts of the river, creating new obstacles to navigation and causing floods upstream.

Figure 4.43a China: The Three Gorges Dam issue (*Source: Time*, 19 December 1994)

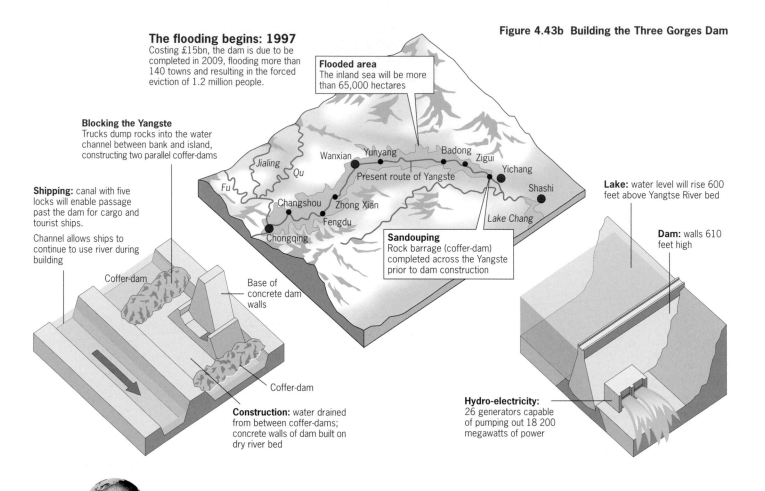

The flooding begins: 1997
Costing £15bn, the dam is due to be completed in 2009, flooding more than 140 towns and resulting in the forced eviction of 1.2 million people.

Figure 4.43b Building the Three Gorges Dam

Flooded area
The inland sea will be more than 65,000 hectares

Blocking the Yangste
Trucks dump rocks into the water channel between bank and island, constructing two parallel coffer-dams

Shipping: canal with five locks will enable passage past the dam for cargo and tourist ships.

Channel allows ships to continue to use river during building

Present route of Yangste

Sandouping
Rock barrage (coffer-dam) completed across the Yangste prior to dam construction

Lake: water level will rise 600 feet above Yangtse River bed

Dam: walls 610 feet high

Coffer-dam

Base of concrete dam walls

Coffer-dam

Construction: water drained from between coffer-dams; concrete walls of dam built on dry river bed

Hydro-electricity:
26 generators capable of pumping out 18 200 megawatts of power

Jialing / Fu / Qu / Wanxian / Yunyang / Badong / Zigui / Yichang / Shashi / Changshou / Zhong Xian / Fengdu / Chongqing / Lake Chang

The Nile basin, Africa: water balance and resource issues

A former UN Secretary General, Dr Boutros Boutros-Ghali, an Egyptian, has prophesied that, 'the next war in our region will be over the waters of the Nile'.

The River Nile and its tributaries drain an area of 2.9 million km^2 and cover nine countries. The source of Nile water is predominantly from the headwater countries, where rainfall is abundant but seasonal, resulting in different runoff patterns of the Nile tributaries (Fig. 4.44). The Nile water is not static in amount or location, and there is evidence that it may be declining due to climatic change.

The Nile is managed by a series of dams and barrages, especially in the Sudan and Egypt. The main purpose of the dams is for low-season water storage for irrigated agriculture, although the Owen Falls Dam on the White Nile at Lake Victoria is primarily for HEP. In the Sudan, the Sennar Dam was built on the Blue Nile in 1925, to irrigate the Gezira area. The Roseires Reservoir expanded this scheme.

The impacts of the Aswan High Dam
The Aswan High Dam was completed in 1963. Prior to the management of the River Nile at Aswan, the regime of the river strongly influenced Egyptian rural life. At the end of July, the rising floodwaters would inundate the fertile **floodplain** agricultural land, replenishing the soil and groundwater stores, and adding a layer of fertile silt. When the floodwaters receded, farmers would plant their crops.

This cycle had sustained Egyptian agriculture for thousands of years, but the country was subjected to droughts or devastating floods when the river's flow varied. In modern Egypt, with a rapidly expanding population, this variable flow and loss of food production during the inundations and low flows posed a major problem. The regulation of the river below Aswan has allowed all-year-round (perennial) irrigation and crop production, e.g. double cropping.

The Aswan Dam has clearly benefited Egypt's 58 million people, but has caused much controversy (Fig. 4.45). The USA refused finance for its building and Egypt nationalised the Suez Canal to raise the capital itself. Eventually financial support was provided by the former USSR. The project was multipurpose. Although irrigation was crucial, the amplitude of the high and low flow fluctuations has been reduced (Fig. 4.46) and the dam is used to generate HEP.

Figure 4.44 The Nile basin: climatic data and mean monthly runoff figures (*Source*: Sutcliffe and Lazenby, 1990)

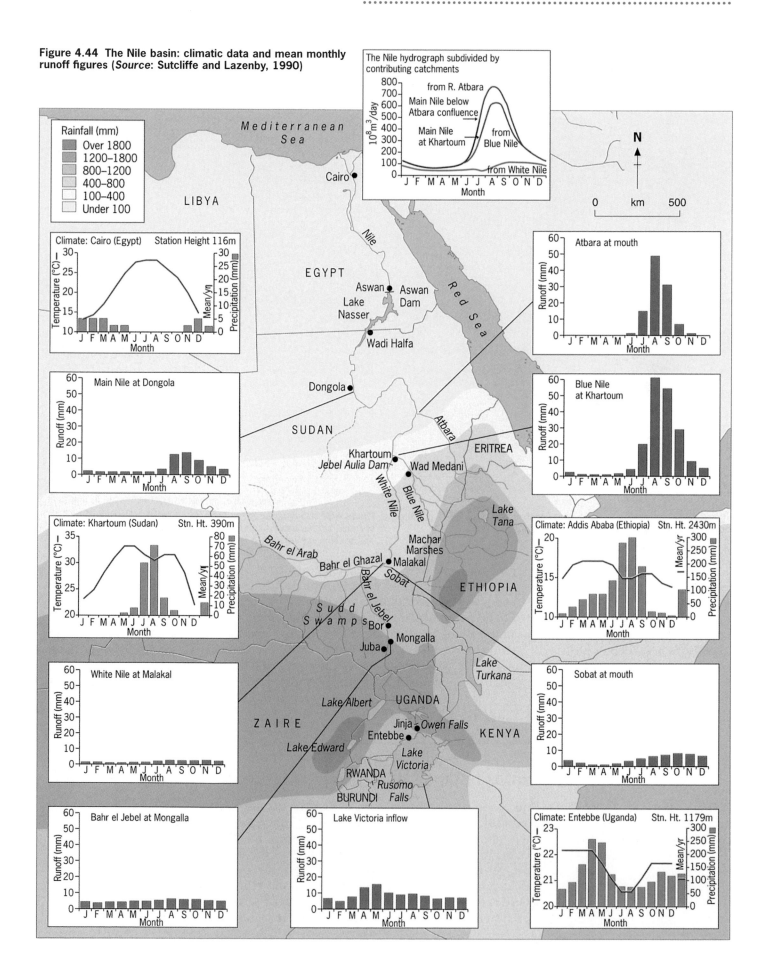

- Lake Nasser fisheries have been successfully developed. Fish is an important source of protein. In Egypt fish is now half the price of meat and poultry.

- The Nile delta fisheries have been greatly reduced. The Nile sediment nutrients do not replenish the delta area and, as a result, the sardine fisheries have declined from 18,000 tonnes to virtually nothing. Thirty thousand fishers have lost their jobs.

- The fertilising and leaching benefits of the annual flood have been lost. The use of artificial fertilisers has increased, which adds to water pollution.

- Fertiliser, chemicals and effluent from towns and industries are not washed away by annual floods, The rodent population has increased. Water quality has deteriorated, but does not represent a health hazard yet.

- Archaeological sites had to be moved when Lake Nasser flooded.

- HEP generation from the dam provides Egypt with 45% of current requirements. However, the full capacity has not been achieved, because the dam has never been full.

- Flood control saved lives in 1964, '67, '75 and 1987, and the costs of flood damage were avoided.

- Nile navigation has improved. This has increased from seasonal to year-round. An important benefit of this is the tourism aspect of the Nile for larger cruise boats.

- Egyptian agriculture has been revolutionised with year-round (perennial) irrigation, a 2.8 million hectare increase in the irrigated area, and an increase in cropping intensity and yields. This has allowed food production to help keep pace with the rapid population increase.

- Storage of water in Lake Nasser protected Egypt from drought in the upper basin during the mid-1980s.

- The groundwater store is under-utilised.

- Lake Nasser inundated the town of Wadi Haifa and flooded fertile agricultural land in Sudanese Nubia. Egypt had to pay compensation to Sudan.

- There is high annual water loss at 10% of the storage capacity of the lake. This is by evaporation and seepage.

- Sedimentation in the lake has reduced the sediment load of the river, The result has been degradation of the river valley below the dam and erosion of the fertile Nile delta (see Chapter 5).

- Year-round (perennial) irrigation has caused waterlogging and rising water tables.

- Irrigation practices have caused an increase in the levels of salt in the soil and water. A pipe drainage scheme, with World Bank finance, is helping to solve some of the problems.

- The still waters of the irrigation canals have led to an increase in diseases such as malaria and schistosomiasis ('sleeping sickness').

Figure 4.45 Impacts of the Aswan High Dam. The vertical aerial photograph shows part of Lake Nasser

Figure 4.46 The impact of the Aswan High Dam on the flow regime of the Nile

Table 4.8 Estimated water use in Egypt (*Source*: Howell and Allan, 1990)

		Volume (billion cubic metres)
Inflow	Aswan release	55.5
Outflow	Edfina to sea	3.5
	Canal tails to seas	0.1
	Drainage to sea and Fayoum	13.9
	Evaporation from water surfaces	2.0
	Sub total	19.5
Water use	Municipal and industrial	2.4
	Irrigation	33.6
	Subtotal	36.0

35a Describe the runoff regimes of the main Nile and its tributaries shown in Figure 4.44.

b Explain these patterns using climate data to support your answer. Think in terms of the water balance equation.

36 The impacts of the Aswan Dam in Figure 4.45 have not been prioritised. Construct a table to arrange these under social,economic and environmental costs and benefits. Give each impact a score between –5 and +5, i.e. high negative impact to high positive impact. Justify your scoring in each case.

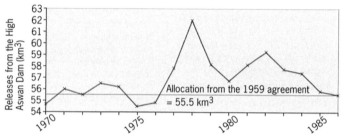

Figure 4.47 Releases from the Aswan High Dam, 1970–86 (*Source*: Howell and Allan, 1990)

Hydropolitical issues

There is a wide diversity of ethnic, religious and political characteristics among the nine countries of the Nile basin and almost all are faced with problems of poverty and high population growth. **Hydropolitical issues** are not crucial yet, but are likely to become more so in the future. The current importance of the Nile waters to the countries of the drainage basin is wide-ranging. The upper basin states of Tanzania, Rwanda, Burundi, Kenya, Uganda and Zaire are using only 0.5 billion cubic metres of Nile water among them. Ethiopia provides 86 per cent of the Nile waters, but only uses 0.6 billion cubic metres at the present time, despite devastating droughts and famines. The key user is the desert state of Egypt, with a demand of 55.5 billion cubic metres (Table 4.8) and the Nile provides 86 per cent of the freshwater supply. The second most important user is the Sudan, with a current consumption of 18.3 billion cubic metres and rising slowly. The external sources of their water raise important management issues.

Egypt and the Sudan currently use 60 per cent of Nile water for irrigation; 10–15 per cent is lost by evaporation and seepage from storage reservoirs; 20 per cent flows north to the Mediterranean to flush out the heavily salinated water at the end of the system. Only 7–8 per cent is currently for urban and industrial uses (Table 4.8). However, this demand will increase as the economics of Egypt and the Sudan develop. Also, the potential for HEP has only just begun to be harnessed. As electricity is an exportable commodity, the likelihood for expansion of HEP schemes is high.

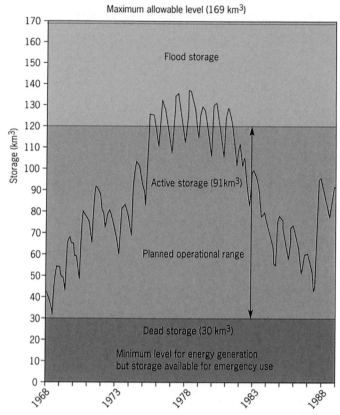

Figure 4.48 Lake Nasser: storage zones and storage levels, 1968–89 (*Source*: Howell and Alien, 1990)

Future water management

Egypt currently uses all the Nile waters it was allocated in the 1959 Agreement (Figs 4.47, 4.48). For the future it will have to look to increase irrigation efficiency.

37 Compare the Nile flow regime (Fig. 4.46) before and after the Aswan Dam. Include details of peak and low flows and the time of year these occur.

38a Use Figures 4.47 and 4.48 to describe the amount of storage in Lake Nasser and the output from the Aswan High Dam.

b The Nile Waters Agreement between the Sudan and Egypt in 1956 allocated 18.5 billion m^3 water to the Sudan and 55.5 billion m^3 to Egypt. In which years were releases to Egypt above the Agreement level? Explain why these higher releases were possible.

c Suggest what the consequences for Egypt might have been if Sudan had taken its full share of Nile water during the mid-1980s.

39 Present the data in Table 4.8 as a proportional flow line diagram.

40a State the evidence for a threatening water shortage between 1982 and 1987.

b Suggest what might have happened without the high inputs to Lake Nasser between 1987 and 1988.

In recent years the releases from Lake Nasser have been in excess of the inputs. It is only the high flood flows of 1987 which saved Egypt from potentially serious water shortages.

International discussion has so far been mainly between Egypt and the Sudan. Future management issues are likely to focus upon the increasing use of water by the upper basin states, especially Ethiopia. Ethiopia has plans to dam the waters of the Blue Nile source at Lake Tana. However, political problems, such as civil war, and economic difficulties in both Ethiopia and the Sudan, have inhibited large-scale projects.

In the White Nile catchment, development is likely to focus on water conservation schemes. At present the flow of the Nile is much reduced by the Sudd Swamps in southern Sudan. If these huge swamps are drained and the water transferred northwards via a canal, there would be important water savings available for the Sudan and Egypt.

In order to safeguard its future interests over Nile waters, especially inputs from the upper basin, Egypt has recently set up a consultative group, called the Undugu Group, of the Nile countries to propose a long-range scheme for Nile development.

4.6 Sediment movement through the drainage basin system

The erosion, transfer and deposition of sediment play significant roles in drainage basin hydrology and management. Sediment in rivers comes from two main sources (Fig. 4.49). The largest inputs are the result of weathering and mass movement on the hill slopes of the drainage basin. The second source, in some cases up to 50 per cent, is bank and bed erosion of the stream channels. (This and the following section (4.7) focus on sediment load in relation to river flow and human activities. You may find it useful to consult relevant chapters in other texts on streamflow – channel form – discharge relationships and fluvial landforms.)

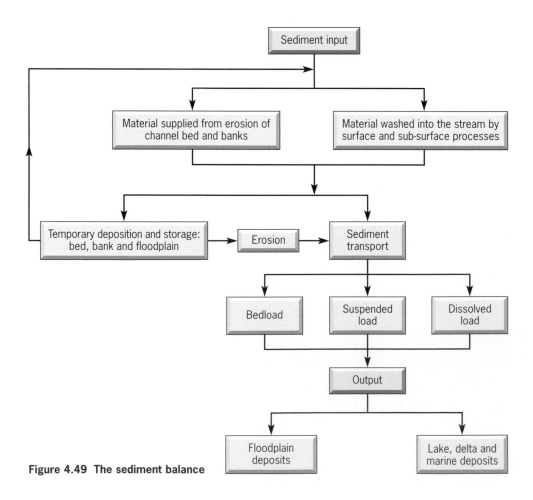

Figure 4.49 The sediment balance

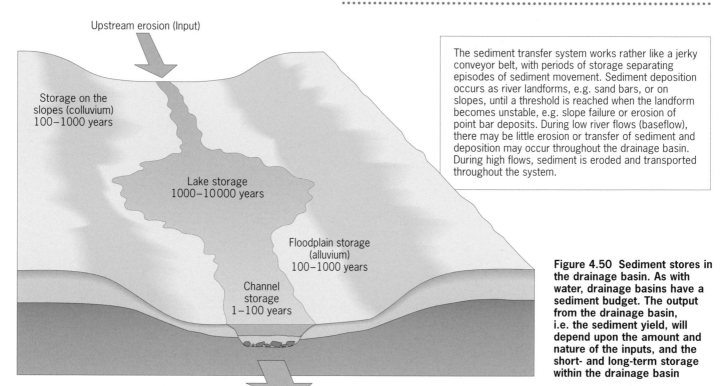

Upstream erosion (Input)

Storage on the slopes (colluvium) 100–1000 years

Lake storage 1000–10 000 years

Floodplain storage (alluvium) 100–1000 years

Channel storage 1–100 years

Sediment yield (Output)

The sediment transfer system works rather like a jerky conveyor belt, with periods of storage separating episodes of sediment movement. Sediment deposition occurs as river landforms, e.g. sand bars, or on slopes, until a threshold is reached when the landform becomes unstable, e.g. slope failure or erosion of point bar deposits. During low river flows (baseflow), there may be little erosion or transfer of sediment and deposition may occur throughout the drainage basin. During high flows, sediment is eroded and transported throughout the system.

Figure 4.50 Sediment stores in the drainage basin. As with water, drainage basins have a sediment budget. The output from the drainage basin, i.e. the sediment yield, will depend upon the amount and nature of the inputs, and the short- and long-term storage within the drainage basin

Table 4.9 Catchment areas, water discharges and sediment yields of selected large rivers (*Source*: Cooke and Doornkamp, 1990)

River	Country	Drainage basin area ('00 km^2)	Mean water discharges (m^3/s)	Sediment yields (tonnes/ km^2/y)
Rhine	Netherlands	160	2 200	17
Po	Italy	54	1 550	280
Vistula	Poland	193	950	7
Danube	Romania	816	6 200	80
Don	Russian Federation	378	830	11
Ob	Russian Federation	2 430	12 200	6
Niger	Nigeria	1 081	4 900	19
Congo	Zaire	4 014	39 600	18
Mississippi	USA	3 269	24 000	91
Amazon	Brazil	6 100	172 000	139
Indus	Pakistan	969	5 500	450
Ganges	India/Bangladesh	955	11 800	1 500
Brahmaputra	India/Bangladesh	666	12 200	1 100
Irrawaddy	Myanmar	430	13 500	700
Red	North Vietnam	120	3 900	1 100
Pearl	China	355	8 000	260
Yangtze	China	1 807	29 200	280
Yellow	China	752	1 370	2 480

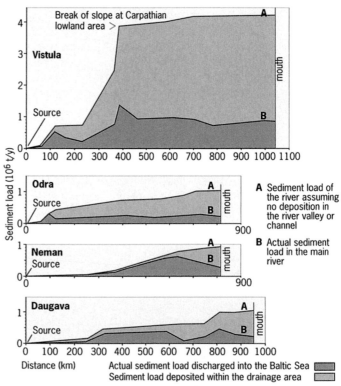

A Sediment load of the river assuming no deposition in the river valley or channel

B Actual sediment load in the main river

Actual sediment load discharged into the Baltic Sea
Sediment load deposited within the drainage area

Figure 4.51 Hypothetical sediment inflow to the main river and actual sediment load for four rivers draining to the Baltic Sea (*Source*: Lajczak and Jansson, 1993)

Sediment supply from weathering, mass movement and erosion does not become an input to the river channel immediately. Much is stored in the drainage basin system for varying lengths of time and moves intermittently through the system (Fig. 4.50). The importance of drainage basin storage is illustrated by data for four rivers flowing into the Baltic Sea (Fig. 4.51). Eventually the material leaves the system as **sediment yield** (output), usually

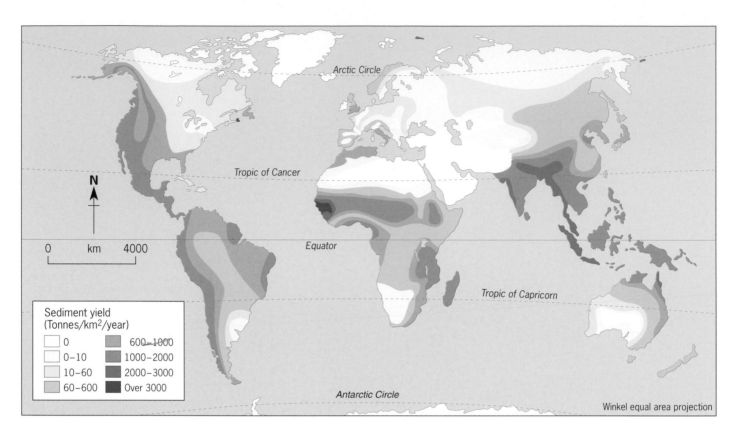

Figure 4.52 World distribution of suspended sediment yield. Estimates are based on the use of annual and monthly precipitation totals and relief factors (height and slope) (*Source*: Cooke and Doornkamp, 1990)

?

41a Suggest three factors that could affect the balance between bedload, suspension load and dissolved load in a river.
b Outline the effects of each of the above factors.

Use the data in Table 4.9 to test the following hypotheses:

42a There is a significant relationship between mean discharge and sediment yield in a drainage basin.
b Drainage basin size has little influence on sediment yield.

measured in tonnes per square kilometre per year (Table 4.9). The yield may also be measured in terms of the total amount, by weight. For example, the total annual sediment yield from the Yellow River (Huang Ho) in China, into the ocean is 1640 million tonnes, or 2480 tonnes/km²/year. However, this is only 24 per cent of the total load, as a further 33 per cent is deposited on the floodplain and 43 per cent in the delta region.

Globally, *suspension load* is estimated to make up approximately 70 per cent of total sediment yield, although there are wide regional variations (Fig. 4.52). *Bed load* contributes a further 10 per cent and *dissolved load* makes up the final 20 per cent. Note that these figures are very general, e.g. in steep mountain streams, bed load may be up to 80 per cent of the total. Furthermore, in any particular river the balance of load components varies over time. For instance, a study of 17 streams in western USA found that 80 per cent of total annual bed load transport occurred in 16 days.

Variables influencing sediment load
The sediment load and hence sediment yield has two main controls. The load may be determined by the available supply of materials, i.e. the load is *supply limited*, or by the capacity of a stream to transport material, i.e. the load is *capacity limited*. In general, the fine-grained suspension load is supply limited, while coarser load components are capacity limited.

Analysis of Table 4.9 reveals that correlations between sediment yield and either drainage basin size or river discharge are poor. Comparison of world distribution of suspended sediment yield (Fig. 4.52) with an atlas map of world climatic regions shows that there is no simple relationship between precipitation total and sediment yield. In other words, drainage basins in moist climates do not necessarily have high sediment loads and yields.

None the less, relatively high sediment yields do occur in the humid tropics and mountainous regions. For example, 20 per cent of the global sediment yield from suspension load is produced by the Ganges-Brahmaputra and Yellow River (Huang Ho) drainage basins. Both have mountainous headstream

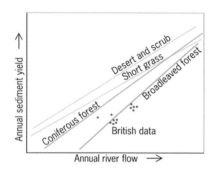

Figure 4.53 Annual sediment yield of world river basins by flow, stratified by vegetation type with British data shown for comparison (*Source*: Newson, 1992)

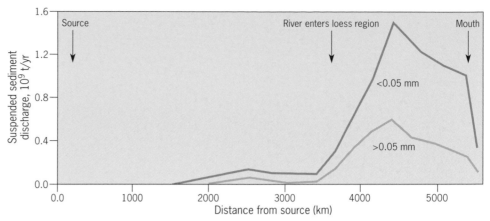

Figure 4.54 Downstream variation in suspended sediment load along the Yellow River (Huang Ho), China (*Source*: Knighton, 1998)

catchments with heavy seasonal precipitation. Except at high altitudes, as precipitation inputs increase, so does the protective vegetative cover, which slows down runoff and sediment supply to streams. Thus, some of the highest sediment yields per km² can occur in semi-arid environments; much of the rainfall occurs in intense, occasional downpours and there is little protective vegetation cover (Fig. 4.53).

Geology, soil types and bed/bank materials are influential variables in sediment load and yield. For example, poorly consolidated silts and sands are highly erodible and readily supply sediment inputs. The enormous sediment load of the Yellow River (China) is explained by the presence of extensive soft loess sediments in the middle basin (Fig. 4.54). During high flood discharges, suspension load in the lower reaches may make up 40 per cent of total discharge by weight – the flow is almost like a soup! Natural events such as the 1980 Mt St Helens eruption may cause fundamental changes to the sediment supply and hence to stream hydrology (Fig. 4.55).

4.7 Human activity and sediment yield

Sediment yields are influenced by changes within the drainage basin and by modifications to river flow (Fig. 4.56). Human activities increase or decrease yields and alter the character and rhythm of yield, with impacts varying over time and space.

Figure 4.55 The 1980 eruption of Mt St Helens (USA) caused abrupt melting of the snow-cap and produced a huge volume of rock clasts, tephra and ash, plus forest debris. The result was a series of catastrophic mudflows down river valleys radiating from the volcano. As the energy of the flood surges declined, the material was deposited, clogging valley floors with sediment up to 50 m deep

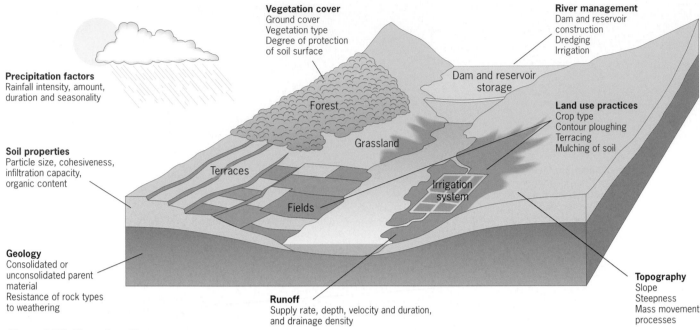

Precipitation factors
Rainfall intensity, amount,
duration and seasonality

Vegetation cover
Ground cover
Vegetation type
Degree of protection
of soil surface

River management
Dam and reservoir
construction
Dredging
Irrigation

Dam and reservoir
storage

Land use practices
Crop type
Contour ploughing
Terracing
Mulching of soil

Soil properties
Particle size, cohesiveness,
infiltration capacity,
organic content

Forest

Grassland

Terraces

Irrigation
system

Fields

Geology
Consolidated or
unconsolidated parent
material
Resistance of rock types
to weathering

Runoff
Supply rate, depth, velocity and duration,
and drainage density

Topography
Slope
Steepness
Mass movement
processes

Figure 4.56 Natural and human factors which affect the sediment yield of a drainage basin

Drainage basin changes

Land use has a signficant influence on erosion rates and sediment supply (Fig. 4.57). Indeed, any change of vegetation cover alters weathering rates and sediment transport. For instance, extensive deforestation will allow accelerated removal of material in hillslope sediment stores and so increase sediment yield (Fig. 4.59). In the experiments of the Maracá project (see Section 3.9), sediment supply from mid-slope sites increased from 200 to 7400 kg/ha after the clearance of virgin rainforest. As the graphs of Figure 4.53 show, for any given river flow, sediment yields from a short grass catchment are likely to be greater than from a forested catchment.

Afforestation tends to reduce sediment yield in the medium and long term. Yet episodes of accelerated erosion and supply do occur during the early and late stages of the afforestation cycle (Fig. 4.60). Over the past 50 years there has been extensive planting of coniferous trees on peat and moorland catchment in upland Britain with high rainfall totals. Studies in Northumberland showed that in the first five years following drainage and planting, soil erosion was equivalent to that achieved in 50 years under natural conditions. At Llanbrynmair in Wales, suspended sediment loads in streams increased by 246–479 per cent after ploughing of the moorland for afforestation.

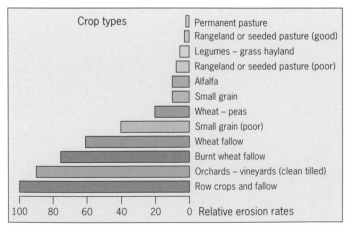

Crop types

☐ Permanent pasture
☐ Rangeland or seeded pasture (good)
☐ Legumes – grass hayland
☐ Rangeland or seeded pasture (poor)
☐ Alfalfa
☐ Small grain
☐ Wheat – peas
☐ Small grain (poor)
☐ Wheat fallow
☐ Burnt wheat fallow
☐ Orchards – vineyards (clean tilled)
☐ Row crops and fallow

100 80 60 40 20 0   Relative erosion rates

Figure 4.57 The influence of crop type on erosion rates in Pacific NW USA (*Source*: Gregory and Walling, 1973)

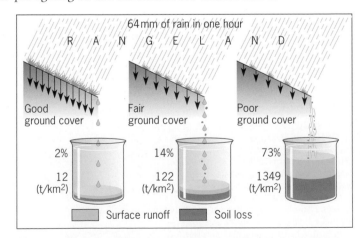

64 mm of rain in one hour

R A N G E L A N D

Good
ground cover

Fair
ground cover

Poor
ground cover

2%
12
(t/km²)

14%
122
(t/km²)

73%
1349
(t/km²)

☐ Surface runoff   ☐ Soil loss

Figure 4.58 The influence of rangeland condition on runoff and sediment yield in Utah, USA (*Source*: Gregory and Walling, 1973)

Figure 4.59 Clifford Pinchot National Forest and Skamania County private lands, Washington State, USA: unsustainable clear-cutting

43 Use the data in Table 4.10 to construct a graph. Comment briefly on the contrasts in sediment load between the natural and controlled river projects.

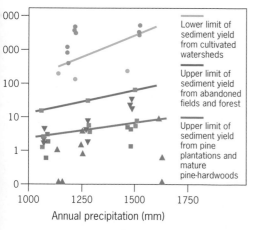

Figure 4.61 The influence of land use on sediment yield from watersheds in hill land of the upper coastal plain in northern Mississippi, USA (*Source*: Gregory and Walling, 1973)

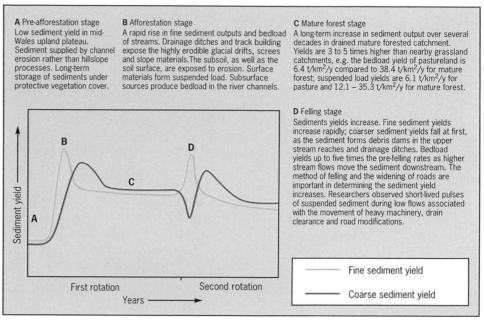

A Pre-afforestation stage
Low sediment yield in mid-Wales upland plateau. Sediment supplied by channel erosion rather than hillslope processes. Long-term storage of sediments under protective vegetation cover.

B Afforestation stage
A rapid rise in fine sediment outputs and bedload of streams. Drainage ditches and track building expose the highly erodible glacial drifts, screes and slope materials. The subsoil, as well as the soil surface, are exposed to erosion. Surface materials form suspended load. Subsurface sources produce bedload in the river channels.

C Mature forest stage
A long-term increase in sediment output over several decades in drained mature forested catchment. Yields are 3 to 5 times higher than nearby grassland catchments, e.g. the bedload yield of pastureland is 6.4 t/km^2/y compared to 38.4 t/km^2/y for mature forest; suspended load yields are 6.1 t/km^2/y for pasture and 12.1 – 35.3 t/km^2/y for mature forest.

D Felling stage
Sediments yields increase. Fine sediment yields increase rapidly; coarser sediment yields fall at first, as the sediment forms debris dams in the upper stream reaches and drainage ditches. Bedload yields up to five times the pre-felling rates as higher stream flows move the sediment downstream. The method of felling and the widening of roads are important in determining the sediment yield increases. Researchers observed short-lived pulses of suspended sediment during low flows associated with the movement of heavy machinery, drain clearance and road modifications.

Figure 4.60 Forestry and sediment yields

Equally important is the quality of land management strategies. For instance, overgrazing of grassland increases erosion rates (Fig. 4.58). In contrast, conservation practices such as contour ploughing and terracing create sediment stores and minimise sediment supply to streams. Increasingly, hilly headwater catchments are being returned to semi-natural vegetation with the aim of reducing erosion, runoff and sediment yield (Fig. 4.61).

River flow and sediment load changes

The components of river regulation schemes, such as dams, barrages, reservoirs and diversion canals transform the sediment storage, throughput and output characteristics of a river, i.e. the **sediment budget**. The most radical change is the deposition of sediment in the reservoir upstream of the dam. In the case of the Sanmenxia Dam on the Yellow River (China), storage capacity of the reservoir was reduced by 40 per cent in only four years (Fig. 4.62). This in turn reduces the downstream supply of sediment, with inevitable impacts upon the erosion–transportation deposition balance and hence upon channel form (see section 5.7 and the Glen Canyon Dam case study, p. 104). The completion of the Aswan High Dam across the R. Nile in Egypt has resulted in a dramatic reduction in downstream sediment load (Table 4.10), the loss of annual

Table 4.10 Silt concentrations in the Nile at Gaafra before and after the construction of the Aswan High Dam (*Source*: Goudie, 1986)

Month	Sediment concentrations (ppm) before the dam, 1958–63	Sediment concentrations (ppm) after the dam	Ratio
Jan	64	44	1.5
Feb	50	47	1.1
Mar	45	45	1.0
Apr	42	50	0.8
May	43	51	0.8
Jun	85	49	1.7
Jul	674	48	14.0
Aug	2702	45	60.0
Sept	2422	41	59.1
Oct	925	43	21.5
Nov	124	48	2.58
Dec	77	47	1.63

?

44 Explain why expansion of settlements, roads, etc. across a drainage basin tends to accelerate water runoff but once construction is complete, is likely to reduce sediment yield.

Figure 4.62 The Sanmenxia Dam on the Yellow River (Huang Ho), China. The bottom sluice gates of the dam are open to flush out the sediment from the reservoir bed behind the dam

supplies of fertile silt across the irrigated floodplain and a serious decrease in sediment inputs to the delta (Fig. 4.63).

Thus, when HEP stations, dams and reservoirs are designed, it is important to build into the environmental impact survey (EIS), predictions concerning sedimentation and sediment yield. This improves calculations of costs and design life for a scheme. The Los Angeles area of southern California is drained by three major rivers – the Los Angeles, the San Gabriel and the Santa Ana. Dams built to regulate these rivers experienced problems of sediment accumulation as the vegetation across the watershed was progressively destroyed. There are now 80 debris dams which trap sediment from upstream canyons. The accumulated material is regularly dredged and much is used for beach nourishment. This replaces the natural supply which used to come as output from the river mouths before dam construction.

In areas of high and increasing sediment supply and sedimentation, where channel capacity is reduced, expensive dredging may be required to control flood risk. Increased sediment yield at river mouths may affect harbours. For example, the Farakka Dam in India was built primarily to divert millions of tonnes of water from the Ganges to the R. Hooghly in order to flush out sediment accumulation from the port of Calcutta.

Water quality

The sediment load may include pollutants from domestic, industrial and agricultural use, which in turn may threaten the quality of water available for further use (Fig. 4.64a, b). For example, in northern England, domestic users supplied from reservoirs fed by flows from peat catchments in the Pennines have complained about the brown tint of their tap water. This has meant the installation of expensive water treatment plants and ongoing research into improved catchment management. Changes in sediment yield can affect stream ecosystems. Studies of afforestation in British uplands found that the increased sediment concentrations reduce light penetration, thereby reducing

Dammed to destruction

THE NILE DELTA, granary of Egypt and still Africa's most productive farmland, is being eaten by the oceans and invaded by the desert. The Aswan dam, hailed in the 1960s as a triumph of engineering and water management, is now seen as a major cause of the region's impending devastation.

The delta is a wedge of highly fertile land the size of northern Ireland where the Nile reaches the Mediterranean. It is composed of layer upon layer of silt, most of it eroded from the highlands of Ethiopia over tens of thousands of years. Each year, 100 million tons of soil slips from the parched lands of Wollo and Tigre, and flows north in a muddy gush as the Blue Nile floods.

What was Ethiopia's loss was Egypt's gain. The silt raised the Nile delta by about one millimetre each year, fertilising it and counteracting natural subsidence and erosion by the sea.

But the dam traps 98 per cent of the Nile silt, which now drops to the bed of Lake Nasser, the reservoir which formed behind the dam. Denied the fertile silt that has sustained farms on the delta for more than 7000 years (longer than anywhere else on Earth), Egypt already uses more fertiliser per hectare than any other nation.

And fertiliser won't protect the delta from the sea. Without a constant supply of silt, it faces eventual destruction as surely as a sandcastle meeting an incoming tide.

As the sea advances, the desert is also invading. Here again, mankind is to blame. Modern irrigation canals no longer bring silt to the fields with the waters of the Nile, but they do bring natural salts eroded upstream and dissolved in the water. In ancient times, when the river flooded fields, the ebbing flood flushed the salts away each year. But modern canal irrigation leaves the salt behind. It is gradually poisoning the soil of this, one of the world's leading cotton-producing regions, and turning it to desert.

Each year, one ton of salt accumulates on each hectare of delta fields. The country is spending tens of millions of dollars each year, laying the largest drainage network in the world in an attempt to flush out the salt. Even so, salt is already reducing crop yields on more than a third of the fields.

Once, much of the delta was composed of marshes and brackish lagoons, protected from the sea by sand bars. Deprived of silt, the sand bars are fast eroding and will collapse. They, and the lagoons form the main defence against the sea for the entire delta. With them gone, the tides will rush inwards ever faster.

Figure 4.63 Impacts of the Aswan Dam, Egypt (*Source*: The *Independent on Sunday*, 6 June 1993)

45 Name and illustrate two ways in which human activity can a) increase, b) decrease, c) alter water quality in a river.

Figure 4.64 Sangre de Cristo Mountains, New Mexico, USA. Spring snow-melt and summer rainstorms cause surges of sediment erosion from mining spoilheaps (*above*), supplying increased suspension load and pollution to tributaries flowing into the Rio Grande (*below*)

photosynthesis by aquatic plants. Furthermore, sediment blanketing the stream bed can kill vegetation and make conditions unsuitable for life forms adapted to clear water and gravelly streambeds, e.g. salmon and filter-feeding molluscs.

Summary

- Each drainage basin has a unique water balance or budget and will experience varying periods of water surplus and deficit.

- The water balance or budget is determined by the relationship between precipitation inputs and the combination of evapotranspiration loss, storage and runoff.

- The main river in a drainage basin has a distinctive regime or annual rhythm of discharge.

- A natural river regime is controlled by the relationship between the pattern of precipitation inputs, the environmental conditions and the processes at work within the drainage basin.

- Streams are grouped into three types according to duration of flow: ephemeral; intermittent; perennial.

- Stream regimes may be simple (uniform and dual) or complex according to the character of the pattern revealed in the hydrograph.

- Human activities are having increasing impacts, both intentional and accidental, upon the water balance and streamflow in drainage basins.

- Sediment is a key output from the drainage basin system and an understanding of the processes involved is important for human management of the drainage basin system.

- The sediment yield of a drainage basin is the result of a complex set of variables related to key natural processes, e.g. climate, vegetation, rock type, and to human activity.

- Sediment is stored within the drainage basin for varying amounts of time as hillslope materials and depositional landforms.

- Human activity can increase the sediment yield of a drainage basin, e.g. land use change, deforestation, afforestation, mining and early urbanisation.

- Human activity can decrease the sediment yield of a drainage basin, e.g. by soil conservation measures, building dams and reservoirs, and the later stages of urban development.

- The mis-management of a drainage basin sediment budget can have important impacts on people, landform processes and ecosystems.

- The management of sediment load of rivers is important to human activity, e.g. for navigation and water supply purposes.

- There is a need for the management of sediment budgets and yields at the scale of the whole drainage basin.

5 Managing channels

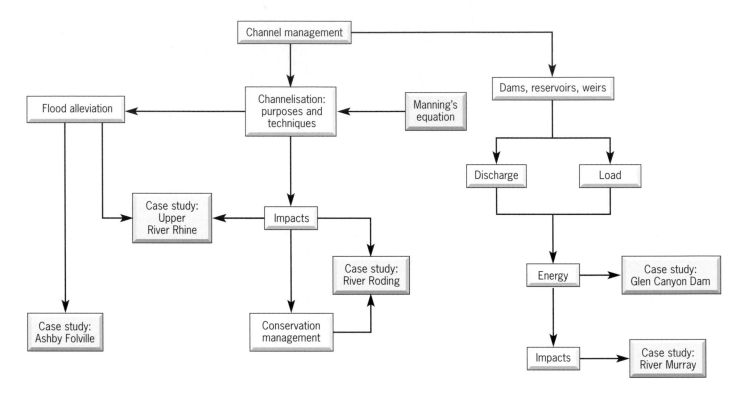

5.1 Introduction

The characteristics of a river channel, e.g. channel width, depth and **sinuosity**, are adjusted to the natural flow **regime** and **bankfull discharge** of the river. There is a **dynamic equilibrium** among these variables, and a change in any one of them will cause changes elsewhere in the **drainage basin** system. People manage river channels by changing some or all of these variables and consequently alter the channel characteristics. For example, we deliberately and directly manage the channel form and sinuosity, or build dams, barrages and weirs, which will alter the flow regime and the **discharge**. The deliberate modification of the river channel for flood control, land drainage, navigation and prevention of erosion is called **channelisation**. A number of channelisation methods are available, and may be applied in an appropriate combination in any particular flood control scheme (see Ashby Folville case study, p. 87 and River Rhine case study, p 92).

In this chapter we shall consider management of the channel itself, but river diversions as flood relief channels and embankments or artificial levées are also forms of channelisation (see Chapter 6).

5.2 Methods of river channelisation

Resectioning or enlarging

We can reduce or prevent flooding by deepening or widening the river channel to increase its cross-sectional area. The channel is often dredged to an energy-efficient trapezoidal cross-section, with a flat bottom and steep banks (Fig. 5.1). This increase in area allows a larger discharge to be contained within the channel. Resectioning also lowers the **water table** on the **floodplain**, which allows wet floodplains to be used for agriculture.

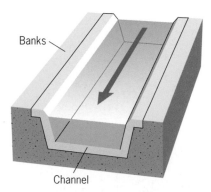

Banks

Channel

A concrete lining improves
the efficiency of flow

Figure 5.1 Resectioning the channel
(*Source*: **Knapp et al, 1989**)

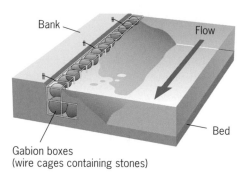

Figure 5.2 Realigning the channel
(*Source*: Knapp et al, 1989)

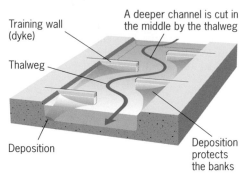

Figure 5.3 Gabion boxes (wire cages containing stones) strengthen the banks (*Source*: Knapp et al, 1989)

Figure 5.4 Groynes or spurs deflect the thalweg, allowing the deposition of sediment in the lee of the groyne, thus protecting the banks from erosion (*Source*: Knapp et al, 1989)

Realignment or straightening

A **meandering** river can be straightened by means of artificial cut-offs (Fig. 5.2). This is known as realignment. The meander may be completely filled in with the dredge spoil as the new channel is cut. The aim is to increase the **long-profile** gradient of the channel in that reach of the river. An increase in gradient increases the flow velocity. Realignment, therefore, reduces the risk of flooding upstream and along the realigned stretch, because water is moved more quickly, helps river navigation and reduces journey times.

Bank protection

Erosion of banks and meander migration cause loss of land and may undermine structures, such as buildings and bridges. We can prevent this by protecting the banks with concrete blocks, steel **revetments**, gabion boxes (Fig. 5.3), **groynes** or spurs (Fig. 5.4).

Lined channels

Often a resectioned length of river is lined with concrete to improve the channel efficiency (Fig. 5.5). Concrete is smoother than the natural soil and pebble materials of the channel. This results in a reduction in energy loss through friction, and an increased flow velocity (see box: calculating channel efficiency, p. 86). However, the accelerated transfer may increase flood risk further downstream (see Section 5.3). The risk of flooding to the upstream and resectioned stretches is reduced because a greater amount of water is carried more quickly. Lined channels are often used in urban areas where access for maintenance is limited or other forms of management are not possible.

Figure 5.5 Twin concrete-lined channels formalised to act as a more effective conduit for flood flows, on the River Erewash at Stapleford, near Derby

?

1 Use the formula for velocity to explain why meander cut-offs will increase flow velocity.

Calculating channel efficiency

The most popular calculation to estimate velocity using the channel form and bed roughness variables is the **Manning equation**, often known as Manning's n:

$$\text{Velocity } (v) = \frac{R^{2/3}\, s^{1/2}}{n}$$

Where: n = Manning roughness coefficient (based on variables such as the size and shape of bed material, the **wetted perimeter**, vegetation in and on the edge of the channel, and discharge)

R = **hydraulic radius**

s = channel gradient.

The Manning roughness coefficient ranges between 0.03 in straight, clean channels and 0.15 for densely vegetated channels. Table 5.1 gives some typical values for natural channels.

Table 5.1 Typical Manning roughness coefficient values (*Source*: Ven te Chow, 1959)

Channel type	Coefficient range
Small mountain stream, pebble and boulder bed	0.041–0.070
Small, clean, straight lowland stream	0.025–0.033
Small weedy stream with deep pools	0.075–0.150
Floodplain stream in pastureland	0.025–0.035
Floodplain stream in heavy woodland	0.100–0.150
Large streams (width >33 m)	0.025–0.060

The Manning roughness coefficient (n) for a concrete-lined channel will be lower than that for a natural channel. If Manning's n in the velocity equation is reduced, the value of average velocity (*v*) will increase, even if the method of channelisation does not change the channel size or shape. Usually the channel is resectioned to a larger trapezoidal shape. This increases the efficiency of the channel and the hydraulic radius (HR). The result is an increase in channel flow velocity, since the value of *R* multiplied by *s* will be higher.

Containment

Culverts are an extreme form of channelisation which contain the channel within concrete arches or pipes (Fig. 5.6). These structures are used where rivers flow under roads or built-up areas. They are more difficult to maintain because of access problems and are limited by a design flood level above which they will fail or cause ponding back of the water and possible floods upstream of the bridge.

Vegetation clearance

A smooth, regular channel can carry up to three times the discharge of a channel of similar size and gradient, which has its banks covered with extensive weed, reeds and other plants. Plants reduce the size of the channel and aid silt deposition, as well as increasing channel roughness (Fig. 5.7). The nature of the plants, e.g. whether they are clump-forming, or the flexibility of their stems, will be important in determining how much they influence channel roughness. In the River Yarrow in Lancashire, for example, there was a 58 per cent reduction in the value of Manning's n, from 0.1484 to 0.0627, following weed clearance. Following tree and debris clearance on the R. Lostock in Lancashire, Manning's n was reduced by 23 per cent, from 0.0662 to 0.0152.

The seasonal cutting of vegetation can be ecologically beneficial, and is an established component in the management of streams. However, the removal of vegetation is normally achieved with great ecological costs (see Section 5.4) and can lead to an increase in bank erosion (Fig. 5.8).

Figure 5.6 East Goscote, Leicestershire: this was a major flood area before the culvert, under the A607, was built. Two tributaries of the R. Wreake join here. The Gaddesby Brook (behind the central wall) and the Queniborough Brook (in the foreground) are confined by concrete in the area where they meet, to the right of the photograph. The culverts carry the two streams under the road

Figure 5.7 Plant growth is removed from channels to reduce roughness, and to prevent culverts and bridges from becoming obstructed or blocked. If they did become blocked, this would pose a serious flooding threat

Figure 5.8 Plant roots bind the soil and protect the banks. This structural protection can be lost by clearance schemes that remove trees and weeds

Dredging

Dredging involves the removal of **sediment** from the channel to enlarge its **capacity**. Dredging machines are required and a suitable site must be found for the removed sediment. Alternatively, bed material is loosened and left in the channel to be entrained and transported by **streamflow**. The removal of sediment reduces the risk of flooding in the dredged section of the river, but it may increase the problem downstream, e.g. if the transferred sediment is deposited in the channel.

Flood alleviation: Ashby Folville, Leicestershire

Ashby Folville has experienced serious flooding on several occasions, most noticeably in 1975, 1979, 1992 and 1993. If you look at the flooded area for the 1993 flood (Fig. 5.9), you will note that the pattern of flooding is unusual. The main area of flooded land is not on either side of the Gaddesby Brook as you might expect, but is concentrated along the main street and around the Brook in the south–east of the village.

This results from a diversion of the Gaddesby Brook around Manor House over 30 years ago. The artificial and unnaturally sharp meander near to Woodford House Farm causes water to build up under high-flow conditions (Fig. 5.13). If the wall is overtopped, the flood waters flow on to the land near the farm and along the main street of the village. The flooding problem is therefore relatively recent and results from human mismanagement of the channel in the past.

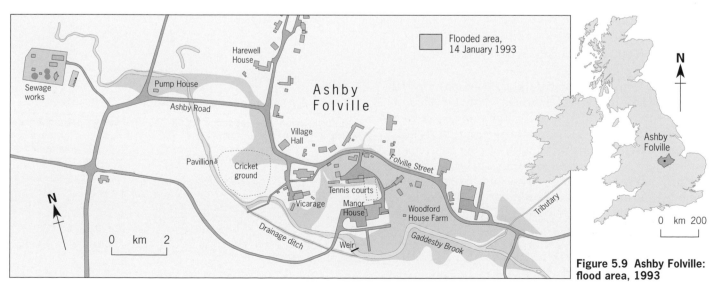

Figure 5.9 Ashby Folville: flood area, 1993

Figure 5.10 (*above left*) **Existing drainage channel looking south-east from the old footbridge (Fig. 5.13).**

Figure 5.11 (*above right*) **The channel has been realigned to remove the sharp bend between y and z in Fig 5.13.**

Figure 5.12 (*left*) **The main channel junction with the drainage channel near the old footbridge (see Fig. 5.13). This has been resectioned and reinforced with gabions**

A flood alleviation scheme

Flood events in Ashby Folville are frequent, and the costs in property damage are high (Table 5.2). In 1992 the National Rivers Authority (NRA) investigated four possibilities for a flood alleviation scheme:

Option 1 'Do nothing'. This would leave 32 properties at risk from flooding. A 1-in-100-year flood would create £550 000 of damage. A viable scheme exists, so this option was rejected.

Option 2 Construct floodwalls, raise an existing wall and regrade some of the channel. Ashby Folville is a conservation area, therefore this option was rejected.

Option 3 Regrade the Brook throughout the village; remove a weir and a short length of new cut; replace and underpin several bridges; and construct a short length of new floodwall and weir on the tributary (Fig. 5.13). Initially this was the favoured scheme. However, a 1994 survey found that the road bridge was unsuitable for underpinning.

Option 4 Build a bypass (flood relief) channel in addition to the existing channel to convey the floodwater. Many trees would have to be removed in an area of tree preservation orders, therefore this option was rejected. However, following the problems with Option 3 discovered in 1994, the value of the trees was reassessed as lower quality species which could be replaced. Hence, Option 4 has become the proposed solution (Figs 5.10, 5.11, 5.12).

Table 5.2 Ashby Folville: flood frequency

Return period flow (years)	Gaddesby Brook (m^3/s)	Tributary (m^3/s)	Number of properties affected
2	10.7	2.48	15
5	16.37	4.01	–
10	19.82	4.90	–
50	28.03	7.00	31
100	31.88	7.99	31
150	40.00	9.00	32

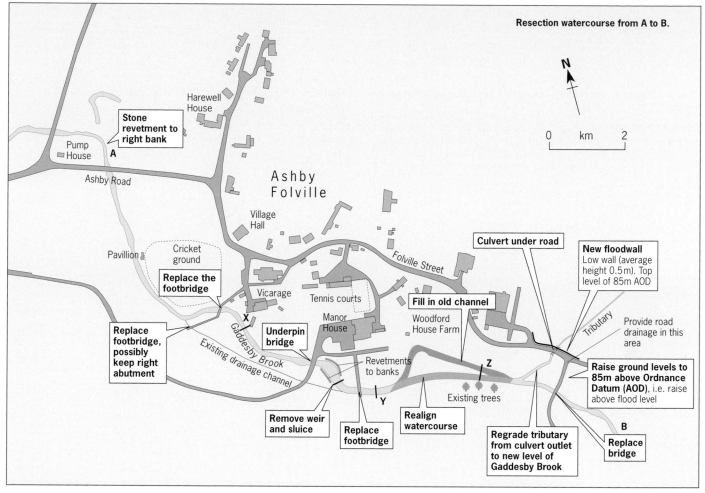

Figure 5.13 Ashby Folville: extent of the proposed flood alleviation works

The cost–benefit analysis

The proposed flood alleviation scheme (Option 3) was investigated for three standards of protection, corresponding to flood return periods of 50, 100 and 150 years. The preferred option from this **cost–benefit analysis** (see Section 6.8) was the 1-in-100-year standard of protection (Table 5.3).

The cost–benefit ratios for this scheme are relatively high because the properties involved are large, and even at the two-year event 15 properties are flooded (Table 5.2). Thus, the scheme would prevent much flooding with events at or below the 1-in-100-year level.

2a Describe the pattern of flooding in Ashby Folville for the January 1993 event. List the land uses affected.
b Suggest the main reason for this pattern of flooding.

3 Use Table 5.2 to draw a flood recurrence interval graph for Gaddesby Brook. Add the tributary to the same graph. Use semi-logarithmic graph paper. Use the logarithmic scale for the return periods and the arithmetic scale for the discharges.

4 Explain fully why the 1-in-100-year protection level was the preferred choice. Remember the cost–benefit analysis and the indicative standards of protection.

Table 5.3 Costs, benefits and the cost–benefit ratio of the flood alleviation scheme (Option 3) for the four standards of protection

	Do nothing	A	B	C
Standard years		50	100	150
Costs (£)	2 000 000	368 504	454 117	539 494
Benefits (£)		1 800 000	1 958 238	1 990 140
Average cost–benefit ratio		1:4.88	1:4.31	1:3.69

The 1-in-50-year protection scheme has the highest cost–benefit ratio and the highest net present value. However, this does not provide the indicative standard of protection for a medium density urban area where 32 properties are at risk (1-in-75-years).

The 1-in-100-year protection scheme has the next highest cost–benefit ratio and net present value. It also has the highest incremental cost–benefit ratio. This is therefore the preferred option.

Channel resectioning and realigning

The scheme is based upon resectioning and the removal of channel obstructions. The channel will be deepened by up to 2 m and consequently the bridges along the Brook will need underpinning or replacing. The artificial meander will be realigned to stop the floodwaters overspilling into the village.

Table 5.4 Channel characteristics before resectioning (original channel)

Cross-section	Width (m)	Average depth (m)	Cross-sectional area (m²)	Wetted perimeter (m)	Hydraulic radius
X	6.1	1.5	9.15	8.35	1.09
Y	7.0	0.8	5.6	7.3	0.77
Z	13.5	1.24	16.74	15.2	1.10

Note: Average depth measurements taken at 50 cm intervals across the channel and averaged.

Table 5.5 Channel characteristics after resectioning (original channel)

Cross-section	Width (m)	Average depth (m)	Cross-sectional area (m²)	Wetted perimeter (m)	Hydraulic radius
X	7.10	2.2	15.62	10.3	1.52
Y	8.4	1.36	11.42	10.0	1.142
Z	8.8	2.01	17.65	?	?

Note: Average depth measurements taken at 50 cm intervals across the channel and averaged.

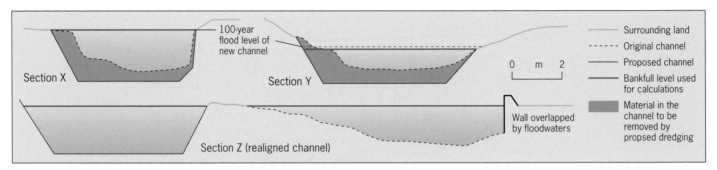

Figure 5.14 Ashby Folville: cross-sections before and after resectioning

?

5 The channel at X and Y is being resectioned, and the channel at Z is to be realigned. Using Table 5.4 and Figure 5.14:
a Calculate the hydraulic radius and the wetted perimeter for channel Z.
b Use the information to describe and fully explain how the new channels will reduce flooding. In your answer refer to channel size and efficiency.

6 Ashby Folville is an attractive conservation village, with many commuters. The work will be disruptive while the scheme is being implemented and the nature of the Brook will be changed. In pairs, one take the role of a resident whose property is affected by flooding, the other the role of a resident who lives above the flood levels. Discuss how your opinions about the scheme differ, giving reasons. Refer to the Environmental Impact Assessment, Appendix 5.

7a Draw a cross-section of a dredged trapezoidal-shaped channel to show low- and high-flow levels.
b Comment on how the hydraulic radius and wetted perimeter of the low-flow levels in the channel will vary.
c Explain why the low flows result in deposition.

5.3 The impacts of channelisation

Resectioning

Researchers have studied the impacts of resectioning on channels at 57 sites in England and Wales. The schemes studied were aimed at enlarging channels by dredging to confine floodwaters within the rivers themselves.

Downstream adjustments

We have seen that resectioning increases streamflow. The studies showed that the higher velocities resulted in greater erosion rates downstream of the schemes. However, over a period of time a **negative feedback** mechanism operated to reduce stream velocity (Fig. 5.15). There was a state of adjustment and self-regulation by the river.

Not all rivers, however responded in the same way. Channel change is dependent on the energy of the river. For example, low-energy rivers in lowland Britain showed little or no downstream channel change, while in

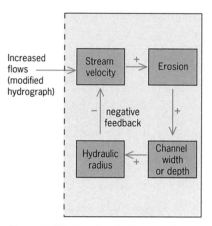

Figure 5.15 Feedback diagram for the adjustment of channel capacity following resectioning (*Source*: Brookes, 1985)

high-energy upland rivers changes in width, rather than depth, were more common. This is explained by the **bed armouring** effect of the channel bedload compared to the smaller sediment and soil material of the banks. Channels which were cut into solid bedrock showed little downstream change.

The studies also showed that channel adjustment fell with distance downstream. Erosion was found to be selective, with reduced rates where trees and other vegetation protected the banks. Erosion was greatest on the outside of meander bends, with little **point bar** deposition on the inside of the bend. The length downstream affected did vary and ranged from a minimum of 120 m on Pickering Beck in North Yorkshire to a maximum of 1950 m for the River Caldew in Cumbria.

On-site adjustments
Resectioned reaches were found to adjust with time. For example, when the R. Thame in Oxfordshire was enlarged as part of a flood alleviation scheme, the channel reverted to its original capacity in under 30 years without maintenance dredging. The enlarged channel was in equilibrium with higher flood flows, but not with the more common low flows. Reduced low-flow velocities and deposition occurred as a result.

Realigning

Changes in the straightened reach
The adjustments by rivers following realigning can be dramatic, especially in high-energy rivers or those with easily eroded sediments. Realigning increases the downstream slope of the channel by shortening the course (Fig. 5.16). The energy budget of the river increases with gradient, allowing more sediment to be transported. In the East and West Prairie Rivers in Alberta, Canada, researchers found that the higher energy available in the newly straightened reach resulted in erosion of the channel bed and encouraged bank collapse. A **knickpoint** was formed in the long profile which moved upstream.

Rivers do not flow in straight lines under natural conditions. If there is sufficient energy available they will try to re-establish their sinuous course by bank erosion. This is particularly the case with high-energy rivers. For example, a section of the R. Severn at Llandinam, Wales, was straightened during the construction of a railway in the early 1850s. There was little bank protection to maintain this new course. Consequently, the river gradually recovered its sinuous course or plan form until, by 1982, the channel had returned to its original long-profile slope.

Figure 5.16 The impact of realigning

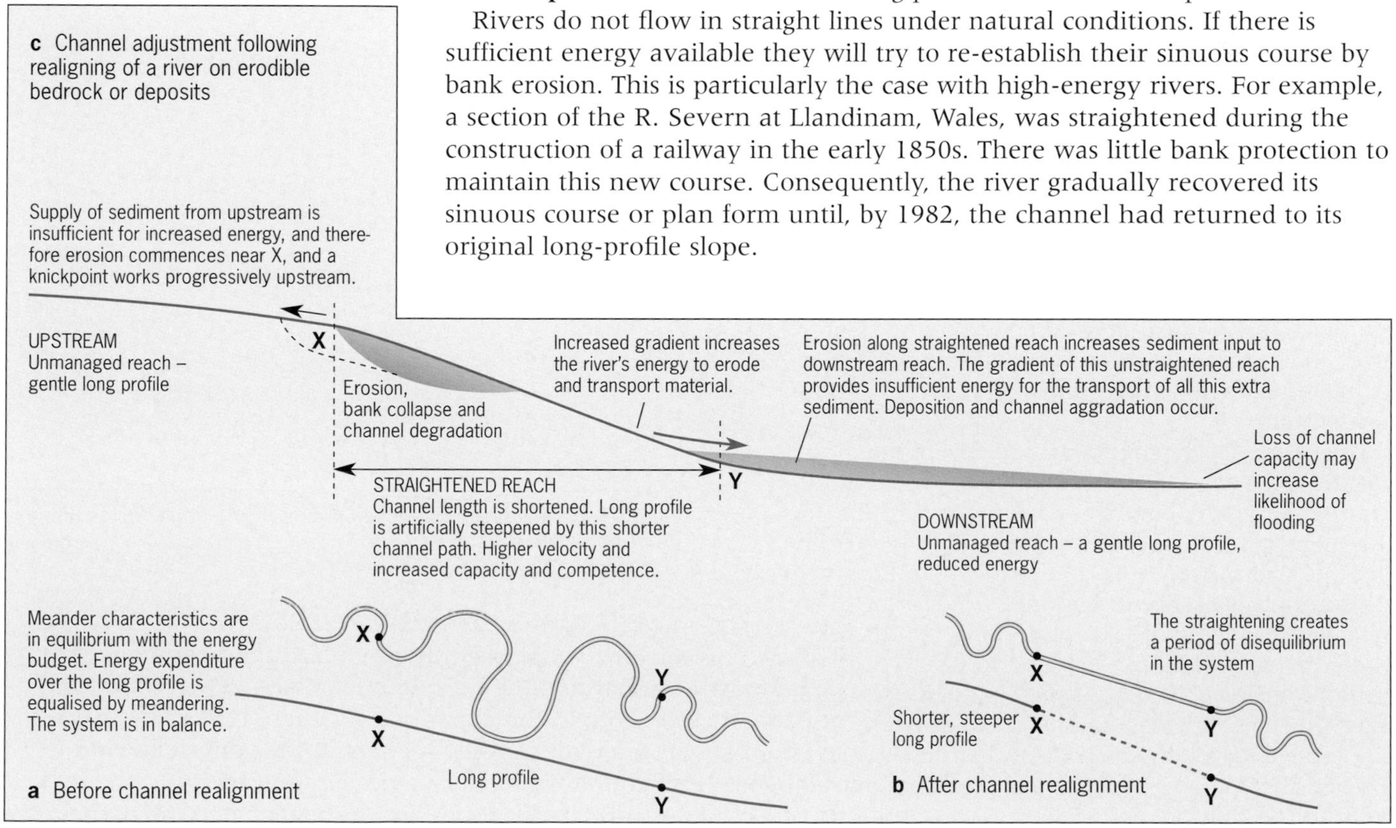

c Channel adjustment following realigning of a river on erodible bedrock or deposits

Supply of sediment from upstream is insufficient for increased energy, and therefore erosion commences near X, and a knickpoint works progressively upstream.

UPSTREAM
Unmanaged reach – gentle long profile

Erosion, bank collapse and channel degradation

STRAIGHTENED REACH
Channel length is shortened. Long profile is artificially steepened by this shorter channel path. Higher velocity and increased capacity and competence.

Increased gradient increases the river's energy to erode and transport material.

Erosion along straightened reach increases sediment input to downstream reach. The gradient of this unstraightened reach provides insufficient energy for the transport of all this extra sediment. Deposition and channel aggradation occur.

Loss of channel capacity may increase likelihood of flooding

DOWNSTREAM
Unmanaged reach – a gentle long profile, reduced energy

Meander characteristics are in equilibrium with the energy budget. Energy expenditure over the long profile is equalised by meandering. The system is in balance.

The straightening creates a period of disequilibrium in the system

Shorter, steeper long profile

Long profile

a Before channel realignment

b After channel realignment

?

8 Draw annotated diagrams to describe and explain how rivers respond to straightening.

Schemes today, therefore, incorporate bank strengthening measures to prevent the river from re-meandering. For example, a 1.5-km stretch of the River Lune at Kelleth in Cumbria was realigned in 1975. The new channel was cut into bedrock rather than sediment, and the banks reinforced with gabions. There has been no subsequent channel adjustment.

Downstream changes

Downstream of the realigned reach, the channel retains its natural, lower gradient. Here, more sediment arrives than available stream energy can remove. The result is deposition and **aggrading** of the bed. Deposition can also result in the formation of large point bars.

The upper River Rhine, western Europe

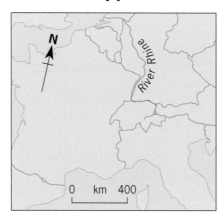

Figure 5.17 The River Rhine, western Europe

Early management

The upper R. Rhine between Basel in Switzerland and Mannheim, Germany (Fig. 5.17), has had severe flooding problems which date back to 1306. The shifting channel caused problems with demarking the border with France. The nineteenth-century German engineer Tulla had the idea of concentrating the water flow of the upper **braided** reach (Fig. 5.18) into one channel. Bed level would be lowered by erosion and the flooding risk reduced. After his work, the river was 100 km shorter and 30 per cent faster in the former braided reach, and over 2000 islands had been removed. In the meandering section of the river, diversion structures were used to train the river to cut its meanders. The banks were stabilised to maintain this new structure.

This work protected against the severe flooding, but the river was still unsuitable for navigation due to irregular gravel bars, i.e. bars of sediment in the channel. Deflector groynes were used to reduce the channel width from 200–250 m to 75–150 m. Increased erosion in this narrower channel scoured the gravel bars. Levées were built for better flood protection. These early regulation works led to nearly 4 m of bed erosion at the beginning of the channelised section. By 1970 the bed levels had been cut down by 7 m. The eroded material was transported downstream and the bed showed aggradation, i.e. deposition of sediment built up the channel bed (Fig. 5.19).

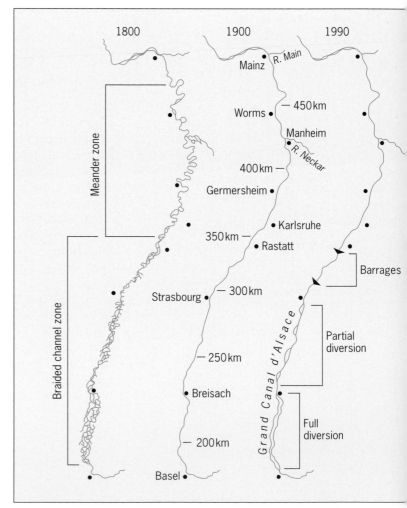

Figure 5.18 The historical development of the upper River Rhine (*Source*: Dister, 1985)

Twentieth-century management

Major river works continued into the twentieth century and the Grand Canal d'Alsace was completed in 1959. In the upper reaches there was a full diversion of the river. This led to a fall in the water table in the surrounding floodplain gravels, and with it came the loss of a large area of wetland habitat. In the partial

Figure 5.19 Bed level development of the River Rhine between Basel and Strasbourg since the beginning of river regulation up to the construction of the river diversions in 1959 (*Source*: Raabe, 1968)

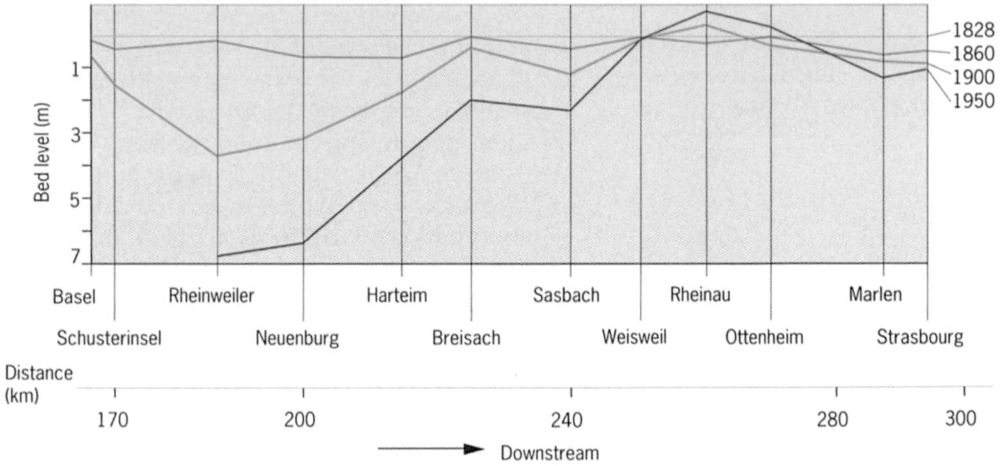

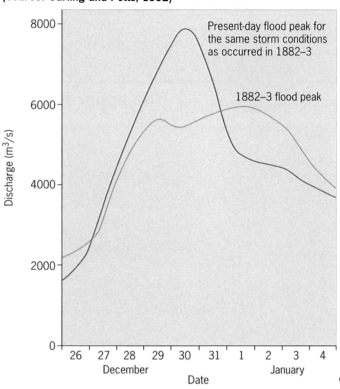

Figure 5.20 Calculated peak discharge under present conditions compared with the historical Rhine flood peak of 1882 and 1883 at the city of Worms (*Source*: Carling and Petts, 1992)

diversion zone (Fig. 5.18), barrages and dams were built to feed power stations and for flow regulation. The downstream erosion effects are now reduced by artificial feeding of sediment into the river.

The diversion works reduced the active floodplain to 40 per cent of its former area. With the loss of this natural storage, the floodwaters built up downstream, giving higher flood peaks. The flood protection defences of Karlsruhe and Mannheim were reduced from the 1-in-200-year flood to the 1-in-50-year flood event. Calculations show that a repeat of the major flood of 1883 under today's conditions would show a clear reduction in lag times and an increase in the flood peak at the city of Worms (Fig. 5.20).

The upper Rhine, therefore, has been subjected to intensive management. This has had serious impacts on the natural flow patterns and ecosystems of the river and its floodplain. Efforts to restore the upper Rhine to a more natural state are now taking place.

?

9 Describe the management of the upper Rhine using the text and Figure 5.18.

10 Describe and explain the changes in the bed level (long profile) shown in Figure 5.19.

11 Explain why the peak discharge has increased and the time lag has been reduced at Worms (Fig. 5.20).

12 Suggest why ways of restoring the upper Rhine to a more natural state are being investigated.

5.4 The ecological impacts of channelisation

River channels and floodplains provide a wide variety of natural habitats (Figs 5.21 and 5.22). Engineered channels lack many of these natural characteristics because there is little flow variability or habitat diversity. Some managed rivers, with high-energy flows or easily eroded sediments, can recover structural and habitat diversity, but engineered reaches in bedrock or in low-energy rivers can not.

We should remember that some rivers are managed with the intention of preventing structural diversity from returning, for example, with constant

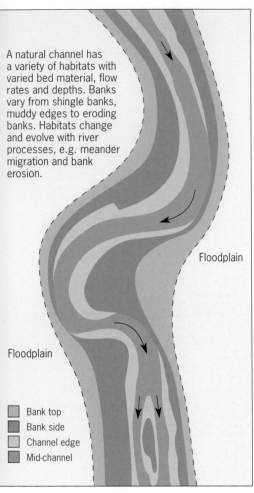

A natural channel has a variety of habitats with varied bed material, flow rates and depths. Banks vary from shingle banks, muddy edges to eroding banks. Habitats change and evolve with river processes, e.g. meander migration and bank erosion.

Floodplain

Floodplain

☐ Bank top
■ Bank side
☐ Channel edge
■ Mid-channel

Figure 5.21 Plan diagram of the habitat types of a typical lowland river (*After*: Lewis and Williams, 1984)

dredging and weed clearance. However, concern about the environmental consequences of channelisation is increasing. Water managers are beginning to value the ecological diversity of natural channels, and modern engineering schemes are more sympathetic to environmental considerations. Most schemes today require an Environmental Impact Assessment (EIA) (see Appendix A5) as well as a cost–benefit analysis before implementation (see R. Roding case study, p. 95).

The impact of realigning

Many river channelisation schemes involve the removal of meanders which can have major impacts on the stream ecology. Meanders provide a wide range of habitats: eroding river cliffs; pools and riffles; turbulent and still water; sun and shade; and sheltered and exposed sites. In the channelisation scheme on the R. Witham, Lincolnshire, the main channel was deepened and slightly widened into a trapezoidal shape. The dredge spoil was used to infill the meanders along the straightened reach. However, one meander was retained at Westborough because of the landowner's objections (Fig. 5.23).

Transition zone between floodplain and channel gradation of soil water content. Supports a wide range of plant types and animal life, e.g. otters, water voles, kingfishers and sand martins.

Low velocities encourage broad-leaved and floating-leaved species, e.g. lilies and pondweed. There are different habitats on riffle-and-pool sequences. Turbulent rivers have mainly mosses, algae and lichen. Fish habitats vary with channel bed materials and water velocities; the wider the variety, the wider the range of fish species found. Wide variety of invertebrates, e.g. stony riffles support mayfly nymphs and river limpets. Pools have a smaller variety of invertebrates.

Figure 5.22 Habitat types of a typical UK lowland river (*After*: Lewis and Williams, 1984)

Plants may be woodland or field edge. Trees and other plants provide shade and nutrients to support the river ecosystem.

Bank top   Bank side   Channel edge

Dry   Damp   Waterlogged

Rich habitat for plants due to low velocities in shoals or shelter by robust plants. Pond-like conditions in the summer low flows. Perennial plants are common, e.g. watercress, reeds. Amphibians, such as newts and toads, breed here. Many birds, e.g. reed warblers, sedge warblers, little grebes, swans, coots. Dragonflies and damselflies.

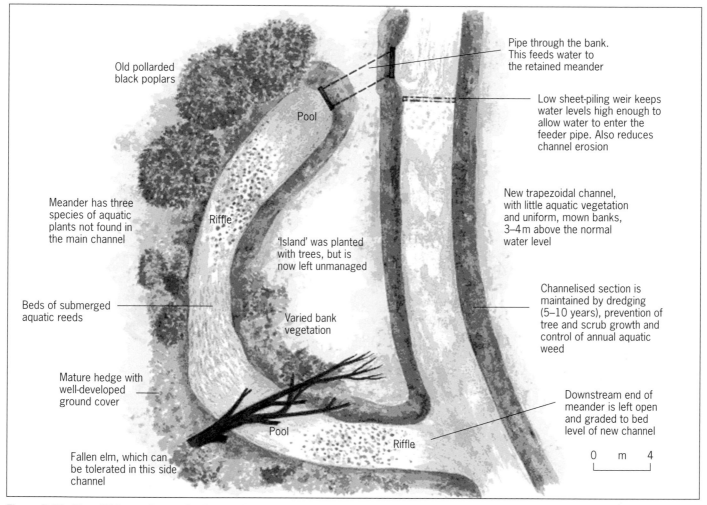

Figure 5.23 River Witham: the retained meander with the new cut-off (*Source*: Lewis and Williams, 1984)

Labels on figure:

Old pollarded black poplars

Pool

Meander has three species of aquatic plants not found in the main channel

Riffle

'Island' was planted with trees, but is now left unmanaged

Beds of submerged aquatic reeds

Varied bank vegetation

Mature hedge with well-developed ground cover

Pool

Riffle

Fallen elm, which can be tolerated in this side channel

Pipe through the bank. This feeds water to the retained meander

Low sheet-piling weir keeps water levels high enough to allow water to enter the feeder pipe. Also reduces channel erosion

New trapezoidal channel, with little aquatic vegetation and uniform, mown banks, 3–4 m above the normal water level

Channelised section is maintained by dredging (5–10 years), prevention of tree and scrub growth and control of annual aquatic weed

Downstream end of meander is left open and graded to bed level of new channel

0   m   4

13a Using Figure 5.23, describe how the River Witham meander was retained.
b Suggest the ecological advantages of retaining this meander.
c Describe how channelisation has affected the ecological structure and diversity of the new channel.

Managing the River Roding, England

The R. Roding in Essex drains a small narrow catchment which is agricultural in its upper reaches and heavily urbanised in the lower reaches as it flows into the R. Thames (Fig. 5.24, Table 5.6). The river has a characteristic lowland meandering pattern, with riffles and pools providing ideal conditions for fish. However, urban development has resulted in changes to the river, and flood control has been necessary.

Flood control management of the river has involved various forms of channelisation, i.e. straightening, dredging, training walls with gabion boxes, sheet piling and concrete blocks, and realignment. The older schemes have had significant adverse impacts on the

river system. However, recent schemes, from 1979 to 1980, have attempted to restore environmental diversity to former channelised reaches.

Table 5.6 River Roding: key facts

		Geology and land use:
Catchment area	342 km²	**Upper reaches** Glacial clay deposits, arable agricultural area with many villages
Length	80 km	
Channel width	5.5–8.5 m	
Banks	Naturally high and steep, cut 1.5–2 m into the floodplain	**Lower reaches** Alluvial deposits on active floodplain. Urban development and transport routes
Long profile	Average gradient 0.001	
Low level flow	2 m³/s	

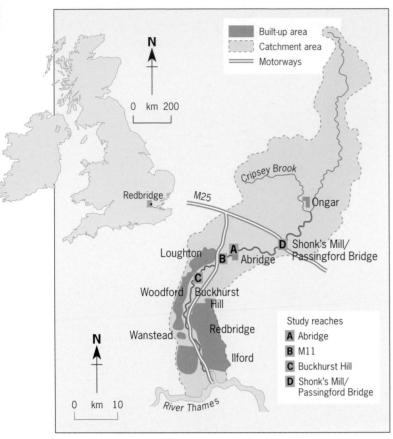

Figure 5.24 The River Roding and its catchment (*Source*: Lewis and Williams, 1984)

Management near Abridge (Reach A)

Between 1979 and 1980 a flood alleviation scheme was needed for the village of Abridge, the B172 road (1-in-70-year flood protection) and the improved pastureland between Abridge and Loughton further downstream (1-in-10-year protection). The scheme involved building a two-stage channel along 3.5 km of the R. Roding (Fig. 5.25). The method of channel management chosen allowed the natural channel to remain as undisturbed as possible. The scheme left more than 90 per cent of the river bed untouched to conserve the chub fishery. Nevertheless, the loss of the two meanders removed deep pool habitats. To compensate, fish shelters were incorporated into the scheme. Overall, habitat diversity has been retained and new habitats created in the higher level channel.

The M11 reach, downstream of Abridge (Reach B)

In 1973, the M11 reach was straightened and reshaped into a trapezoidal channel for the motorway to be built. The length of channel was shortened from 700 m to

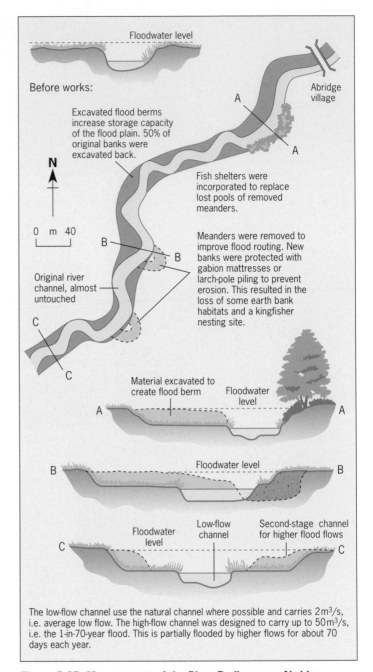

The low-flow channel use the natural channel where possible and carries 2m³/s, i.e. average low flow. The high-flow channel was designed to carry up to 50m³/s, i.e. the 1-in-70-year flood. This is partially flooded by higher flows for about 70 days each year.

Figure 5.25 Management of the River Roding near Abridge

500 m, and the stream gradient consequently increased by 40 per cent. The channel was lined with concrete blocks and river flow became shallow, fast and uniform.

Water managers took the new 1979–80 flood alleviation scheme as an opportunity to upgrade this reach and introduce a more environmentally sensitive scheme (Fig. 5.26).

?

14 Explain why a two-stage channel was developed near Abridge.

15 Suggest reasons why the flood engineers decided to remove the two meanders as part of the flood alleviation scheme.

?

16 Study Figure 5.26. Explain how the deflector groynes give areas of variable velocities and erosion and deposition in the channel.

17 Draw two annotated diagrams of the channel cross-sections in Figure 5.26, one at the site of the groynes and one between the groynes to show the changes in channel profile which result from the scheme.

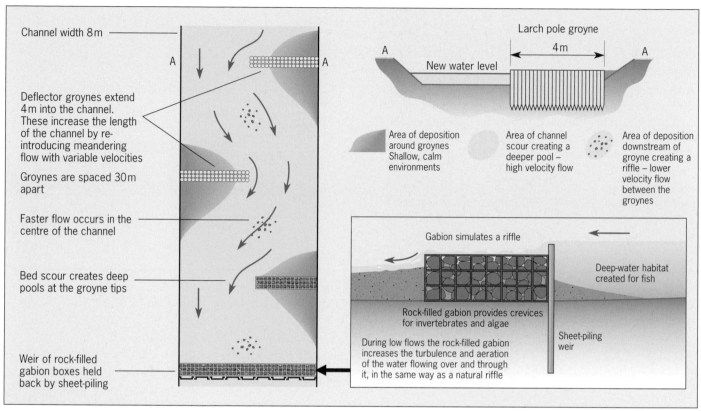

Figure 5.26 The 1979–80 upgrading of the M11 reach

The effect of the management schemes on habitat diversity

Figures 5.27 to 5.29 show in-channel vegetation in straightened reaches.

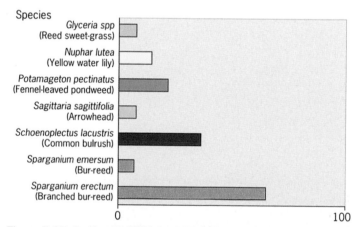

Figure 5.27 At Shonk's Mill (reach D) 880 m of river was straightened in 1750 to provide power for a mill. The reach was shortened by 330 m, Its gradient increased by 60 per cent and the channel was cut as straight and narrow as possible. There is a gently meandering thalweg, but due to the resistant clay river bed there has been little morphological recovery

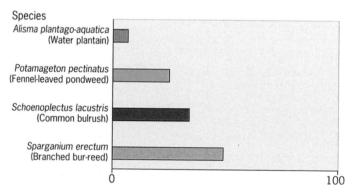

Figure 5.28 The channel at Buckhurst Hill (reach C) was straightened in 1975 to allow people to extract gravel from the floodplain. The river was shortened by 250 m, the gradient increased by 25 per cent and the width by 6.75 m. The river flow is shallow, fast and uniform. There has been bed erosion upstream, resulting in bank collapse and lateral instability. This upstream section has had to be dredged to prevent deposition of the newly eroded sediment. Downstream, increased sedimentation means that maintenance dredging has become necessary

Figure 5.29 In the M11 reach (reach 2) deflector groynes and a weir have had a major impact on the quantity and diversity of fish species and the vegetation. In 1978 a survey showed that there were large numbers of small fish, such as stone loach, typical of shallow steams. A year after the groynes were installed, the fish population showed a wider variety, with more medium and large-sized species, such as chub, dace, roach, gudgeon, pike and large eels

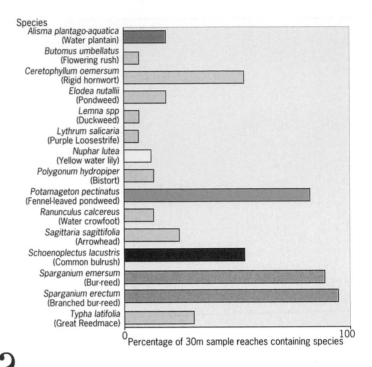

Management of Shonk's Mill, Passingford Bridge (reach D)

In 1982, the R. Roding at Passingford Bridge required a similar diversion to that which had taken place for the M11 in 1973. This time it was for the building of the M25. The impacts on the river ecosystems from the 1973 scheme and the necessary upgrading were considered when planning this work. A whole channel realignment was needed; a suitable stretch of river was found 4 km downstream of Passingford Bridge. The realigned channel (Fig. 5.30) has been designed to maintain habitat diversity as much as possible.

?

18a Compare the in-channel vegetation for the three reaches of the Roding shown in Figures 5.27 to 5.30. Comment on changes in biomass and ecosystem diversity.
b What implications do the three vegetation surveys have for the fluvial ecosystems?

19 In what other ways has the channel upgrading improved opportunities for wildlife in the area?

20a Describe the upstream and downstream effects of channelisation in the Buckhurst Hill reach.
b Explain why maintenance dredging became necessary.

21 Use Figure 5.30 to describe how the engineers have designed the realigned channel to simulate a natural river and its ecosystems.

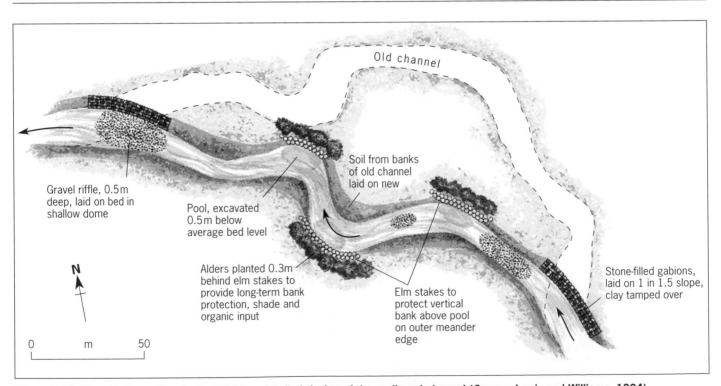

Figure 5.30 River Roding at Passingford Bridge: detailed design of the realigned channel (*Source*: Lewis and Williams, 1984)

5.5 River regulation and channel processes

In Chapter 4 we saw that river regulation schemes have important impacts on flow regimes, sediment budgets and available energy. High dams and huge reservoirs in mountain environments are the most spectacular regulation structures (Fig 5.31), but low barrages and weirs are far more numerous and are found across a wide diversity of drainage basins (Fig. 5.32 and River Murray case study, p. 101).

Upstream effects

As a river with high capacity and competence flows into a reservoir, the available energy is abruptly reduced. The resulting sedimentation spreads progressively across the reservoir floor as a delta-like deposit (Fig 5.33). The reservoir acts as a local base level and the river bed is aggraded upstream. This increases the likelihood of flooding unless releases through the dam lower the reservoir level during high discharge events.

Figure 5.31 Hoover Dam and Lake Mead (USA), from an altitude of 10 000 m. The deep, hard-rock canyon across which the high dam has been built can be seen beyond the reservoir which has filled the upstream canyon

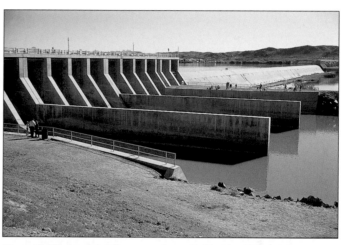

Figure 5.32 Imperial Dam, southern California. This low barrage across the lower Colorado River controls releases into diversion canals for the irrigation system of the arid Coachella Valley

Downstream effects
Clear water erosion

Downstream of the dam, water emerges with a reduced sediment load of 8–50 per cent. The Aswan High Dam (Fig. 4.44) traps 98 per cent of the Nile silt. The river has increased energy as a result of this reduction, and erosion of the channel results especially in reaches immediately below a dam. This channel incision is called **clear water erosion**. In the case of the Hoover Dam on the R. Colorado, USA, vertical incision lowered the river bed by 6.1 m over an 11-km stretch in four years. Rivers with a naturally high sediment load show dramatic results. The Sanmenxia Dam on the Yellow River in China (Fig. 4.62) has caused 4 m of bed degrading over 68 km in only four years.

Clear water erosion can cause **rejuvenation** of tributary channels as they adjust their long profiles to the newly degraded main channel. Continued vertical down-cutting can undermine bridges and other structures along the river. To reduce these effects, some river engineers artificially feed channels with sediment. However, the increased erosion is not all bad. In northern China, the incision of some river channels has reduced the strain on levées and consequently reduced the need for increasing levée heights.

Increasing sediment load

One of the main reasons for building dams is to regulate the flow regime. Thus, the discharge regime of the river downstream has changed from the pre-dam

Figure 5.33 The upstream and downstream effects of a dam on the long and cross profiles (*After*: Goudie, 1990)

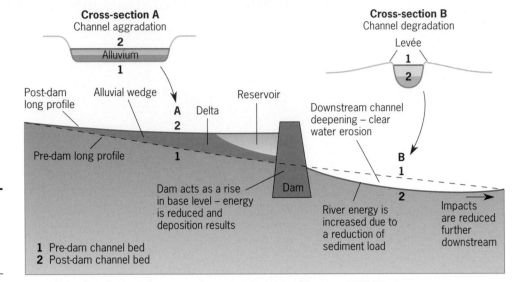

23 Draw a large copy of Figure 5.33. Add detailed notes on the upstream and downstream effects of a dam.

flow (see Chapter 4). Water abstraction for irrigation and municipal use will reduce the discharge of the river. As a result, the river may have a reduced flow which has insufficient energy to carry any sediment load supplied by undammed tributary rivers. The effect is the opposite to clear water erosion. For example, downstream of the Glen Canyon Dam on the River Colorado, USA, the extremes of flow have been reduced (see the case study on p. 104). The main channel is no longer capable of removing the sediment supplied by flash-flooding tributaries. As a result, deposits of up to 2.6 m thick have accumulated in the upper Grand Canyon (the opposite effect to the clear water erosion downstream of the Hoover Dam).

Reducing channel size

The decreased maximum discharges downstream of dams result in reduced channel sizes, especially if the river is not competent to carry the sediment load supplied by tributaries. Reductions of 30–70 per cent have been recorded. For example, the Elephant Butte Dam on the Rio Grande in the USA, has resulted in a 50 per cent channel capacity loss; the Ladybower Reservoir on the River Derwent in Derbyshire has caused a 40 per cent loss. Discharge reductions of 10–30 per cent in the North and South Platte Rivers in the USA resulted in changes in channel form. The North Platte River was 760–1220 m wide in 1890 and today has a reduced width of 60 m. Both rivers had a braided course before dam construction, but today the river flows in one narrow, well-defined channel. When channel slope stays the same but discharge reduces, the channel is more likely to meander than be braided. Indeed, sinuosity of the North and South Platte rivers has increased. The channel forms have adjusted to a new dynamic equilibrium with the new conditions.

The impact on landform development

Our study of the Aswan High Dam in Chapter 4 looked at the consequences of controlling flooding. Without flooding, there will be no further deposition of sediment on the floodplain or building of natural levées. The lack of sediment transport downstream means that delta regions are not supplied with sediment. Erosion by the sea continues and the delta is eroded away. There is a reduction in soil fertility and an increase in **salinisation**. Channel and floodplain morphology will have to reach a new equilibrium with the changed sediment and discharge conditions. For example, as the case study of the Glen Canyon Dam shows, the controlled flows have resulted in channel bed aggradation, but have also led to the erosion and shrinking of flanking sand bars. There has been

Study Figure 5.34.

24 Describe and explain the terrace development in the Grand Canyon before the Glen Canyon Dam was built.

25 Describe and explain how the changed regime of the river has affected the terraces.

26 You are a water engineer advising a planning authority on the feasibility of building a dam. Outline a programme of fieldwork and other data that you would need before you could assess the likely impacts of the dam on the river system.

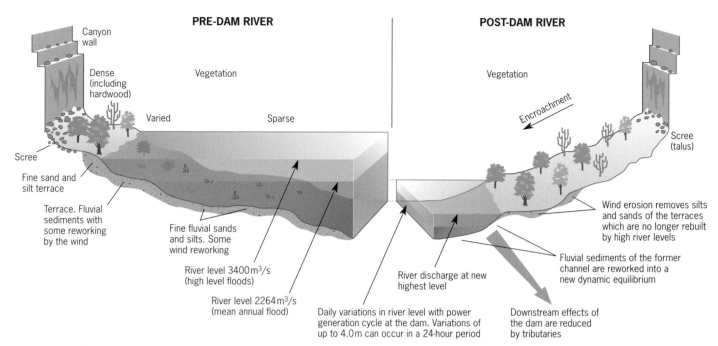

PRE-DAM RIVER

Canyon wall

Dense (including hardwood)

Vegetation

Varied

Sparse

Scree

Fine sand and silt terrace

Terrace. Fluvial sediments with some reworking by the wind

Fine fluvial sands and silts. Some wind reworking

River level 3400 m³/s (high level floods)

River level 2264 m³/s (mean annual flood)

POST-DAM RIVER

Vegetation

Encroachment

Scree (talus)

Wind erosion removes silts and sands of the terraces which are no longer rebuilt by high river levels

Fluvial sediments of the former channel are reworked into a new dynamic equilibrium

River discharge at new highest level

Daily variations in river level with power generation cycle at the dam. Variations of up to 4.0m can occur in a 24-hour period

Downstream effects of the dam are reduced by tributaries

Figure 5.34 The effects of the Glen Canyon Dam on the alluvial morphology and ecology of the Grand Canyon

a significant change in the **alluvial morphology** of the channel (Fig. 5.34).

The effects of channel morphology change downstream are reduced as distance from the dam increases and the human management variables of flow regulation and sediment loss are reduced by tributary rivers. There is also a reduction in impacts over time, for two reasons:

1 Downstream degrading flattens the channel slope so much that there is insufficient energy to transport the available sediment.

2 Reduced peak flows lessen the competence of the river. Thus, only the finer particles are transported, leaving behind a coarser bedload. This eventually forms a protective armour on the river bed, which reduces further erosion.

The River Murray, South Australia

The R. Murray has its source in the Snowy Mountains and flows north-west to South Australia (Fig. 5.35). It has an extended long profile due to the low gradients downstream of the Snowy Mountains.

River regulation

Regulation of the Lower Murray began in 1929. Weirs were built (Fig. 5.37) which reduced floods, but increased flows to near channel capacity. Today the weirs are used to maintain flows for irrigation. They provide a steady flow of water upstream, but downstream water levels vary erratically with changes of up to 2.6 m recorded in one day. Estimates suggest that up to 73 per cent of the river's sediment load is retained by the dams and weirs along its course.

Figure 5.35 The River Murray channel has a low-energy and meandering form. Flow is controlled by upstream dams and reservoirs. The river receives no major tributaries downstream of the River Darling junction (*Source*: Carling and Petts, 1992)

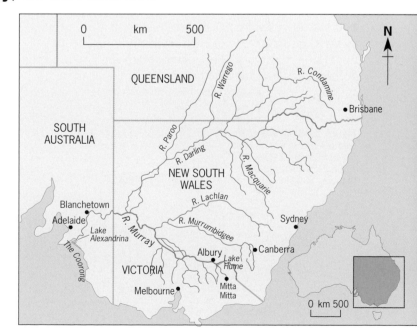

Changes in channel form

The lower Murray is a low-energy river due to its gentle gradient (55 mm/km) and there have been no changes in channel planform as a result of regulation. However, fluctuating water levels from weir operations have increased bank erosion downstream, even in relatively cohesive sediment (Fig. 5.36). As the water levels fall with the operation of the weir, the banks are left saturated and there is collapse. The small, but frequent changes in water level may undermine the bottom of the bank, making it more vulnerable to collapse. Immediately below weir 4, bank slopes increased from 65 to 81 degrees between 1988 and 1989.

27a Use Figure 5.36 to describe the effects of the weirs on bank erosion.
b Explain why increased bank erosion occurs and describe the impacts on bank slope.

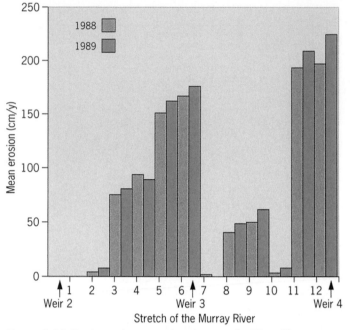

Figure 5.36 Bank erosion at twelve sites on the River Murray between weirs 2 and 4, 1988–9 (*Source*: Thorns and Walker, 1992)

Changes to the long profile

The long profile has shown significant changes which are similar to those downstream of dams. There is an increased gradient due to aggrading in the upper region of the profile. The long profile has become stepped in form, with the individual steps corresponding to the weirs. These changes are shown by mean bed elevation (i.e. height above sea level). Four regions of response have been distinguished, as shown in Figure 5.38.

On a local scale, the impacts of the weirs on the long profile can be identified (Fig. 5.39). Degrading of the bed has occurred below each weir varying from 4–19 km. The downcutting below weir 5 occurred within 18 km of the weir. In the first kilometre downstream the bed was lowered by 2.4 m, but by only 0.8 m in the next 9 km. Upstream of each weir, there has been aggrading of the bed. The material deposited behind the weirs builds up into a delta-type feature and then migrates downstream towards the next weir.

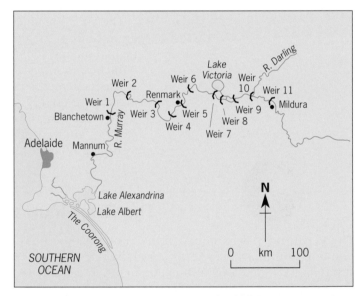

Figure 5.37 Eleven weirs were built in the 830 km stretch of the River Murray, initially for navigation purposes (*Source*: Carling and Petts, 1992)

Figure 5.38 Changes in bed elevation of the lower River Murray, 1906–88 (*Source*: Thorns and Walker, 1992)

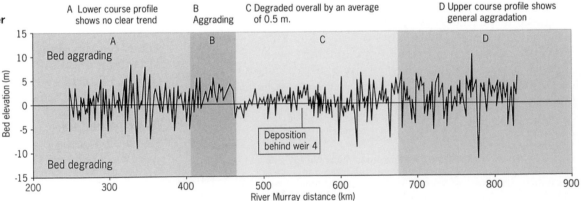

?

28a Study Figure 5.38. Describe the changes in bed elevation (i.e. the long profile) shown in the lower Murray. Give reasons for your observations.
b Suggest why the low-energy budget of the river might explain the unclear response in the lowest reaches (Section A).

29 Use Figure 5.39 to describe and explain the overall changes in the long profile of the lower Murray.

30 Draw an annotated long profile of the River Murray to describe and explain the changes in bed level observed between the weirs.

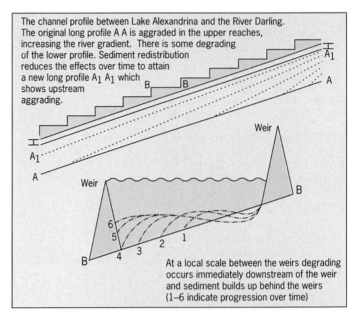

The channel profile between Lake Alexandrina and the River Darling. The original long profile A A is aggraded in the upper reaches, increasing the river gradient. There is some degrading of the lower profile. Sediment redistribution reduces the effects over time to attain a new long profile $A_1 A_1$ which shows upstream aggrading.

At a local scale between the weirs degrading occurs immediately downstream of the weir and sediment builds up behind the weirs (1–6 indicate progression over time)

Figure 5.39 A model of the changes to the long profile of the Lower River Murray over time (*Source*: Thorns and Walker, 1992)

Changes in cross-sectional area

Earlier in the chapter we saw that below dams clear water erosion causes channel enlargement. This erosion is rapid at first and then slows down until a new equilibrium is reached with the managed flow and sediment regime. The weirs on the R. Murray cause a similar response. There is channel enlargement, which is then followed by reduction in channel size as the new equilibrium is reached. The managed section of the Murray is near the mouth of the river and therefore receives a constant supply of fresh sediment from upstream. However, coarse sediments are trapped behind the upland weirs and, consequently, sediment size has decreased by 32 per cent overall. Recent research on the cross-sectional area of the channel downstream of the weirs has identified three groups of responses (Figs 5.40 to 5.42).

31a Using Figures 5.40 to 5.42, list the changes which have occurred in the size of the river channel. Explain the three types of response shown by the river.
b What changes would you expect to occur in the eroding and fluctuating channels in the future? Explain your answer.

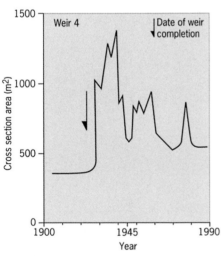

Figure 5.40 Stabilising, e.g. weir 4. After an initial period of erosion and fluctuation, the channel cross-section reaches a new dynamic equilibrium, 30–40 years after the building of the weir, with channels larger than before regulation. After initial clear water erosion, there is infilling or aggrading as sediment deposits behind each weir are reworked by the river

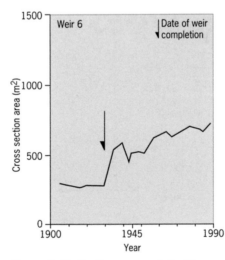

Figure 5.41 Eroding, e.g. weir 6. After initial fluctuations, erosion has continued to enlarge the cross-sectional area since the 1950s

Figures 5.40–5.42 (*Source*: Thoms and Walker, 1992)

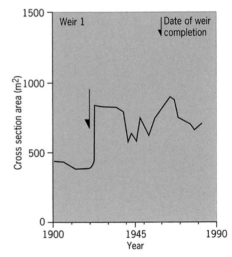

Figure 5.42 Fluctuating, e.g. weirs 1 and 2. There is no clear pattern of adjustment and the changes do not appear to be related to discharge. It is interesting that the two weirs in this group are located the furthest downstream. Possibly the impacts of management have not resulted in any new dynamic equilibrium in the lowest reaches, because the time scales are insufficient for this low-energy river environment

?

32 Make a list of the principal impacts of dams and other control structures upon the character and function of river systems. Illustrate each of your points from examples you have studied.

33 The key to successful river management is an understanding of river processes and channel dynamics.

34 Describe and explain each of the four human activity impacts, bulleted below, in terms of:
a sediment supply to the channel
b erosion (degrading) or deposition (aggrading) in the channel
c channel size
d likelihood of increased flooding
e changes in landform development, e.g. floodplains and meander development.
(Think about channel form and discharge–sediment relationships.)

• Urbanisation causes an increase in discharge and a reduction in sediment load.
• Deforestation causes an increase in discharge and sediment load.
• Mining activity can lead to a large input of additional sediment to the channel.
• Soil conservation measures reduce the discharge and sediment load of a river.

35 Essay: A major debate taking place in many countries, e.g. the UK, the USA and Germany, is whether to restore rivers to a more unmanaged state which maintains wetlands and other habitats and enhances their amenity value. Suggest why early river management schemes have been so damaging to rivers and examine how future management can preserve, restore or enhance the natural environment. Use a range of examples which you have studied to exemplify the points you make.

Impacts of the Glen Canyon Dam, Colorado River, USA

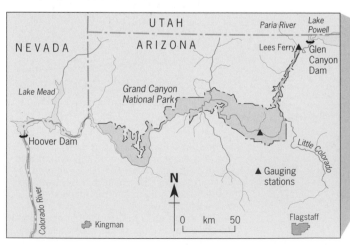

Figure 5.43 Running the Colorado. The US National Park Service restricts numbers to about 22 000 visitors a year, all travelling with licensed operators, and the total revenue exceeds $60 million

One of the most popular recreational activities in the Grand Canyon National Park is river running or whitewater boating down the Colorado River (Fig. 5.43). In addition to the excitement of 'running' the river through the mighty canyon, one of the key attractions is camping on sandbars flanking the river.

Figure 5.44 The Colorado basin and Glen Canyon Dam

More than 200 sandbars are used by the boating groups in a 365-km stretch through the national park. The problem is that these sandbars have been shrinking and disappearing since the building of the Glen Canyon Dam upstream of the Grand Canyon (Fig. 5.44).

The Glen Canyon Dam

The Colorado River is one of the most intensively regulated rivers in the world. The total reservoir capacity along its course is more than four times the mean annual flow of 17 billion cubic metres. The largest reservoir, Lake Powell behind the Glen Canyon Dam, has a storage capacity of 30 billion cubic metres (Fig. 5.44). This multi-purpose dam and reservoir scheme has fundamentally changed the river regime at a range of time-scales (Fig. 5.45a–d).

Releases through the Glen Canyon dam are determined by:

- the snowmelt flow surge in May–June and the storage capacity of the reservoir, e.g. the high volume releases of 1983 after heavy snowfalls during the previous winter (Fig. 5.45b)
- the requirement to supply 9.25 billion cubic metres into the lower Colorado basin
- the generation needs of the HEP plant at the dam (plant capacity 930 cumecs)
- downstream flood control
- the requirement to maintain environmental quality and values within the Grand Canyon National Park.

Impacts upon sediment transport

During the pre-regulation regime, the mean annual suspended load at Lees Ferry was 66 million tonnes.

At the Grand Canyon gauging station, 150 km downstream, the total was 86 million tonnes. Thus, 20 million tonnes were delivered by tributary rivers, especially the Paria and Little Colorado (Fig. 5.44).

Today, almost all sediment entering Lake Powell is deposited on the reservoir bed. The dam releases clear water and the available energy allows the water to entrain and transport load. As a result, fine sediment has been scoured from the channel bed and a bed armour of coarse gravel and cobbles has developed for the first 20 km below the dam. Continued inputs from the Paria and Little Colorado tributaries maintain the sediment load 150 km downstream, at 25 per cent of the pre-dam amount. All of this sediment input has been removed and there has been bed aggradation. Within a decade of the start of regulated flows, the sandbars along the river in the Grand Canyon shrank significantly. Research suggested four main reasons:

- decreased sand supply from upstream
- a reduction in annual peak discharges that built up the sandbars
- increased diurnal flow variations that accelerate erosion
- increased human usage of the sandbars.

Rebuilding the sandbars

Two main factors have influenced the sediment budget of the sandbars. First, the sandbars are built up by strong eddies that spill laterally from the main flow. As velocity in the eddies decreases, sediment is deposited. Under the controlled regime, flows are rarely powerful enough to create these sediment-bearing eddies. Second, the daily rise and fall of river level

Figure 5.45 Flow regimes along the Colorado River at Lees Ferry gauging station (*Source*: Andrews and Pizzi, 2000)

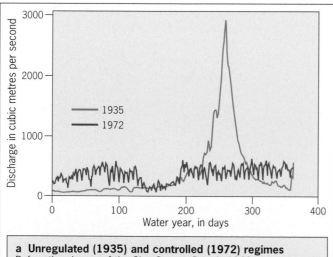

a Unregulated (1935) and controlled (1972) regimes
Before the closure of the Glen Canyon Dam in 1963, the seasonal regime was dominated by the May–June flood discharges fed by snowmelt from the mountainous headwater catchments. The controlled releases remove the flood peak but maintain higher flows through much of the year.

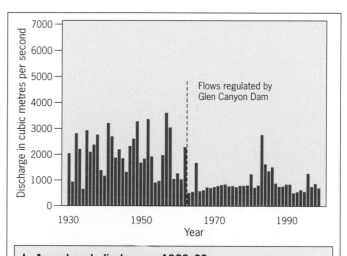

b Annual peak discharges, 1930–99
The huge Lake Powell reservoir of 30 billion cubic metres allows peak controlled releases to be kept within the permitted maximum of 920 cumecs, except in years of exceptional snowmelt, e.g.1983. The mean unregulated peak flow was 2420 cumecs.

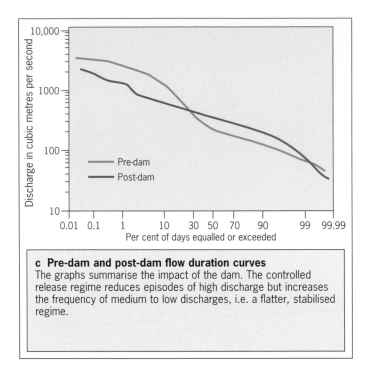

c Pre-dam and post-dam flow duration curves
The graphs summarise the impact of the dam. The controlled release regime reduces episodes of high discharge but increases the frequency of medium to low discharges, i.e. a flatter, stabilised regime.

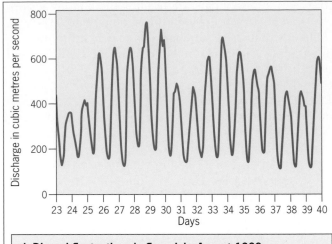

d Diurnal fluctuations in flow, July–August 1988
Although the controlled releases dampen year-to-year and seasonal variations in flow, daily fluctuations have increased. This is the result of day–night and weekday–weekend variations in electricity demand. Releases through the dam HEP plant reflect this varying demand and cause river levels to rise and fall by up to 4 m in a 24-hour period.

causes repeated soaking and slumping of the flanks of the sandbars (Fig. 5.45d). The slumped material is then removed by the main channel flow. As a result, since 1992, the release regime has been adjusted to:
a decrease daily and annual peak flows in order to retain a sand supply in the river bed
b decrease daily fluctuations in order to reduce sandbar erosion.

Studies have also shown that much of the sediment carried by flood discharges along the Little Colorado and Paria tributaries is stored in the bed of the main Colorado channel. This provides a valuable potential supply for sandbar rebuilding when flow is vigorous. Thus, the water managers are experimenting with occasional increased releases, e.g. a seven-day release of 1275 cumecs in 1996. The aim is to increase available stream energy and so to entrain and transport bed material for redeposition on the sandbars.

Summary

- People manage river channels by the deliberate action of channelisation for flood control, land drainage, erosion prevention and navigation.

- Channelisation involves resectioning, realignment, bank protection, lining channels and containment, vegetation clearance and dredging, as well as flood relief channels, embankments and levées.

- Channelisation aims to increase channel efficiency, size or gradient, so that flow velocities are increased in the channelised reach.

- Channelisation can have major impacts on channel processes and form, both in the altered reach and downstream.

- Channelisation can have major ecological impacts. Many modern schemes try to reduce the adverse effects and restore channels to a more natural state.

- Dams have important impacts on river channel forms and processes, both upstream and downstream of the dam site.

6 Flooding and human responses

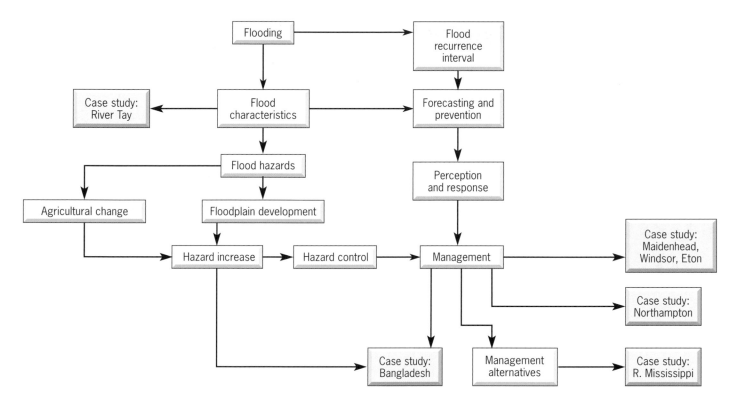

6.1 Introduction

Most of the time, a river's water and **sediment** load are transported in the river channel itself. The function of the **floodplain** is to act as a temporary store at times of higher flows. Floods occur with similar frequency in different environments, with **bankfull discharges** occurring on average every 1.5 years, with a range of 0.5–2 years. Overspill is therefore a normal event, and the floodplain and river channel are closely linked parts of the same **fluvial system**. In semi-arid areas, **alluvial fans** have a similar function.

Most floods are caused by a large input of water to the river by **quickflow processes**. Although there are rare events, such as landslides or dam failures, most river floods result from a downpour of very heavy rainfall, or prolonged rainfall giving high antecedent soil moisture conditions or rapid snowmelt. The severity of the flooding is related to the degree of quickflow-forming processes (see Chapter 3).

Floods as hazards

Floods are the cause of 40 per cent of all deaths due to natural disasters and, throughout the world, this figure is increasing. Between 1965 and 1990, 100 000 deaths worldwide were caused by flooding, and three-quarters of a billion people were distressed or had their lives disrupted in some way. Since floods are a frequent natural process in fluvial systems, we might ask why they are also the most common environmental or natural hazard.

Floods become a hazard when they interact with human activity. It is this interaction which distinguishes a natural process from a natural hazard. However, is it our misunderstanding and misuse of rivers and their floodplains that create the hazard (Fig.6.1)?

1 Read Figure 6.1.
a Suggest why floods are described as disasters which are people's own fault.
b Explain why Professor Thorne suggests that rivers should be allowed to flood.
c Give reasons why it would be difficult to restore floodplains and water meadows to their water storage function.

Who's soggy now?

After a decade of dryish winters broken by occasional severe downpours in a few regions, the British weather has gone back to basics. And it is still only January, the start of the usual wet season.

The Severn, Britain's longest river by a short head from the Thames, meets the Avon at Tewkesbury. Normally it's a quiet affair conducted below serious riverbanks but for 37 of the last 39 days it's been a passionate, public mingling of juices collected from as far away as the Black Country and Stratford.

What excites Jim Bourton, the former mayor of Tewkesbury, and many old timers is that these rains are nothing unusual. They're very widespread, yes, but not really severe.

'We've built on everything,' Jim says. 'One reason for all the floods now is that we've built so much on the flood plains. Water has to go somewhere. You stop one area getting flooded and another one floods.'

Last year Tewkesbury built a Safeway's hypermarket on many acres of the Severn flood plain; it built on St John's Island, it built new roads and over the years it has partly filled in the 'ham', all areas that used to flood. 'And they haven't maintained their sluices,' Jim says. 'I've warned them. Nothing a river likes more than flooding. It's nature's drainage. Can't stop it. Sometimes shouldn't try.'

But it's worse than that. Floods are more likely even in moderate rains these days, he says, because we've grubbed up the hedges, felled the trees, filled the ditches and turned the water meadows to cereal growing. 'The water runs off more now than it used to, see?'

A mature tree, Jim says, takes up 150 gallons of water a day and Dutch elm disease took out thousands near the town.

Colin Thorne, professor of geography at Nottingham University, a flood man who has advised the Bangladeshis on how to mitigate the monsoons and the Brahmaputra river, says: 'It's much better to work with nature and where possible leave rivers to overflow.' Study after study shows that urbanisation is directly linked to flooding. 'Floods are becoming more peaked. Rivers are rising faster, their periods of concentration are becoming reduced and they fall back more quickly – even if the volume of water is the same.'

A river is not just water, he says. 'It's full of sediment, too, and we've become much better at managing the water than the sediment. But if you disturb the dynamics between water and landscape, things start happening and it becomes very unpredictable. Your channels will start naturally to silt in and the only way to stop that is to dredge. Thousands of miles of river dredging take place each year.'

Not only that, we've tried to manage some of our rivers almost to death. Massively expensive, heavy-handed concrete drainage works along many British rivers are testament everywhere to people's arrogance over nature, developers' profit motives and farmers' desires to drain every last inch of lowland ground in the name of subsidies. Some British rivers are today little more than concrete drainage channels designed to take water away as quickly as possible.

Thorne advocates not quite a tearing down of the river flood defences (we spend some £250 million a year on them) but a gradual compensating of farmers and others and a grand taking back of the floodplains and restoration of the water meadows.

'Rivers are meant to flood,' he says. 'They must have room to move. Ideally it should be three times as wide as their lowest channels.'

Figure 6.1 UK floods, January 1994 (*Source: The Guardian*, 10 January 1994)

2 Study Figure 6.2.
a Describe the trends shown in damage and loss of life in the USA from 1940 to 1993.
b Suggest reasons for the wide yearly variations.

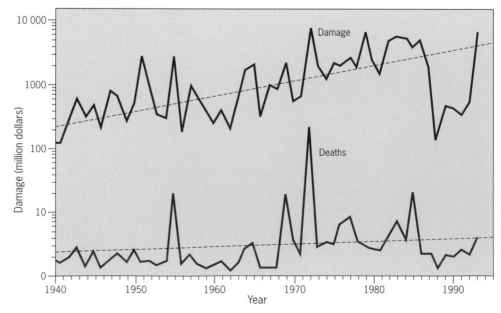

Figure 6.2 USA: annual deaths and economic losses caused by flooding, 1940–93. Damages are in millions of US$, adjusted to 1990 values. (*Source*: Smith, 1993 and US Corps of Engineers, 1996)

Tide of death sweeps Mozambique

GOVERNMENT APPEALS for help as just five helicopters battle to save thousands stranded in the flood.

Dozens, possibly hundreds of people were swept to their deaths by surging flood waters in Mozambique yesterday as too few rescue helicopters battled to save survivors clinging to trees and roofs, and crammed into ever shrinking strips of high grounds.

The Mozambican government appealed for more aircraft to back up five South African military helicopters which are battling to save thousands of people from surging river waters.

Up to 60 000 people were yesterday attempting to flee the town of Chokwe, where waters rose by about six feet in a few hours and were predicted to surge significantly higher with a new bout of flooding. Surrounding low-lying villages have completely disappeared.

One helicopter pilot wept as he described his desperation at being able to save just a few dozen at a time.

'People are just disappearing. We can't get to them all in time. We see people stuck and when we fly back they've gone,' he said.

One helicopter crew said they had flown over a cluster of houses with people waving for help. When they returned later, the homes had vanished into a vast lake broken only by the tips of a few tall trees and telegraph poles. The people were nowhere to be seen.

Figure 6.3 Flooding in Mozambique (*Source*: *The Guardian*, 28 February 2000)

Countries in the economically developing world typically experience the greatest loss of life and damage to crops and property, but the trend is clear even in developed nations such as the USA (Fig. 6.2). Research suggests that developed nations suffer only 5 per cent of fatalities from floods, but 75 per cent of the costs from natural hazards, whereas the economically developing world suffers 95 per cent of the deaths but 25 per cent of the costs.

The reasons for this increasing damage to life and property are interrelated, but they can be divided into three factors:
• changing agricultural activity on floodplains which is not compatible with flooding
• development of floodplain areas with urban uses; this is called floodplain encroachment
• human activity changing the location, magnitude, frequency and duration of flooding.

There is evidence that serious floods are becoming more frequent as a result of increases in extreme weather events, e.g. the prolonged rains that caused the disastrous floods across south-east Africa in February 2000 (Fig. 6.3). Scientists believe this is one effect of global warming.

6.2 Increasing the hazard: changing agricultural activity

Flooding can sustain agricultural productivity by renewing soil fertility. Silt is deposited on the floodplain, and floodwaters wash away any salt build-up in the soil. In semi-arid areas, people develop irrigated agriculture along the courses of **perennial streams** which provide a vital water supply.

Many of the world's river floodplains have high population densities on the fertile agricultural land. Examples are the Nile in Egypt, the Mississippi in the USA, the Ganges in India, the Yangtse and Yellow Rivers (Huang Ho) in China (Fig. 6.4), the Tigris–Euphrates in the Middle East and the Rhine in Europe. In some of these areas, the seasonal agricultural processes are linked with the flooding pattern and the society has adjusted to the flooding **regime**, as with the R. Nile before the Aswan Dam and in Bangladesh today. It is the extreme events in these increasingly densely populated areas which result in loss of

?

3 From the information in Figures 6.3 and 6.4:

a Outline the scale and effects of the floods.

b What are the main problems in attempts to protect and rescue people?

c What causes are suggested for the floods?

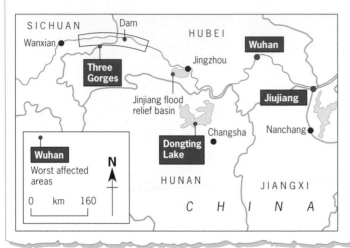

Storms bring misery to China

The home and lives of millions of Chinese are threatened by the worst floods on the Yangtze river for more than 40 years, authorities in Beijing warned yesterday.

President Jiang Zemin has intervened personally to order reinforcement of river dykes in the central Yangtze region which could collapse at any moment.

More than 134 000 people are reported homeless in rural Boyang county near the city of Jiujiang. In the three river provinces of Hubei, Hunan and Jiangxi, 157 deaths have been confirmed, 29 towns have been flooded, three railways have been cut off and 450 000 houses destroyed.

Some of the water threatening the central region could, in theory, be diverted into a huge relief basin at Jinjiang, excavated in the 1950s. But 300 000 people have settled in the area since then

and would have to be evacuated.

The Beijing-based China Daily said yesterday 230 000 people had been mobilised to protect the Dongting lake area downstream. If the dykes are breached there, 10 million people in southern Hunan province will be at risk.

Sweeping on, the flood has threatened Wuhan, the provincial capital of Hubei, where some streets are waist-deep in water. Embankments at Jiujiang, in the neighbouring province of Jiangxi, are being shored up in a desperate struggle to protect 1.5 million residents.

Explanations for the floods – which have also hit other parts of China – range from global warming to the effects of El Niño. But Chinese experts believe the real causes are local deforestation, uncontrolled building and neglect of flood control.

Figure 6.4 Flooding in China
(*Source: The Guardian*, 23 July 1998)

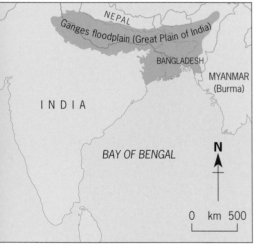

Figure 6.5 The Great Plain of India is 650 000 km^2 of alluvium which has been deposited on the Ganges floodplain. It supports over 100 million people. The land nearest to the river was traditionally used as pasture and during flood events could be easily evacuated. After 1947, these areas were occupied by Hindu refugees from the newly created Islamic West Pakistan and used for subsistence and commercial arable farming. Although homes on the floodplain have raised platforms, flooding has become a hazard to people's lives, homes and property, including crops. Even the normal, seasonal floods are now a hazard rather than a benefit, and extreme events could result in a disaster

life and property. Increasing population pressure and economic development mean that people need to reduce river flooding over time, because the hazard increases as the traditional economic and social systems which work with the river begin to break down. This combination of increased population pressure and economic change has intensified flood hazards across the Ganges floodplain (Fig. 6.5).

6.3 Increasing the hazard: floodplain encroachment

Floodplains provide areas of flat land with a ready water supply and are, therefore, ideal locations for urban development. In upland areas, river valleys provide a natural routeway for roads and railways. However, as development increases, the flooding hazard also increases. The flood risk varies among individual countries.

The United Kingdom

In England and Wales, less than 2 per cent of the population live in floodplain areas, compared to 10 per cent in the USA. Many areas in Britain which were affected by widespread flooding in 1947 have since seen further, substantial urbanisation (Figs 6.7 and 6.8). Much of the lower Thames floodplain has become developed, especially at Maidenhead (Fig. 6.6), and between Windsor and London, despite opposition from the EA and its predecessors. In Nottingham, the floodplain of the R. Trent has been developed behind embankments which are now considered to provide a lower standard of protection than when they were built. Serious flooding that recurred across much of England between October 2000 and February 2001 highlighted the hazards from floodplain encroachment. The government has reacted by strengthening planning controls (Fig. 6.9).

It is this floodplain enroachment which is the crucial factor in determining the flood hazard from extreme events, since most urban land uses are not compatible with flooding (Figs 6.7 and 6.8).

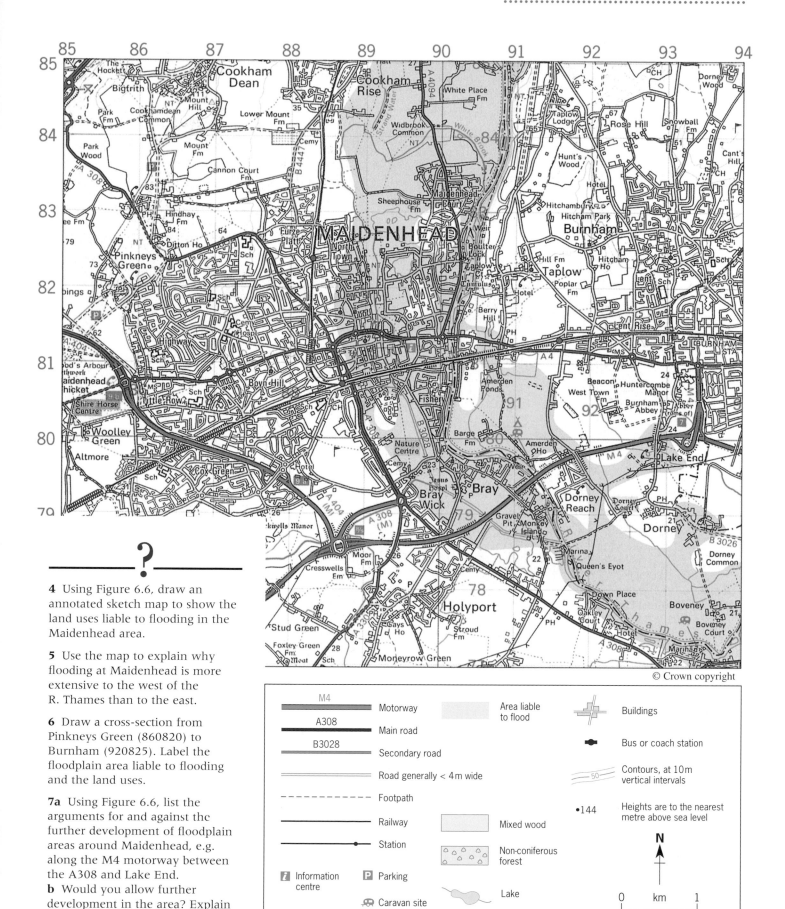

© Crown copyright

?

4 Using Figure 6.6, draw an annotated sketch map to show the land uses liable to flooding in the Maidenhead area.

5 Use the map to explain why flooding at Maidenhead is more extensive to the west of the R. Thames than to the east.

6 Draw a cross-section from Pinkneys Green (860820) to Burnham (920825). Label the floodplain area liable to flooding and the land uses.

7a Using Figure 6.6, list the arguments for and against the further development of floodplain areas around Maidenhead, e.g. along the M4 motorway between the A308 and Lake End.
b Would you allow further development in the area? Explain your answer.

Legend	
M4 Motorway	Area liable to flood
A308 Main road	Buildings
B3028 Secondary road	Bus or coach station
Road generally < 4m wide	Contours, at 10m vertical intervals
Footpath	•144 Heights are to the nearest metre above sea level
Railway	Mixed wood
Station	Non-coniferous forest
i Information centre	P Parking
Caravan site	Lake
	0 km 1

Figure 6.6 1:50 000 Ordnance Survey extract of the Maidenhead and Windsor area

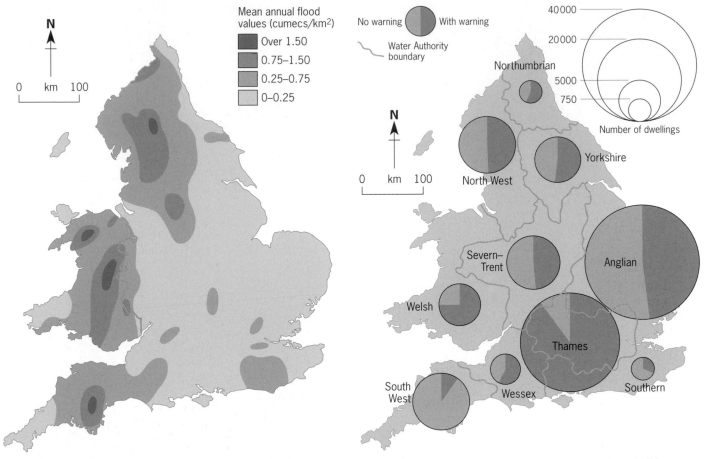

Figure 6.7 **England and Wales: best estimate of mean annual flood values** (*Source*: **Ward and Robinson, 1990**)

Figure 6.8 **England and Wales: dwellings within the 1-in-50-year to 1-in-100-year floodplain** (*Source*: **Penning-Rowsell and Handmer, 1988**)

6.4 Increasing the hazard: human-induced flooding

Within an individual drainage basin there are a number of flood-intensifying factors or conditions that are stable over time, e.g. rock type, slope, altitude and drainage network, which will make some river basins more likely to flood than others. However, there are also key **variable** flood-intensifying conditions, such as vegetation cover, fires, urban development, channel load and shape, soil **porosity** and land drainage. The variable conditions are subject to change as a result of human activity. If change results in increased quickflow processes, there is consequently an increase in the size and frequency of flooding (Fig. 6.1). Human activity can, therefore, result in flooding in areas which were not previously threatened, or increase the size and frequency of flood events.

Changing the seasonality of flooding

In addition to changing the location, magnitude and frequency of floods, human activity can also result in a change in the seasonality of flooding. Data from 77 000 flood records held on a database at the Institute of Hydrology, show that for the UK as a whole, flood hazard is greatest in the winter (Fig. 6.10). However, drainage basins in the north and west have a dominant flood season in the autumn, when soils become **saturated** earlier. Further to the south and east, the dominant flood season is winter, because lower rainfall than in the north and west of the country means that soil saturation is delayed.

Hydrologists have also shown that, in central and south-east England, there are a low number of catchments with a summer modal month of flooding

8 Study Figure 6.7. Describe and explain the pattern of mean annual flood values for England and Wales.

9 Using Figures 6.7 and 6.8, give reasons for the contradiction in the pattern of number of dwellings at serious risk from flooding and the flood runoff.

10 Describe and suggest reasons for the regional variations in the availability of flood warning systems shown on Figure 6.8.

Thousands of new homes to be built on flood plains

DEVELOPERS ARE PLANNING to build hundreds of thousands of new homes on areas at serious risk from flooding, the Environment Agency has revealed.

Research by the agency predicts that the amount of housing to be built on flood plains by 2020 will increase the number of people at risk from floods from 4 million to 6 million.

This weekend an internal report from the agency showed that in the six months up to April this year it had advised local authorities to refuse 190 planning applications because of the risk of flooding. In 83 (44%) of the cases, however, the local authority granted permission regardless.

'If these kinds of developments go ahead then serious flooding will become a regular event,' said Ray Kemp, a spokesman for the agency. 'We have been warning local authorities and the government about this risk for years.'

He said that the agency has repeatedly warned local authorities that Lewes and Uckfield, in East Sussex, were at great risk of serious flooding. However, the local flood defence committees – which are controlled by local authorities along with the Ministry of Agriculture, Fisheries and Food – had decided it would cost too much to strengthen the river banks. The agency has no statutory powers.

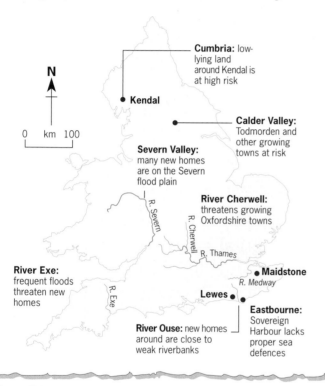

Cumbria: low-lying land around Kendal is at high risk

Kendal

Calder Valley: Todmorden and other growing towns at risk

Severn Valley: many new homes are on the Severn flood plain

River Cherwell: threatens growing Oxfordshire towns

R. Severn

R. Cherwell

R. Thames

River Exe: frequent floods threaten new homes

R. Exe

Maidstone

R. Medway

Lewes

Eastbourne: Sovereign Harbour lacks proper sea defences

River Ouse: new homes around are close to weak riverbanks

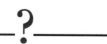

New guidelines

Building on river banks, water meadows and flood plains is to be restricted to reduce the number of new homes at risk from flooding.

Guidelines to be issued to local authorities by Nick Raynsford, the Planning Minister, will "presume against" developments in flood-prone areas. New homes will be allowed on at-risk sites only in exceptional circumstances and after full planning inquiries.

The policy's first big test is expected to be at Ashford, Kent, where thousands of new homes are planned south-west of the town on the flood plain of the River Stour.

Geoff Mance of the Environment Agency said that it was hoped that the new guidance would "stack the cards against the developers" and in favour of the agency. It is pressing for the Ashford homes to be built to the east and north-west on higher, safer ground.

There are an estimated two million houses inland, valued at some £35 billion, that have been built on flood plains and are currently at risk from flooding. Insurers and the Environment Agency believe that the number of properties at risk could rise sharply as a result of global warming and increased stormy weather.

They are also alarmed at the prospect of three to 4.4 million new houses being built in England by 2016. They fear that a large number could end up on river banks, water meadows and in other flood risk areas of southern England. Builders prefer to construct on flood plains because they are flat and cheaper to develop.

Figure 6.9 At risk from flooding (*Source: The Times* 14 October 2000)

?

11 Study Figures 6.10 and 6.11.
a Describe the pattern of river floods for these two examples.
b Explain the seasonal pattern of UK flooding.

12 Suggest why small drainage basins with a high degree of urban development respond with a distinctive seasonal pattern of flooding, e.g. Beverley Brook (Fig. 6.11).

(MMF). These catchments are small with a predominantly urban land use, e.g. Beverley Brook at Wimbledon, which has 81 per cent of its catchment area urbanised (Fig. 6.11). The catchments respond to localised high-intensity summer rainfall. Urban development increases the likelihood and intensity of convection storms. As drainage basin size increases, the proportion under urban use is decreases and the diversity of other land uses increases.

Dam failure

Other human-induced causes of flooding include the rare but dramatic effects of dam failure. In 1928, the St Francis Dam in California, USA, collapsed, killing 500 people. In 1963, the Vaiont Dam disaster in northern Italy was caused by a landslide into the reservoir behind the dam, destroying several villages and killing 2000 people. In 1972, 238 deaths occurred in Rapid City, South Dakota, where a dam failure resulted in catastrophic flooding.

Table 6.1 Critical physical characteristics of floods (*After*: Cooke and Doornkamp, 1990)

1. How deep is the flood water? (Magnitude)
2. What area is flooded?
3. How long does the flooding last? (Duration)
4. What is the velocity of flow?
5. How often does the flooding occur? (Recurrence interval)
6. What is the lag time between the flooding over the banks and the peak flow?
7. When does flooding occur during the year? (Seasonality)
8. What is the peak flow? (Magnitude)
9. How fast does the river flow rise and fall? (Time lag and recession limb)
10. What is the sediment load?
11. How much water is stored on the floodplain? (Flood runoff)

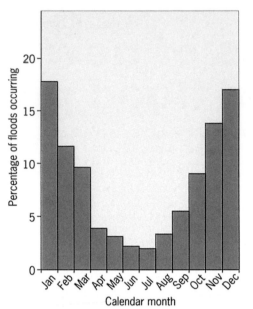

Figure 6.10 UK: the percentage of floods occurring in each calendar month (*Source*: Institute of Hydrology)

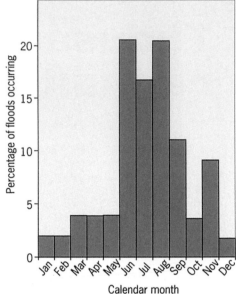

Figure 6.11 Beverley Brook, Wimbledon: percentage of floods in each calendar month (*Source*: Institute of Hydrology)

6.5 Physical characteristics of floods

Every flood event is the result of a unique set of variables but eleven critical characteristics of floods can be identified (Table 6.1). These are important in evaluating flooding in terms of the magnitude, frequency and duration of the flood event. There are two key flood documents: the flood **hydrograph** (see Section 3.3) and the flood frequency or flood recurrence interval graph.

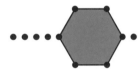

The flood recurrence interval graph

Two vital questions that water managers ask are, 'How often can we expect a flood?' and 'How severe will the flood be?'. We can calculate the likelihood or statistical probability of flooding from flood frequency graphs (Fig. 6.12). We rank the records of a river's discharge over the longest time available, from the largest peak to the lowest discharge recorded. We then calculate the recurrence interval as follows:

$$\text{Recurrence interval (years)} \text{ of discharge } z \text{ m}^3/\text{s} = \frac{\text{number of peaks in the list} +1}{\text{ranked position of discharge } z}$$

If we plot the recurrence intervals, or return periods of a number of discharges, against discharge as a graph on semi-logarithmic graph paper, it is possible to extrapolate the data to give recurrence intervals for floods which have not been recorded. Using these graphs, we can make statements about the statistical probability of flood events. The longer and fuller the flood records, the more confidence we can place in this extrapolation. Thus, in Figure 6.12, a discharge of 110 m^3/s or more is likely to recur on average every 10 years. Another way of putting this is to say that there is a 10 per cent chance of a discharge of 110 m^3/s or more occurring in any given year.

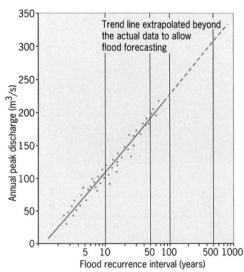

Figure 6.12 Flood recurrence intervals and discharge (*Source*: Clowes and Comfort, 1987)

You must remember that the statistical prediction of flood recurrence intervals is only an indication of probability based upon *past* records. As events happen, the statistical prediction will change. It is therefore important for hydrologists to update records as events happen. You should also remember that this information does not forecast a flood for a particular year.

River Tay, Scotland

The R. Tay at Ballathie (Fig. 6.13) illustrates how flood records used by water managers must be constantly updated. In the period 1989–93, events in Scotland have caused a reassessment of the River Tay's flood recurrence intervals.

In mid-January 1993, the River Tay and its tributaries were in flood with a record flow of 2200 m³/s. This surpassed the previous highest flow on the National River Flow Archive. Hundreds of properties in Perth were flooded and there was severe disruption of the transport network (Fig. 6.14). What surprised hydrologists was that only three years had passed since the last major flood on the River Tay, in February 1990 (maximum discharge of 1043 m³/s). Both the 1990 and 1993 floods were greater in magnitude than the previous highest record from 1952, and the expected flood return periods have consequently had to be reduced (Table 6.2 and Fig. 6.15).

The short time between such extreme events raises the question of climatic change or whether these events are just part of our 'normal' changeable climate. The R. Tay example shows clearly the need for continued monitoring and research by institutions such as the Institute of Hydrology.

Figure 6.13 River Tay, Scotland

Table 6.2 Variation in flood quantities for the River Tay

Period of record (Ballathie gauging station)	Number of annual maxima	100-year flood (m³/s)	Return period for 2000 m³/s flood (y)
1952–89	38	1540	>1000
1952–93	42	1990	105

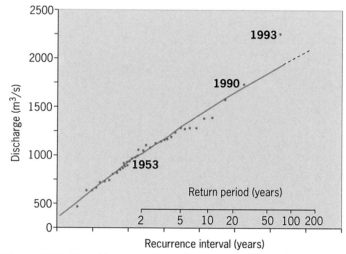

Figure 6.15 River Tay: revised flood recurrence intervals, 1953–93, and the extreme 1990 and 1993 events (*Source*: Institute of Hydrology, 1993)

13 Use Table 6.2 and Figure 6.15 to describe the significance of the 1990 and 1993 floods to flood forecasting on the River Tay.

Figure 6.14 Flood damage near Dalguise, Tayside, January 1993

6.6 Flood forecasting and prevention

Water managers use flood recurrence interval graphs as a key tool to assess the flood hazard and, thus, the nature and cost of possible flood prevention measures. Flood prevention is expensive. It is related to the degree of risk, and also to the land uses involved, i.e. the potential costs of the flood event in terms of the risk to life and property. The design flood is the flood recurrence that defence measures are designed to cope with. The Ministry of Agriculture, Fisheries and Food (MAFF) issue guidelines to organisations, such as the Environment Agency (EA) and local councils on the degree of protection to be considered for different land uses (Table 6.3). MAFF recommends, for example, that a high-density urban area is protected against the 1-in-100-year flood event where possible, but that there should be a lesser degree of protection against the 1-in-10-year flood for arable farming with isolated properties. Grassland and low-productivity agricultural land with few properties should not be protected from flooding.

?

14 Study Table 6.3.
a Why do MAFF recommend that high-density urban areas and areas subjected to tidal flooding should have a higher degree of protection than rural areas?
b Suggest what may happen to the degree of protection recommended for rural land uses if there was a shortage of food production in the future.

Table 6.3 Indicative standards of protection (*Source*: MAFF, ©Crown copyright, 1994)

Current land use	Indicative standard of protection (return period in years)	
	Tidal	Non-tidal
High-density urban area containing significant amount of both residential and non-residential property.	200	100
Medium-density urban area. Lower density than above, may also include some agricultural land.	150	75
Low-density or rural communities with limited number of properties at risk. Highly productive agricultural land.	50	25
Generally arable farming with isolated properties Medium-productivity agricultural land.	20	10
Predominantly extensive grass with very few properties at risk. Low-productivity agricultural land.	5	1

Forecasting the timing and location of flooding

Water managers also use hydrological data to calculate the likelihood of a river flooding at a particular time of year. This can be useful in the planning and allocation of resources for flood protection or in the timing of repairs and maintenance. They relate the flood recurrence interval and the discharges involved to the area likely to be flooded (Fig. 6.16). Smaller floods will only

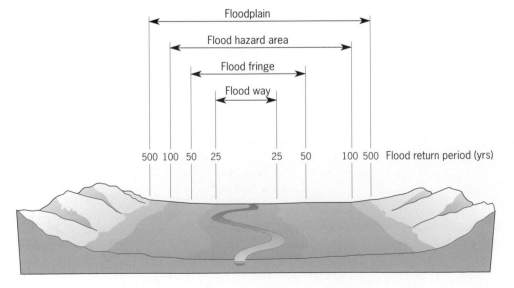

Figure 6.16 Hazard zones on the floodplain (*Source*: Knapp et al, 1989)

Figure 6.17 Floodplain zoning, along the Bow River, Calgary, Canada. The flood fringe remains under semi-natural vegetation; the flood hazard zone is used for roads and recreation. The CBD is built on the bluff beyond the floodplain

affect the area near to the river channel itself. However, the larger, rare events will flood a greater area of the floodplain.

The **floodway** is that area of the floodplain needed to transmit a selected flood. This area will experience a high frequency of flooding and thus potential loss of life and property damage. The flood fringe is only affected by the rare, higher floods. Although the fringe is still within the flood hazard area, the degree of risk is lower. This difference can be used for land-use zoning of the floodplain (Fig. 6.17).

Evaluating responses to the flood hazard: cost–benefit analysis
A common method of assessing the feasibility of a public flood control programme or hard engineering structure, such as a dam, is a **cost–benefit analysis**. Water managers compare the options available using the costs involved and the benefits to be gained by the alternative flood control measures. The costs are essentially the engineering costs and are relatively straightforward. The project benefits are more difficult to measure. They are the same as the expected flood damage in the 'without project' situation, minus the expected annual damage in the 'with project' situation.

Criteria for choosing flood management options (see Appendix A3)
1 The economic cost–benefit analysis
2 Technical feasibility of the solution available
3 The environmental impacts of the schemes.

6.7 Flood perception and response

A key factor determining how a society responds to floods depends upon how the hazard is perceived. The frequency of flooding is a vital factor. Human behaviour is more likely to adjust to flood events if they are frequent occurrences. This adjustment can vary depending upon how people use the area of flooding, the nature of the flood event and how the flood is perceived. Cultural influences are important. Some groups of people are more likely to see floods as 'Acts of God' and as a result are more prepared to endure them and bear the loss. Other societies, especially the more technically advanced societies of western Europe and the USA, are more likely to wish to control floods.

Figure 6.18 Information sets, perception and human responses to the flood hazard (*After*: Park, 1983)

15 Group activity: Figure 6.18 is a form of *flow diagram* or *critical path diagram*. It follows the process from recognition of a flood hazard to the decision on how to deal with this hazard. The sequence may be divided into six phases (A–F). At each phase, decision-makers need reliable information. The following exercise helps you to consider what information is important, why it is important, and why the decision may be imperfect.

a Phase B

• Devise a brief questionnaire to find out what floodplain residents think about flood hazards.

• Make a list of the types of information water managers need when considering how to manage flood hazards.

b Give examples of how the perceptions of residents and managers (Phase C) may lead to different interpretations of flood hazard (Phase D).

• How might information gathered at Phase B be useful in reducing conflicts that arise at Phase D?

c Using examples, explain why the action decision (Phase F) may be a compromise between the differing priorities of elements in Phase E.

Note: You may find the understandings of case studies in Chapters 4 and 5 useful.

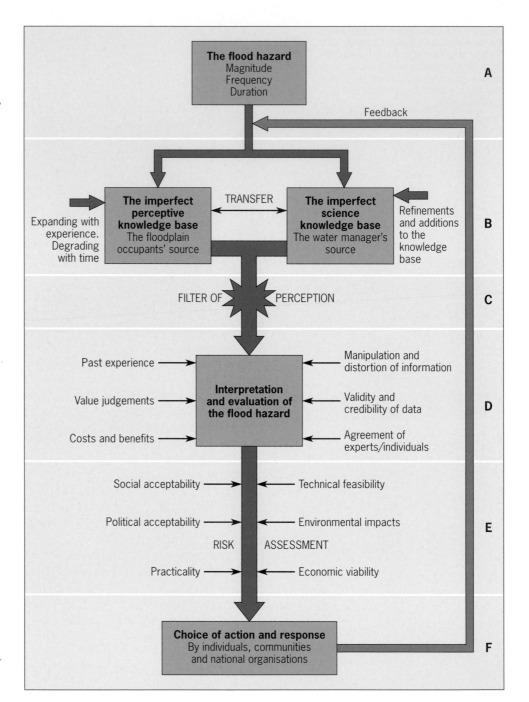

Perceptions of floodplain occupants and water managers

Individual perceptions of the flood hazard vary from those directly affected by flooding (the floodplain occupants), to the water managers involved in decision-making (Fig. 6.18). The water manager's view is more objective, but still incomplete, because most decisions are made using past flow records and hydrological data. The floodplain occupant's perception of the hazard is based on direct experience. Research suggests that public expectations in the UK are rising and even very occasional flooding is considered unacceptable. This is especially so when the floodwaters are polluted, e.g. with discharges from sewage treatment works and urban storm drains.

Although economic costs of floods are important in decision-making and influence the manager's actions and responses, the intangible damages caused to floodplain occupants are of the greatest importance. In Southgate, London, people were asked to rate the impacts of a flood event on a scale of 1 to 10

Left page (partial, p.121)

es will meet just
4bn damage

...ept through
...t insurers up to
...f the country's

...bill of £4 billion,
...ho were not
...he cost of the

...e main insurance
...to be the
...saster. A
...at £2 billion,
...insured.
...rs had been
...which had
...f £2 billion
...s when storms
...anuary 1990.

The largest pay-out for flooding in recent times was for £137 million in April 1998, when thousands of people had to leave their homes in the Midlands and East Anglia.

Homeowners will want compensation, not only for structural damage and the destruction of property, but also for the cost of temporary accommodation. The average claim is likely to be about £12 000.

Factors that determine the insurance premiums include flood defences and frequency of flooding in the area. Proximity to a river is not penalised.

As many as 30 per cent of people in the worst-hit regions are thought to be uninsured. They will be forced to pay for their own repairs, which could run into thousands of pounds.

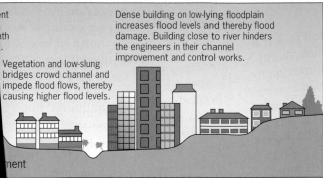

Dense building on low-lying floodplain increases flood levels and thereby flood damage. Building close to river hinders the engineers in their channel improvement and control works.

Vegetation and low-slung bridges crowd channel and impede flood flows, thereby causing higher flood levels.

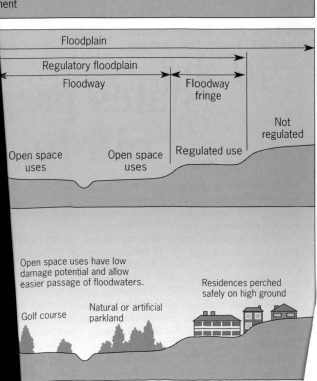

Floodplain

Regulatory floodplain

Floodway | Floodway fringe

Open space uses | Open space uses | Regulated use | Not regulated

Open space uses have low damage potential and allow easier passage of floodwaters.

Residences perched safely on high ground

Golf course | Natural or artificial parkland

Right page (p.119)

Figure 6.19 Southgate, Enfield, England: rating scale for the effects of flooding (*Source*: Penning-Rowsell and Handmer, 1988)

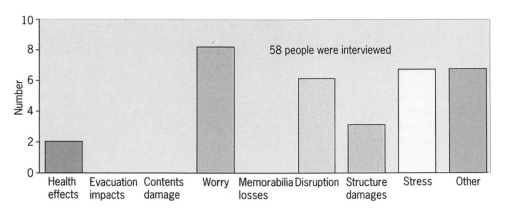

(Fig. 6.19). Economic losses received a lower score than the effects on mental health and physical well-being. At Tooting and Ruislip in London, people affected by flooding showed continuing anxiety or a feeling of helplessness several years after their flood experience. Other research links longer-term adverse health effects with major flood events. Following the 1986 floods in Bristol, researchers found a 50 per cent increase in the number of deaths from homes that had been flooded, with cancer forming a significant element in this increase. There was also an increase in doctor's surgery attendances and hospital admissions.

Table 6.4 Flood management solutions with their advantages and disadvantages

Method	Advantages	Disadvantages
A Water and land-use control measures	Promote soil and water conservation. Reduce flood levels without affecting river ecosystems. Floodplain development could continue.	May be very expensive. Only affect minor floods. Needs cooperation of many groups and organisations. Drainage basins may be international in scale; need international planning. Slow to take effect.
B Non-structural control measures		
Bearing the loss	Cheap. Allows floodplain development.	Individuals bear the burden of flooding. Applicability depends upon society's perception of the flood hazard.
Public relief/emergency action	Costs only involved if there is a flood event.	Costs may be very high if there is a catastrophic flood or large numbers of people involved.
Flood warnings	Relatively cheap. Prevent loss of life. Reduce damages if warning time is insufficient. Floodplain can continue in use.	Community response is uncertain. Require accurate and continuous information. Damage potential to property remains high. Effectiveness may diminish over time.
Floodplain zoning	Low cost for undeveloped areas of floodplain. Prevents/reduces future damage effectively. Some land uses require floodplain location/large water supply.	Existing floodplain damages are not reduced. May reduce development in the area; located elsewhere.
Flood insurance	Helps promote community involvement. Inexpensive to policy holders. Raises an awareness of the flood hazard. May encourage floodplain development.	Flood damages are not reduced. May not be available in high-risk areas. Insurance cover may be limited in cost/property.
C Structural measures		
Storage of floodwaters, e.g. dams, basins and relief channels	Reduce flood losses. Protect property already in the risk area. Dams, etc. may be multi-purpose. Increase development in the area. Some harmful environmental impacts. Flood may be worse if defences fail.	High cost to build and maintain. Proper site needs to be available. Have a design level; may encourage a false sense of security.
Change the channel	Relatively cheap. Does not affect existing land uses. Suitable site not required. Channel enlargement requires room; not suitable for highly developed areas.	Needs to be maintained. Harmful environmental impacts to channel and bank ecosystems.
Flood proofing	Reduces damages. Can remain at site. Lowers flood insurance costs.	Damage is still likely/possible. Only applicable to certain types of structures. May be costly with a false sense of security.

?

16 For each of the flood hazard adjustments in table 6.4, draw up a matrix to evaluate their appropriateness to:
a a Thames floodplain area in Greater London
b an agricultural area on the Ganges floodplain in India.

6.8 Managing the flood

Management options fall into three broad categories, whose characteristics are summarised in Table 6.4 (see Maidenhead case study, p. 125).

Water and land-use control measures

The aim of this method of flood abatement is to modify the cause of the flooding within the drainage basin itself. Land-use practices which minimise the quickflow processes in the catchment area aim to slow or reduce the delivery of water to the river channel. Soil conservation measures, especially afforestation, generally help to reduce runoff (see Section 4.2). However, there are problems in establishing forests in areas of grassland cover. In the initial stages, at least, there may be increased flooding, because pre-afforestation ditching is required to drain the land before planting.

Flood abatement involves widespread planning and it may not be possible to control land uses effectively. Whole-catchment planning is hampered by administrative and political difficulties, because many river catchments are international in scale or cross local authority boundaries. Two other limitatio with this approach are that the flood risk is only likely to be reduced for smaller scale floods and that these measures are slow to take effect.

Non-structural control measures

This group of measures involves a variety of responses, with the overall air of redistributing the losses. The responses vary: simply bearing the loss; pu relief from family and friends, to government and international aid; or

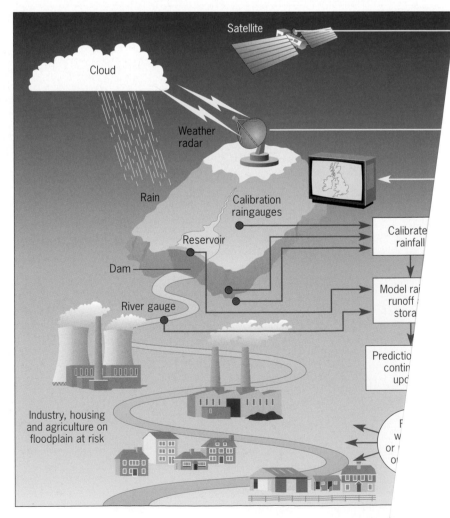

Figure 6.20 The structure of a flood forecasting system. Continued research is taking place to try to provide more realistic models of how drainage basins respond to rainfall, runoff and storage in order to increase the accuracy of flood warnings and the length of time between the warning and the flood event (*Source*: National Environment Research Council, 1994)

Figure 6.21b Floods: who pays? (*Source: The Times*, 14 October 2000)

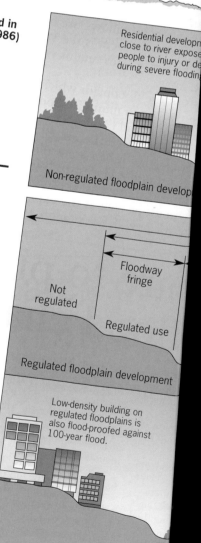

Policie half £4

The flooding which has s southern Britain could cos £2 billion, making it one costliest natural disasters.

Experts predicted a tota with hundreds of people, w insured, having to pay for damages themselves.

Jeffrey Salmon, one of t assessors, said: "It is going country's costliest natural d conservative estimate puts i [but] many owners were no

He said many homeowne deterred by high premiums, resulted from the huge bill o faced by insurance compani swept across the country in

Figure 6.22 Floodplain zoning management approach as applied in New Zealand (*Source*: Eriksen, 1986)

Residential developm close to river expose people to injury or de during severe floodin

Non-regulated floodplain develop

?

Read Figure 6.21a.
17 In which ways did European governments and authorities act to reduce injury and loss of life?

18 State two reasons why people did not have flood insurance. Give an example in each case, and explain why there was no insurance cover.

19 From the information given in Figures 6.21a and b, summarise:

• the short-term problems faced by homeowners and businesses

• the longer-term problems they are likely to face.

20 Describe the causes of economic losses for businesses in the flooded area.

21 List the arguments for and against insurance and government aid as a flood hazard response.

Floodway fringe

Not regulated

Regulated use

Regulated floodplain development

Low-density building on regulated floodplains is also flood-proofed against 100-year flood.

Figure 6.19 Southgate, Enfield, England: rating scale for the effects of flooding (*Source*: Penning-Rowsell and Handmer, 1988)

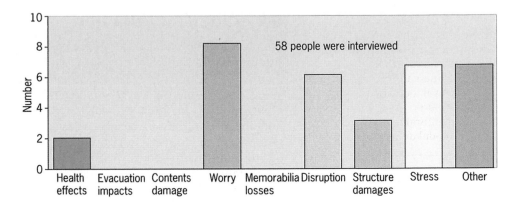

(Fig. 6.19). Economic losses received a lower score than the effects on mental health and physical well-being. At Tooting and Ruislip in London, people affected by flooding showed continuing anxiety or a feeling of helplessness several years after their flood experience. Other research links longer-term adverse health effects with major flood events. Following the 1986 floods in Bristol, researchers found a 50 per cent increase in the number of deaths from homes that had been flooded, with cancer forming a significant element in this increase. There was also an increase in doctor's surgery attendances and hospital admissions.

Table 6.4 Flood management solutions with their advantages and disadvantages

Method	Advantages	Disadvantages
A Water and land-use control measures	Promote soil and water conservation. Reduce flood levels without affecting river ecosystems. Floodplain development could continue.	May be very expensive. Only affect minor floods. Needs cooperation of many groups and organisations. Drainage basins may be international in scale; need international planning. Slow to take effect.
B Non-structural control measures		
Bearing the loss	Cheap. Allows floodplain development.	Individuals bear the burden of flooding. Applicability depends upon society's perception of the flood hazard.
Public relief/emergency action	Costs only involved if there is a flood event.	Costs may be very high if there is a catastrophic flood or large numbers of people involved.
Flood warnings	Relatively cheap. Prevent loss of life. Reduce damages if warning time is insufficient. Floodplain can continue in use.	Community response is uncertain. Require accurate and continuous information. Damage potential to property remains high. Effectiveness may diminish over time.
Floodplain zoning	Low cost for undeveloped areas of floodplain. Prevents/reduces future damage effectively. Some land uses require floodplain location/large water supply.	Existing floodplain damages are not reduced. May reduce development in the area; located elsewhere.
Flood insurance	Helps promote community involvement. Inexpensive to policy holders. Raises an awareness of the flood hazard. May encourage floodplain development.	Flood damages are not reduced. May not be available in high-risk areas. Insurance cover may be limited in cost/property.
C Structural measures		
Storage of floodwaters, e.g. dams, basins and relief channels	Reduce flood losses. Protect property already in the risk area. Dams, etc. may be multi-purpose. Increase development in the area. Some harmful environmental impacts. Flood may be worse if defences fail.	High cost to build and maintain. Proper site needs to be available. Have a design level; may encourage a false sense of security.
Change the channel	Relatively cheap. Does not affect existing land uses. Suitable site not required. Channel enlargement requires room; not suitable for highly developed areas.	Needs to be maintained. Harmful environmental impacts to channel and bank ecosystems.
Flood proofing	Reduces damages. Can remain at site. Lowers flood insurance costs.	Damage is still likely/possible. Only applicable to certain types of structures. May be costly with a false sense of security.

16 For each of the flood hazard adjustments in table 6.4, draw up a matrix to evaluate their appropriateness to:
a a Thames floodplain area in Greater London
b an agricultural area on the Ganges floodplain in India.

6.8 Managing the flood

Management options fall into three broad categories, whose characteristics are summarised in Table 6.4 (see Maidenhead case study, p. 125).

Water and land-use control measures

The aim of this method of flood abatement is to modify the cause of the flooding within the drainage basin itself. Land-use practices which minimise the quickflow processes in the catchment area aim to slow or reduce the delivery of water to the river channel. Soil conservation measures, especially afforestation, generally help to reduce runoff (see Section 4.2). However, there are problems in establishing forests in areas of grassland cover. In the initial stages, at least, there may be increased flooding, because pre-afforestation ditching is required to drain the land before planting.

Flood abatement involves widespread planning and it may not be possible to control land uses effectively. Whole-catchment planning is hampered by administrative and political difficulties, because many river catchments are international in scale or cross local authority boundaries. Two other limitations with this approach are that the flood risk is only likely to be reduced for smaller scale floods and that these measures are slow to take effect.

Non-structural control measures

This group of measures involves a variety of responses, with the overall aim of redistributing the losses. The responses vary: simply bearing the loss; public relief from family and friends, to government and international aid; or

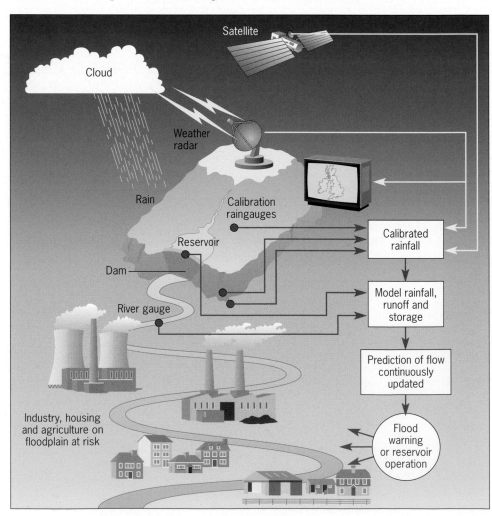

Figure 6.20 The structure of a flood forecasting system. Continued research is taking place to try to provide more realistic models of how drainage basins respond to rainfall, runoff and storage in order to increase the accuracy of flood warnings and the length of time between the warning and the flood event (*Source*: National Environment Research Council, 1994)

emergency action, where people and property are removed from the flood hazard area. Emergency action relies on an adequate flood warning system if it is to be effective. The effectiveness of emergency action improves with increased warning time (Fig. 6.20).

Insurance

Flood insurance is another possible response, where a premium is paid over time to spread the costs. An issue with flood insurance as a stategy is that it may encourage people to live on the floodplain rather than developing land elsewhere. In areas of above-average chance of flooding, the financial risk for insurance companies is too high and flood insurance may not be available (Fig. 6.21b). Government and international action is likely to be needed in such circumstances, e.g. in northern Europe during December 1993 and January 1994 (Fig. 6.21a).

Zoning

Floodplain zoning involves dividing the floodplain into areas which experience different degrees of flood risk (Fig. 6.16). It also involves regulating land use to take account of the nature of the flood hazard (Fig. 6.22). In the highest-risk areas, development is excluded, except for land uses which have a low damage potential. Land uses which retain the floodplain as a natural floodwater storage area and wetland also help to reduce the flood risk downstream. In urban areas, recreational uses allow the valuable provision of open space which maintains wetland habitats but allows use by residents for most of the time. An example of such a development is the Watermead Country Park to the north of Leicester city centre. This retains wetland open space on the floodplain of the R. Soar.

In the outer areas of the floodplain which are at a reduced risk of flooding there would be regulations to minimise flood problems, e.g. flood-proofing of buildings, flood insurance and contingency planning. Floodplain zoning is a successful management technique because it is cheap and effective. Unfortunately it is not realistic for existing urban areas (Fig. 6.23). Relocation of structures would be effective, but might be resisted by owners who lose the advantages of a floodplain location. Also, the cost is prohibitive because people will need compensation payments as well as the expense of re-building. In reality, zoning is only appropriate for new developments (see Northampton case study, p.126).

Figure 6.21a Flood damage, northern Europe 1994 (*Source*: The *European*, 31 December 1993)

States prepare to pick up bill for flood chaos

GOVERNMENTS across northern Europe are preparing to pay out millions of dollars in compensation following the devastation of thousands of homes and businesses in the worst flooding northern Europe has seen for more than 50 years.

It will be weeks before the true extent of the devastation is known as businesses in France, Germany, Belgium and the Netherlands begin to assess the damage.

In the Netherlands, where 12 000 people were evacuated from their homes in the province of Limburg over Christmas weekend, the government offered an initial aid package of 20m guilders.

Dutch insurers have refused flood cover ever since thousands died in the worst floods in living memory when the sea engulfed Zeeland in 1953. 'With half the country below sea level, insurers maintain that it is too expensive to insure against flooding,'

said Gert Kloosterboer, spokesman for the Dutch insurers' association, VVY

The European Commission released emergency aid worth $565 000 for the four worst-hit countries.

Ulrich Bockrath, spokesman for Colonia Versicherung, a German insurer, said: 'We introduced insurance against natural disasters but the number of policies is small. Most people are not insured against flood damage.'

This is a severe blow for small businesses now facing bankruptcy as the toll of cleaning up adds to lost sales.

In Belgium, the government has opened a disaster fund to compensate families, farmers and businesses after damage was estimated to have exceeded well over Bfr50m ($1.4m) – the government minimum for declaring a disaster area.

Figure 6.21b Floods: who pays? (*Source: The Times*, 14 October 2000)

Policies will meet just half £4bn damage

The flooding which has swept through southern Britain could cost insurers up to £2 billion, making it one of the country's costliest natural disasters.

Experts predicted a total bill of £4 billion, with hundreds of people, who were not insured, having to pay for the cost of the damages themselves.

Jeffrey Salmon, one of the main insurance assessors, said: "It is going to be the country's costliest natural disaster. A conservative estimate puts it at £2 billion, [but] many owners were not insured.

He said many homeowners had been deterred by high premiums, which had resulted from the huge bill of £2 billion faced by insurance companies when storms swept across the country in January 1990.

The largest pay-out for flooding in recent times was for £137 million in April 1998, when thousands of people had to leave their homes in the Midlands and East Anglia.

Homeowners will want compensation, not only for structural damage and the destruction of property, but also for the cost of temporary accommodation. The average claim is likely to be about £12 000.

Factors that determine the insurance premiums include flood defences and frequency of flooding in the area. Proximity to a river is not penalised.

As many as 30 per cent of people in the worst-hit regions are thought to be uninsured. They will be forced to pay for their own repairs, which could run into thousands of pounds.

Figure 6.22 Floodplain zoning management approach as applied in New Zealand (*Source: Eriksen, 1986*)

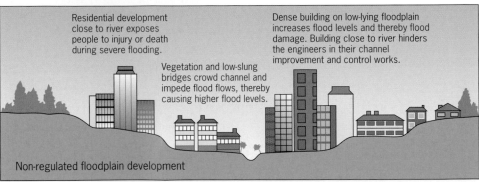

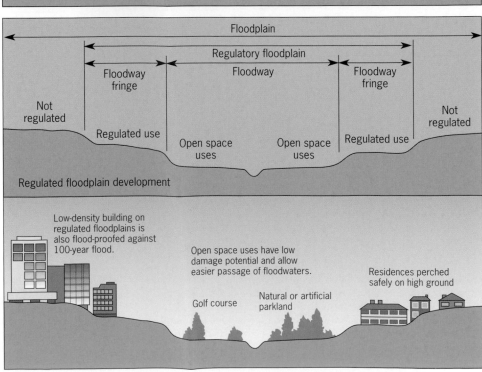

Read Figure 6.21a.

17 In which ways did European governments and authorities act to reduce injury and loss of life?

18 State two reasons why people did not have flood insurance. Give an example in each case, and explain why there was no insurance cover.

19 From the information given in Figures 6.21a and b, summarise:

• the short-term problems faced by homeowners and businesses

• the longer-term problems they are likely to face.

20 Describe the causes of economic losses for businesses in the flooded area.

21 List the arguments for and against insurance and government aid as a flood hazard response.

Figure 6.23 Urban impact of October 2000 floods; Ouse riverfront, York

Structural control measures

Structural measures aim to control the flood and prevent floodwaters from reaching developed or sensitive areas. These hard engineering solutions can centre on the flood site or on upstream storage of floodwaters. They can be divided into four main groups:

• Storage of floodwaters in reservoirs behind dams or flood storage basins. Dams provide the advantage of multi-purpose water uses, e.g. a public water supply, irrigation potential, HEP and recreational uses. There are, however, some serious environmental implications (see Sections 4.4 and 4.6). Flood relief channels and flood storage basins are used as temporary stores for excessive flows.

• Changing the channel by cutting a new channel for the excess water while leaving the original channel for the 'normal' flow, or by modifying the channel by realigning, resectioning or smoothing it (see Section 5.2).

• Building defences such as floodbanks or heightened levées along the channel (Figs 6.26 and 6.29).

• Flood-proofing the area at risk of flooding, e.g. constructing buildings on stilts, sealing walls or having flood-control gates on underground structures.

'Softer' approaches

In recent years there has been a trend away from hard engineering solutions. This is partly on the grounds of cost, but also because they may not be effective in extreme situations. This was demonstrated vividly by the disastrous 1993 floods along the R. Mississippi (see Mississippi case study, p. 128). Increasingly, engineers favour 'softer' approaches, based upon floodplain zoning. Such schemes designate sections of floodplains and deltas as temporary stores for floodwaters and control land uses accordingly.

It is clear therefore, that there may be several potential solutions to a specific problem. The choice is likely to depend on a cost–benefit analysis that includes economic, social and environmental factors (Fig. 6.24). Whatever the choice, we must never forget the message of the 1993 Mississippi floods and those across England in November 2000: floodplains and deltas are meant to flood, and are hazardous areas, even in rich MEDCs. In LEDCs, the combination of population pressure and poverty can result in catastrophe, as the recurring floods in Bangladesh demonstrate (see Bangladesh case study, p. 130).

22 Using Figure 6.22, define:
a the floodway
b the floodway fringe
c the regulatory floodplain.

23 Explain how the development of the non-regulated floodplain increases the flood hazard.

24 Describe how floodplain land use is regulated.

25 List the advantages and disadvantages of this method of flood control for flood managers and urban land users.

Choosing a method of flood control

Figure 6.24 The main methods of flood control in the UK (*After*: Cooke and Doornkamp, 1990)

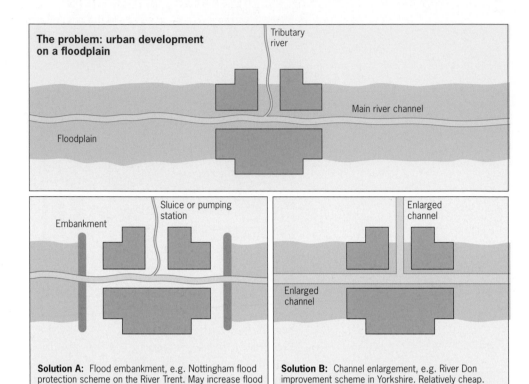

The problem: urban development on a floodplain

Tributary river

Main river channel

Floodplain

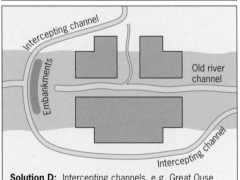

Embankment

Sluice or pumping station

Solution A: Flood embankment, e.g. Nottingham flood protection scheme on the River Trent. May increase flood levels upstream and/or downstream.

Enlarged channel

Enlarged channel

Solution B: Channel enlargement, e.g. River Don improvement scheme in Yorkshire. Relatively cheap. Channel enlarged to increase capacity. As the whole channel is rarely used, weeds grow. May be difficult to enlarge channel if there is a high degree of development.

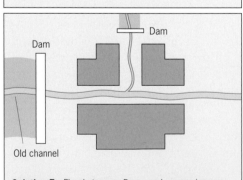

Sluice

Bypass channel

Sluice

Flood relief channel

Solution C: Flood relief channels, e.g. River Welland improvement scheme which bypasses Spalding. Excess flood waters are diverted from the urban area. Very expensive.

Intercepting channel

Embankments

Old river channel

Intercepting channel

Solution D: Intercepting channels, e.g. Great Ouse protection scheme in the Fens. These channels divert part of the flow from the urban area but retain some river flow. May have commercial impacts if the economic activity is based on river traffic.

Dam

Dam

Old channel

Solution E: Flood storage. Dams and reservoirs may have multiple uses, e.g. for water supply and recreation as with the Bala Lake scheme. Expensive to implement, may be loss of homes and high-quality land left behind the dam. Other important environmental impacts.

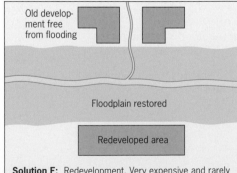

Old development free from flooding

Floodplain restored

Redeveloped area

Solution F: Redevelopment. Very expensive and rarely used due to resistance by land owners.

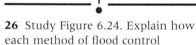

26 Study Figure 6.24. Explain how each method of flood control works. Evaluate each method.

27a Which scheme would you choose for:
• a large urban area with a high amount of industrial and residential development close to the river channel?
• a small market town with little industrial development and low-density housing along the floodplain?
b Justify your choice in each case.
c What other information would be helpful in making your choice?

The Maidenhead, Windsor and Eton flood alleviation scheme, England

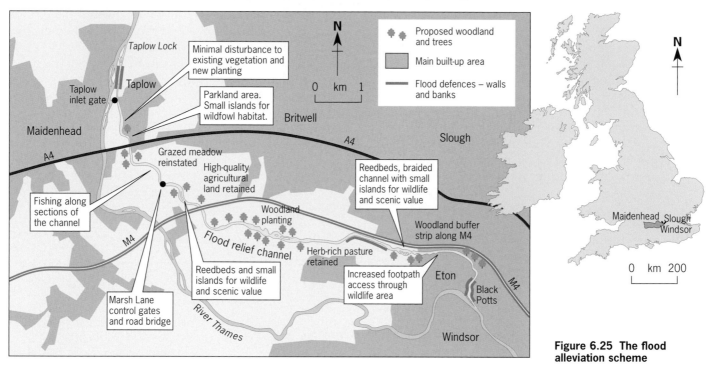

Figure 6.25 The flood alleviation scheme

The towns of Maidenhead, Eton and Windsor, and nearby villages (Fig. 6.25) have a long history of flooding by the R. Thames. Major flooding occurred in 1894, 1947, 1979 and 1990. The 1947 flood was particularly severe and widespread, and lasted for many weeks. A repeat of a flood of this scale today would affect more than 5500 properties and severely disrupt services and communications. Extreme conditions would close the M4 motorway.

To reduce the flood risk, Thames Water considered 492 combinations of options, some of which included widening the R. Thames. The preferred option was an 11.8 km flood relief channel (Fig. 6.25). Planning proposals were submitted in January 1991 and approval was given in November 1994, following a public inquiry in 1992.

The flood relief channel scheme

The flood relief channel leaves the Thames upstream of Taplow Lock, Maidenhead, and rejoins it downstream of Black Potts Viaduct, Windsor. It will look like a natural river. Water levels will be maintained by six low weirs. The scheme is designed to contain flows of 515 m³/s, i.e. the 1-in-65-year flood. At flows over 515 m³/s, there is the risk of flooding from the Thames, but its magnitude would be much reduced by the scheme. There is no risk of flooding from the flood relief channel.

The flood relief channel has been designed with wider aims than simply flood relief. The scheme also aims to enhance the local environment and provide increased amenity for residents, e.g. with public-access common land, new woodland, club fishing, cycleways and footpaths. In some areas, low flood banks and walls are required to ensure flood protection.

The construction costs of the scheme were estimated originally at £45 million. The costs of flooding over the 65-year life of the scheme lie between £41 million and £69 million. These flooding costs, which would not be incurred if the scheme were built, become the benefits in the cost–benefit ratio. The average cost–benefit ratio was calculated at 1:1.2. However, by the time the scheme was completed in 2001, the construction costs had risen to £90 million and there was still some flooding in November 2000.

28 Using Figure 6.25, describe the route of the flood relief channel.

29 How has the scheme been designed to enhance the area's environmental and amenity value?

30 Suggest why flood defences (walls and embankments) are needed in some locations.

Flood defences in Northampton, England

Northampton is situated on the R. Nene. The town suffered serious flooding in 1937, 1939 and 1947. The New Towns Act, 1965, designated Northampton as a growth area, with a planned population increase from 30 000 to 230 000 by 1981. This urban expansion, with much new development on the floodplains of the Nene and its tributaries, meant that flood defences in the town were unlikely to be adequate. The increased flood risk results from two factors. First, the development would cover a larger area with impermeable surfaces. Secondly, there would be a loss of storage water capacity on the floodplains as the area was developed. Three main problem areas were identified (Fig. 6.28).

The Washlands scheme

The Washlands storage basin on the River Nene floodplain covers 103 ha within curved earth embankments, varying in height from 2 m to 5 m. The scheme was completed in 1980 at a cost of nearly £3.5 million (Figs 6.26, 6.27). In their calculations, water managers had to consider three factors:

1 the water generated by extra runoff from the new urban development (1. 1 million m^3)

2 a high-intensity storm over the area (Table 6.5) (up to 0.96 million m^3)

3 the loss of storage capacity of floodwaters on the floodplain itself after development (1.29 million m^3).

The storage capacity of the Washlands scheme needs to cope with a combination of factor 3 with either factor 1 or 2, i.e. a maximum capacity of 2.39 million cubic metres of water. The Washlands actual storage capacity is 2.34 million m^3. However, this is adequate because the channel has storage space and the sluices can release water from the reservoir.

Figure 6.27 Aerial view of the Washlands

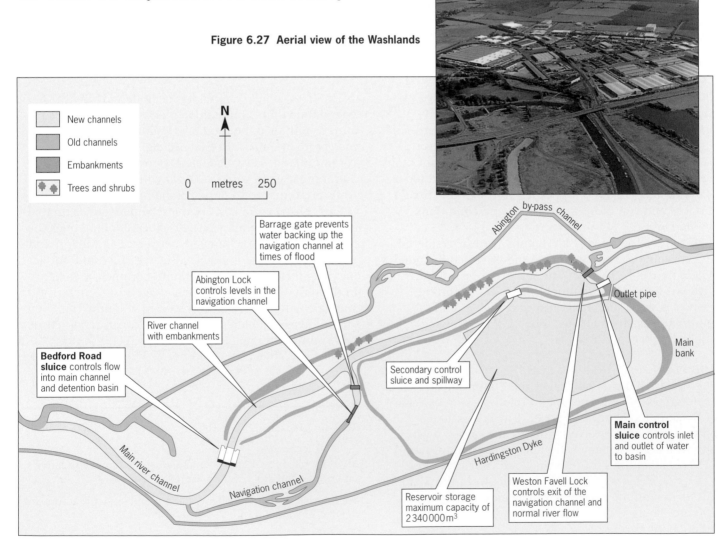

Figure 6.26 Northampton Washlands scheme.

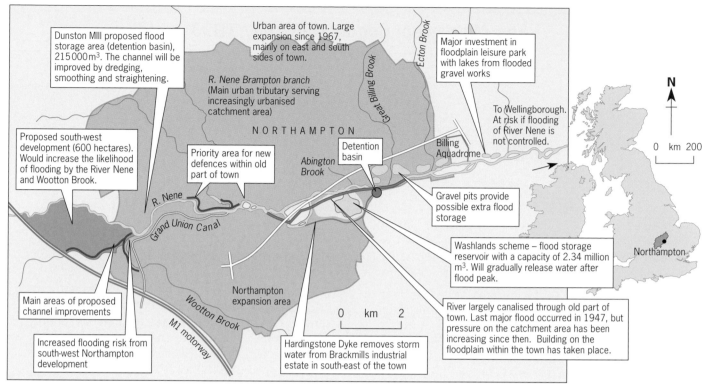

Figure 6.28 Northampton: river improvements. Costs were £750 000, benefits were £5 million, giving a cost–benefit ratio of 1:6

Table 6.5 Storage demand due to an intense urban storm

Storm duration (hours)	Storage demand pre-development (million m³)	Storage demand post-development (million m³)	Increase in storage demand (million m³)
4	0.82	1.38	0.56
8	0.87	1.54	0.67
12	0.81	1.55	0.74
15	0.73	1.52	0.79
20	0.56	1.41	0.85
24	0.40	1.29	0.89
30	0.14	1.08	0.94
33	0	0.96	0.96
34	0	0.92	0.92

Water enters the Washlands through the new Bedford Road Sluice. Under non-flood conditions, the water flows west to east along a new embanked channel to leave via the outlet control at Weston Favell Lock. At times of flood, the Bedford Road Sluice diverts water into the Washlands and the water is released slowly by the main control sluice. If the storage volume of the reservoir is effective, the outflow can be reduced to 82.5 m³/s instead of the 170 m³/s of the 1-in-50-year flood. The main sluice and emergency spillway could discharge 620 m³/s in an emergency. Navigation rights are maintained through the Washlands scheme.

?

31 Draw an annotated sketch map to show the flood prevention measures employed by Anglian Water (now NEA Anglian region).

32 Using Figure 6.26, describe how the Washlands scheme works.

33a Draw a graph to illustrate the information in Table 6.5. Plot storm duration on the x axis and storage demand on the y axis. Draw two lines: one to show storage demand before the development and one to show storage demand after the development.

b Shade the area between the two lines and label it, 'Increase in storage demand after development'.
c Give your graph a key and annotate it with details of why there was an increase in storage demand.

34 Explain how the water managers calculated the size requirements for the Washlands.

35a How was the scheme paid for?
b Do you consider that this scheme is an appropriate way to use public money? Explain your answer.

The Mississippi floods, USA, July 1993

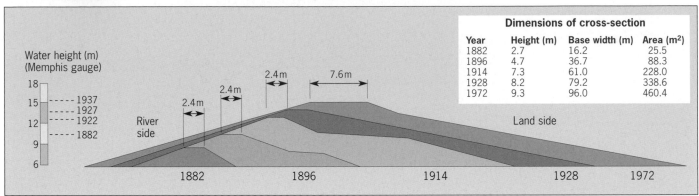

Dimensions of cross-section			
Year	Height (m)	Base width (m)	Area (m²)
1882	2.7	16.2	25.5
1896	4.7	36.7	88.3
1914	7.3	61.0	228.0
1928	8.2	79.2	338.6
1972	9.3	96.0	460.4

Figure 6.29 How the Mississippi levées have grown, 1882–1972 (*Source*: The Independent, 27 July 1993)

Flood damage

The Mississippi Basin has one of the most sophisticated and costly flood control and defence systems in the world. Yet in July 1993, the Mississippi floodplain was affected by a catastrophic flood which was over the 1-in-100-year flood event (Fig. 6.31). Towns and seven million hectares of farmland were flooded, communications disrupted and the R. Mississippi closed to shipping for two months upstream of St Louis.

The timing and location (Fig. 6.31) of this flood were unusual. Normally, flood flows occur in spring and in the lower course of the river south of Cairo, Illinois. Unusual weather conditions caused a change in this pattern and resulted in an estimated US$10 billion worth of damages despite desperate emergency efforts (Fig. 6.30). Although 50 lives were lost, the death toll was prevented from being higher by good warning systems.

Flood defences

Flood defences along the Mississippi are the responsibility of the US Army Corps of Engineers.

Defences have centred upon building levées with dams, reservoirs and barrages, i.e. hard engineering solutions. The 1993 flood has started a debate about these solutions, even though the defences were not built to cope with such a catastrophic flood. Water managers hoped that the levée defences would confine the river channel into artificial 'canyons'. Some are set back from the river to provide a larger storage capacity. The policy of levée-building has undoubtedly been effective up until 1993, but there are three main problems with this strategy:
- With each successive flood, the levées grow higher and wider (Fig. 6.29), increasing the land required and the costs involved.
- The river flow confined by the levées rises above the level of the surrounding floodplain at times of flood flows. This increases the damage by floods if the levées are breached.
- The levées increase the flood peaks because water is channelled between the levées and there are higher flow velocities. The storage capacity of the natural floodplain is lost.

Figure 6.30 Many levées were reinforced by local people building them higher as the floodwaters rose

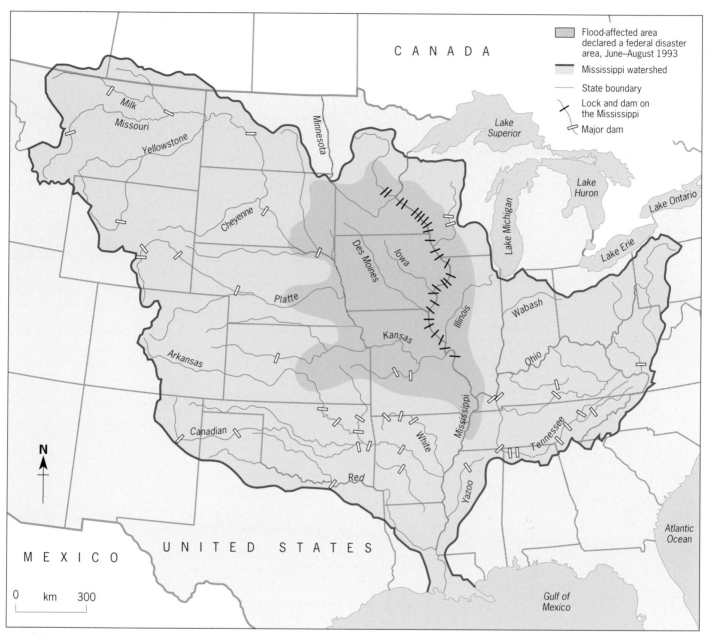

Figure 6.31 The Mississippi floods of 1993

Future plans

The debate taking place in the USA is similar to that following the 1994 floods in the UK. Should rivers be allowed to flood and floodplain wetland environments be maintained as natural water storage areas, or should the levées be rebuilt and reinforced to continue the hard engineering flood protection policy?

Hard engineering solutions have been relatively successful along the Mississippi and have allowed major urban and agricultural development to occur along the river. Nevertheless, the 1993 flood illustrates the effects of a flood above the design level of the hard engineering structure, with the associated human misery and economic cost.

?

36a Using Figure 6.29, describe how the levées along the Mississippi have grown.

b What have been the advantages of the levées?

37a List the arguments for and against rebuilding and reinforcing the Mississippi levées.
b Would you advise the US government to rebuild the levées? Justify your answer.

Flood hazards in Bangladesh

Background

Bangladesh lies in the lower floodplain and delta built by the convergence of three great rivers, the Ganges, Brahmaputra and Meghna (Fig. 6.34). Each year these rivers, fed by snowmelt in the Himalayas and the summer monsoon rains (Fig. 6.33) reach their peak discharge in July–August. In a 'normal' year, about 25 per cent of Bangladesh is covered by up to 1 m of water during this flood season. Bangladeshis have adapted to this seasonal rhythm, planting their main crops as the floods recede (Fig. 6.32).

However, Bangladesh is vulnerable to much larger flood surges. For instance in 1988 and 1998, up to two-thirds of the country was flooded; the floods were deeper and lasted longer than normal. These major floods killed thousands of people, made millions homeless, caused health problems and disrupted the economy, thereby adding to the country's poverty. In 'normal' years the snowmelt flood peaks arrive in the delta up to a month before the monsoon rain discharges peak, thus 'flattening' the flood hydrograph. It is when the two surges arrive together, as in 1988 and 1998, or when the monsoon rains are unusually heavy, that abnormal floods occur.

The following resources (Figs 6.33–6.40) provide the physical and human framework within which the 1998

Figure 6.32 Bangladesh is essentially a low-lying fluvial environment, with more than 80 per cent of the land lying less than 6 m above mean sea level

floods occurred; the extent of these floods; the current government flood control policy, and indications that this 'hard' engineering approach may not be effective.

38 Take each resource in turn and summarise what it tells you.

39 Relate the location and extent of the floods (Fig 6.35) to
a the landform distribution (Fig 6.37)
b the population distribution (Fig 6.38).

40 Do the 'hard' engineering schemes (Fig 6.36) appear to have influenced the distribution of flooding?

41 Compare the population distribution and flood risk maps (Figs 6.38 and 6.39).

42 Write a brief report summarising the distribution and impacts of the 1998 floods and assess the effectiveness of the current government strategy.

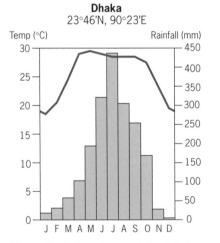

Figure 6.33 Climate graph for Dhaka, Bangladesh

The catchment basin of the three rivers covers almost 2 million km². Only 7.5% of this catchment area lies within Bangladesh.

Note: The Brahmaputra river is called the Jamuna in Bangladesh.

Figure 6.34 Bangladesh: catchment area of rivers entering Bangladesh

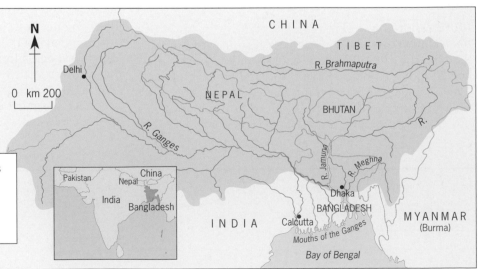

Weight and sea

FLOODING IN BANGLADESH has crippled the country and left millions homeless. Was this year's severe flooding a freak occurrence or could Bangladesh face worse in the future?

The simple answer is that Bangladesh is sinking. Over three-quarters of Bangladesh is within the deltaic region formed by the confluence of the mighty Ganges, Brahmaphutra and Meghna rivers. More than half of the country is less that 5 metres above sea level; so flooding is a common occurrence.

During the summer monsoon a quarter of the country is flooded. These floods, like those of the Nile, bring with them life as well as destruction. The water irrigates and the silt fertilises the land. So successful is this combination that the fertile Bengal Delta supports one of the world's most-dense populations – more than 110 million people in 140 000 sq km.

But the floods in Bangladesh are getting worse because the whole country is sinking. Every year the Bengal Delta should normally receive more than 1 billion tons of sediment and 1000 cubic km of freshwater. This sediment load balances the erosion of the delta both by natural processes and human activity.

However, the Ganges River has been diverted in India into the Hooghly Channel for irrigation. This reduced sediment input is causing the delta to subside. Exacerbating this is the rapid extraction of freshwater from the delta for agriculture and drinking water.

In the 1980s, 100 000 tube wells and 20 000 deep wells were sunk in the delta, increasing the freshwater extraction by six-fold. Both these projects, which were aimed at increasing the region's economy, have produced a subsidence rate of over 2.5 cm per year in parts of the country.

From these estimates of subsidence, the World Bank has estimated that by the middle of the twenty-first century, the relative sea level in Bangladesh could rise by as much as 1.8 metres.

They estimated that this would result in a loss of up to 16 per cent of land, supporting 13 per cent of the population and producing 12 per cent of the current gross domestic product (GDP).

The figures are frightening and do not take account of accelerated subsidence which would be caused by dams on the Ganges and the Brahmaputra proposed by India and Bangladesh, nor the effects of global warming on the monsoon system.

Solutions have been put forward, such as the Flood Action Plan, funded by the World Bank and western governments, which set out to construct embankments along all the major rivers to contain the floods. This has not helped, as the floods are so powerful that many of the puny embankments are washed away, or they divert waters to other parts of the country.

Bangladesh must persuade its neighbours to maintain the sediment inflow into the Bengal Delta. Moreover, there is an urgent need to return to the widespread, low-tech irrigation canals and dykes which provided Bangladesh ample flood protection prior to colonisation.

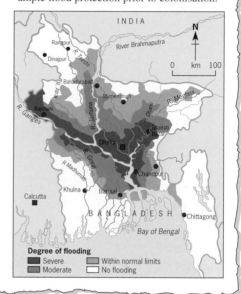

Figure 6.35 Key flood issues in Bangladesh (*Source: The Guardian* 23 September 1998)

Unnatural disaster
Although the principal cause of the excessive flooding has been the torrential monsoons, a catalogue of human error, thoughtlessness and corruption has made the situation a great deal worse than it otherwise might have been.

River diversion
In India, the Ganges has been diverted into the Hooghly Channel for irrigation purposes. This means that a great deal of the river sediment that used to pour into Bangladesh is no longer transported into the delta, which is effectively sinking each year, something it cannot afford as half the country is less than 5 metres above sea level.

Corruption
Many Bangladeshis believe that officials have helped themselves to government money that should have been used for flood prevention. Just recently, an anonymous piece appeared in the *Bangladesh Independent*, claiming that a planned embankment that might have protected part of Dhaka was never built due to corruption.

Deforestation
The removal of many trees in the Himalayan uplands has meant that water the might otherwise have been absorbed into the ground and taken up by the vegetation has been free to run to the lowlands of Bangladesh.

Inadequate overseas aid
A Flood Action Plan was established by the World Bank to build embankments along the major rivers. These have been largely ineffectual; many have been washed away or have merely diverted water to other parts of the country.

Fresh water wells
During the 1980s some 100 000 tube wells and 20 000 deep wells were sunk in the delta to provide drinking water for the rapidly growing population. These wells have altered the water table and added to the country's subsidence at a rate of 2.5 cm per year.

Figure 6.36 Factors affecting Bangladesh floods

Figure 6.37 Bangladesh: landforms and flood areas

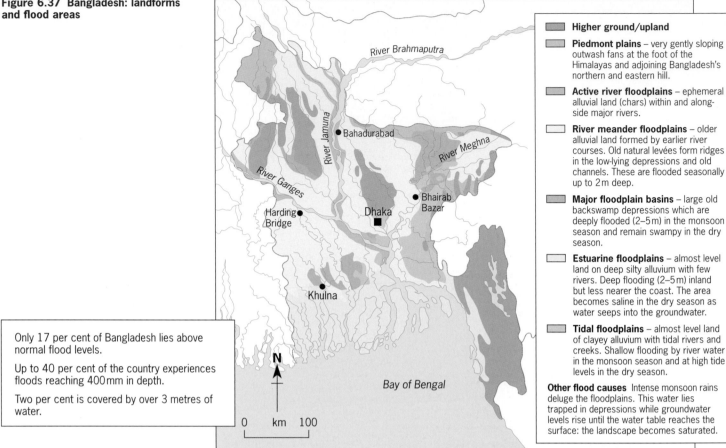

Higher ground/upland

Piedmont plains – very gently sloping outwash fans at the foot of the Himalayas and adjoining Bangladesh's northern and eastern hill.

Active river floodplains – ephemeral alluvial land (chars) within and along-side major rivers.

River meander floodplains – older alluvial land formed by earlier river courses. Old natural levées form ridges in the low-lying depressions and old channels. These are flooded seasonally up to 2m deep.

Major floodplain basins – large old backswamp depressions which are deeply flooded (2–5m) in the monsoon season and remain swampy in the dry season.

Estuarine floodplains – almost level land on deep silty alluvium with few rivers. Deep flooding (2–5m) inland but less nearer the coast. The area becomes saline in the dry season as water seeps into the groundwater.

Tidal floodplains – almost level land of clayey alluvium with tidal rivers and creeks. Shallow flooding by river water in the monsoon season and at high tide levels in the dry season.

Other flood causes Intense monsoon rains deluge the floodplains. This water lies trapped in depressions while groundwater levels rise until the water table reaches the surface: the landscape becomes saturated.

Only 17 per cent of Bangladesh lies above normal flood levels.

Up to 40 per cent of the country experiences floods reaching 400mm in depth.

Two per cent is covered by over 3 metres of water.

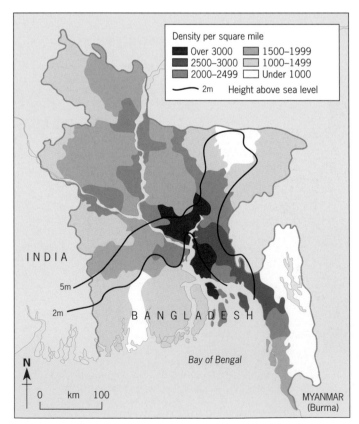

Figure 6.38 Population density and land elevation (*Source:* Newson, 1998)

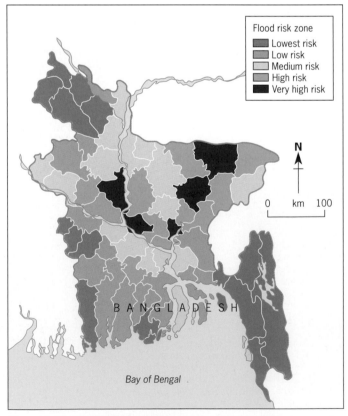

Figure 6.39 Flood risk by administrative districts (Risk assessed by frequency and depth of floods)

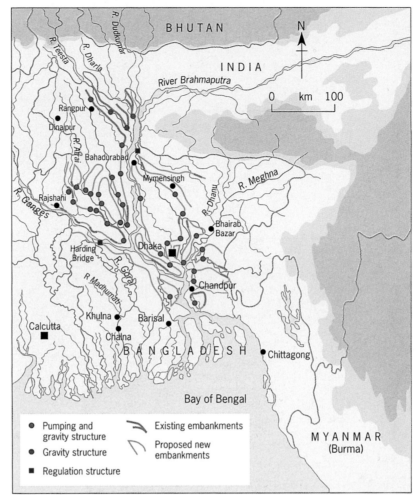

Figure 6.40 Existing and proposed embankments (*Source*: *Geographical Magazine*, August 1992)

Summary

- The floodplain acts as a temporary store for runoff at times of higher streamflow.

- The floodplain and river channel are closely linked parts of the same fluvial system.

- Flooding is a natural event and can be beneficial, e.g. it renews soil fertility, washes away any salt build-up from the floodplain.

- Human activity, such as changing agricultural practices and urban development, can cause a change in the location, magnitude and frequency of flooding. The flood event can consequently become a disaster.

- Water managers forecast flood events using past hydrological data and flood characteristics, such as the hydrograph and recurrence interval graph. Information must be continually updated.

- A range of flood control and management strategies are now used.

- There is a trend away from 'hard' engineering solutions to flood problems towards 'softer' techniques that retain the natural role of floodplains as temporary water stores.

7 Water supply and the role of groundwater

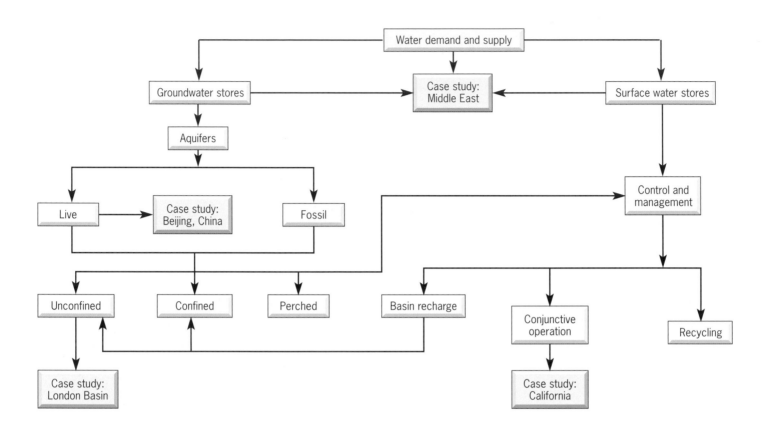

7.1 Introduction

Throughout the world, people's demand for water is increasing and is pressing against the limits of supply. An aim of every government is to ensure a sustainable water supply which is sufficient in both quantity and quality. Achieving this may create international as well as internal tensions. For example, access to precious water resources has been an important element in the long-running conflict between Israel, and Palestinian communities and neighbouring Arab countries in the Middle East (see case study, p. 135). Water conservation, i.e. improved efficiency in the storage and usage of water, is a high-profile environmental, economic and political issue (Fig. 7.1).

Water stores
Water resource managers organise supply by drawing upon surface water stores – rivers, lakes, reservoirs – and subsurface stores, e.g. Israel. The balance between the two stores varies from one environment to another, but all management systems integrate both sources. In its broadest sense, 'groundwater' refers to all water below the ground surface. However, hydrologists divide this subsurface water into four zones (Fig. 7.6). In this chapter we shall concentrate on the zone below the **water table**. Water managers call this zone the **groundwater store**. First, we shall illustrate the growing importance of the groundwater store in water supply. In later sections we shall examine how the groundwater store works, and how it is both managed and mismanaged as a water resource.

Figure 7.1 Florida has a water shortage. Irrigation water to this huge vegetable field is expensive and is metered. Only the minimum amount required by the plants is fed into the shallow channels. Plastic covers are used to reduce water loss by evaporation

The conflict over water resources in the Middle East

The most common cause given for the long-running conflicts between Israel and its Arab neighbours has been the complex dispute over land. However, in this arid region of the Middle East, the control of precious surface water and groundwater resources is equally important. This is illustrated vividly by three elements of the 1967 Six Day War: the capture by the Israelis of the Golan Heights from Syria (A on Fig. 7.2) and of the West Bank from Jordan (C on Fig. 7.2). Israel held onto both tenaciously throughout the long peace negotiations. The third element was the bombing of a dam being constructed by Jordan on the River Yarmuk (B on Fig. 7.2).

The Golan Heights

The R. Jordan drainage basin has five main components (Fig. 7.4). The upper basin [1] provides at least two-thirds of the total runoff and sustains Lake Tiberias (Sea of Galilee)[2]. Since 1964, this lake has been a vital component in Israel's national water grid: the National Water Carrier aqueduct abstracts 400 million m^3/yr, supplying Tel Aviv and irrigated agriculture of coastal districts (Fig. 7.3). While Syria controlled the Jordan headstreams in the Golan Heights that feed Lake Tiberias, Israel felt threatened, hence the 1967 invasion. A key issue in the negotiations for the Israeli withdrawal from the Golan Heights has focussed on ensuring water inputs to Lake Tiberias.

The River Yarmuk basin

The Yarmuk catchment (3 on Fig. 7.4) lies in Syria and Jordan, and gives the largest input of water to the main Jordan valley [4]. It is a seasonal stream, but discharges up to 400 million m^3/yr into the R. Jordan and is an important source of irrigation water for Israel. A dam inside Jordan would threaten this supply. As a result, Israel bombed the dam being built in 1967, and strongly opposed any further construction intil the Israel–Jordan peace agreement of 1994. Today Jordan abstracts 375 million m^3/yr from the Yarmuk, largely to supply the capital, Amman. (This surface supply replaces the groundwater aquifers beneath the city that have been seriously over-exploited, and are forecast to become exhausted by 2020.)

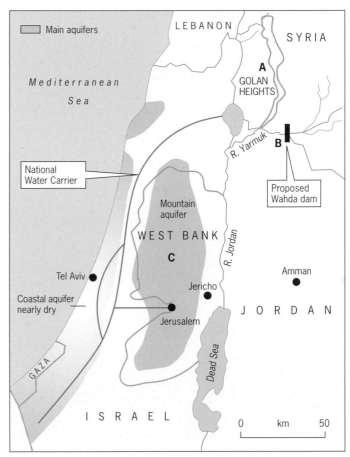

Figure 7.2 Strategic elements in the River Jordan basin

The outcome of these water abstractions is that of a mean flow of over 1300 million m^3/yr along the upper Jordan, only 600 million m^3/yr reaches the Dead Sea [5]. As a result, the highly saline inland sea (salinity ten times that of sea water) is shrinking and is affecting regional tables (Table 7.1). Jordan has proposed the 'Red–Dead' canal to recharge the Dead Sea. This project would build a canal to bring Red Sea water northwards into the Dead Sea, with associated HEP generation and large-scale water desalination plants.

The West Bank

The sedimentary strata that make up the hilly terrain of the West Bank contain important aquifers, dipping steadily westwards beneath the coastal plain. By the 1960s, this groundwater store had become a major water source for Jerusalem and the expanding coastal settlements. However, the West Bank hills, then within Jordan, were also home to Palestinian communities, who were sinking increasing numbers of wells. Thus, the 1967 occupation by the Israelis involved not only control of these militarily important hills and space for new Jewish settlements, but was also to secure the groundwater resource.

Table 7.1 The shrinking Dead Sea

Year	Level (m.b.m.s.l.)	Area (km²)
1958	395	1000
1998	411	645

m.b.m.s.l. = metres below mean sea level
The Dead Sea is the lowest continental place on earth.

After 1967, Israel established a number of settlements in the West Bank and the Palestinian population was banned from sinking further wells. By 1995, Israel was pumping 600 million m³/yr, which was 30 per cent of the country's total demand. At least 30 million m³ went to the 130 000 Israeli West bank settlers (230 m³/person); 115 million m³ went to the 1.4 million local Arabs – an allocation of only 82 m³/person. The rest went to Jewish cities such as Jerusalem and Tel Aviv. Understandably, this led to an intensifying dispute between the Palestinian and Jewish communities, and has been a crucial issue in the struggle to establish a Palestinian state (Fig. 7.5).

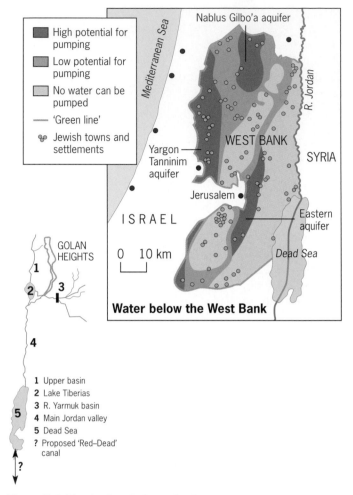

Water below the West Bank

Figure 7.3 Irrigation near Jerusalem, Israel

1 Upper basin
2 Lake Tiberias
3 R. Yarmuk basin
4 Main Jordan valley
5 Dead Sea
? Proposed 'Red–Dead' canal

Figure 7.4 The Jordan drainage basin

Palestinians thirsting for justice on tap

The waters trickling through the limestone aquifers below the West Bank provide a powerful undercurrent to the peacemaking process. Water is easily the most immediate problem facing ordinary Palestinians.

In the village of Eza'im, in the eastern lee of the Mount of Olives, 8000 Palestinians wonder where their water supply will come from. Eza'im is set in a kind of West Bank no-man's land, bordering Jerusalem and between rapidly growing Jewish settlements.

Mutasam Fahlan, aged 24, said that the summer had been truly miserable. 'Sometimes we only got water once a week, in the middle of the night. I was waiting until 3 a.m. with the tap open to see the water run.'

A local wealthy Palestinian contractor – or 'collaborator' as the villagers call him – has a deal with the Israeli-controlled Jerusalem municipality to run a water pipe. Mr Fahlan said: 'The Israelis control the pipe, so one day they open it and another they close it. Most closures happen in the summer so they can keep it to themselves. In winter they don't care because there is plenty of water.'

Haim Gvirtzman, a settler living at Dolev, north of Jerusalem, is one of Israel's leading hydrologists. His maps of 'Israeli interests in Judea and Samaria' – the West Bank – could be vital in the final status negotiations.

Study of the maps shows a pattern of settlement construction since the 1970s along ridges and edges of aquifers, suggesting that this strategic consideration was part of the Jewish pattern in populating the area.

Dr Gvirtzman admits that the West Bank's water sources, known as the Mountain aquifer, is the largest and most important reservoir for Israel. Some 600 million cubic metres are produced in an average year, about a third of Israel's water consumption.

Dr Gvirtzman argues: 'The vital need to prevent wildcat drilling by Palestinians, and the need to ensure the supply of good quality water, requires exclusive Israeli control of the vital pumping areas.'

But Jad Isac, of the Applied Research Institute of Jerusalem, has conducted exhaustive surveys of water use by Palestinians and Israelis. He found that Israel exploits more than 80 per cent of what he calls Palestine's water.

Irrigated agriculture constitutes less than 6 per cent of the total Palestinian cultivated areas. Some 39 per cent of the total water for agricultural use is extracted by Jewish settlements in the West Bank, while 26 per cent of Palestinian homes have no water.

Each Israeli consumes an average of 370 cubic metres of water a year, compared with each Palestinian's 107.

Agriculture provides only 6 per cent of Israel's GDP and 3.5 per cent of employment, yet 47 per cent of the country's cultivated land is irrigated. All but 6 per cent of Palestinian land is purely rain-fed, yet agriculture accounts for nearly a third of its GDP.

Figure 7.5 Water: Palestinian and Israeli viewpoints (*Source*: The *Guardian* 2 November 1998)

1a Using the terms, 'inputs', 'stores' and 'outputs', construct a systems diagram to show the storage and transfer of water through the environment of Figure 7.6.
b In what ways would you expect the techniques illustrated in Figure 7.1 to influence the working of the system you have drawn?

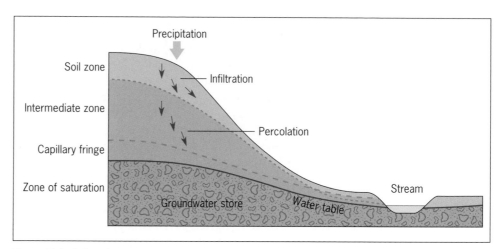

Figure 7.6 Subsurface water zones (*Source*: Ward and Robinson, 1990)

7.2 The global store

Groundwater is the earth's largest accessible store of fresh water (Fig. 1.1), accounting for over 90 per cent of the total. (The volume locked up as ice is excluded because it is not regarded as being readily accessible.) One half of this store lies within 800 m of the ground surface and is, therefore, relatively accessible for human and **ecosystem** use. It is difficult for us to grasp the scale of this groundwater store, but one way is to visualise the whole of the world's land surface covered to a depth of 60 m by water.

Groundwater is one component of the global **hydrological cycle** (Fig. 1.5). On average, a drop of water spends 300 years in the groundwater store, and so may reduce the impacts of climatic change. For instance, today's arid regions may contain groundwater reserves from wetter periods. Under the Sahara there are reserves which are estimated at 500 000 km³ of water.

A surprising proportion of the world's human population depends on groundwater stores. For example, in south-east England, which has a moist, temperate climate, 70 per cent of urban water supplies are drawn from groundwater stores. In Denmark the proportion reaches 90 per cent.

The groundwater store is a component of the **drainage basin** system (see Chapter 2). However, for the purposes of this chapter, we shall regard it as an open system in its own right. It has inputs, a main store, several pathways and outputs. Throughout our study, we should keep the key questions of Figure 7.7 in mind.

2 In south-east England groundwater provides 70 per cent of the water supply. In Wales and Scotland the figure drops to 10 per cent. With the help of your atlas, suggest reasons for this contrast. (Compare rainfall, temperature, land use, relief and population distribution maps.)

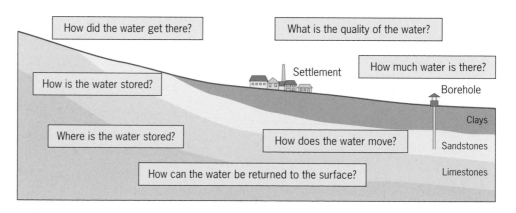

Figure 7.7 Groundwater: key questions we should ask

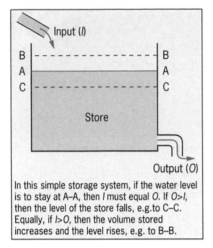

In this simple storage system, if the water level is to stay at A–A, then *I* must equal *O*. If *O>I*, then the level of the store falls, e.g.to C–C. Equally, if *I>O*, then the volume stored increases and the level rises, e.g. to B–B.

Figure 7.8 A simple storage system

7.3 Understanding the groundwater store

Wherever and whenever a groundwater reservoir is used, the most important message should always be, 'You can't take out more than is put in'. The groundwater store works like any other reservoir (Fig. 7.8). In economic terms, if demand continues to exceed supply, the reserve will shrink.

Aquifers and aquitards

Geological formations vary in their water-holding capability. Rock formations or layers of unconsolidated deposits which hold substantial volumes of water are known as **aquifers,** i.e. water-bearing materials. They are permeable and can transmit and store water effectively. Rock formations which are less permeable and transmit water more slowly are known as **aquitards** (Figs 7.9 and 7.10). Notice from Figures 7.9 and 7.10 that these terms are relative. In Figure 7.9 the fine-grained silt beds are the aquitards and in Figure 7.10 they act as the aquifers.

Most aquifers are composed of **sedimentary deposits** which have well-developed systems of interconnected pore spaces (gaps. between the rock particles) of a range of sizes. For example, the groundwater reservoir for Beijing, in China, is made up of an alternating series of sands and clays (see Fig. 7.13). The depth and size of this groundwater store vary, because of the uneven surface of the impermeable bedrock (see Beijing case study).

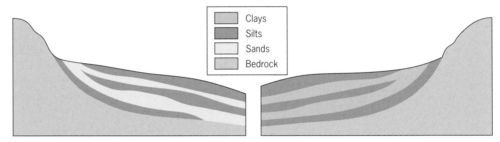

	Clays
	Silts
	Sands
	Bedrock

Figure 7.9 Silts as aquitards   **Figure 7.10 Silts as aquifers**

Aquifers in Beijing, China

The population of Beijing, China's capital city, doubled to six million between 1961 and 1981. Because Beijing lies at the junction between mountains and sedimentary plains, the city draws its water supplies from both groundwater and surface reservoirs (Figs 7.11 and 7.12). The groundwater store is a series of alternating sands and clays (Fig. 7.13). Until recently, it was the dominant water store. However, as demand has grown, the balance has been shifting.

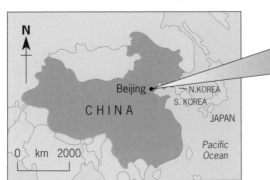

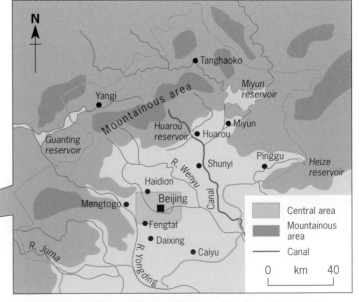

Figure 7.11 Beijing: water reservoirs In the city and suburban area (*Source*: Volker and Henry, 1988)

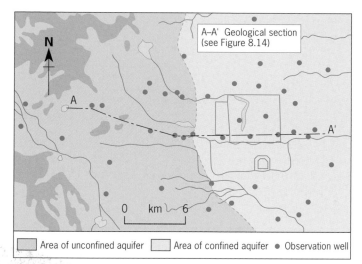

Figure 7.12 Distribution of observation wells around Beijing
(*Source*: Volker and Henry, 1988)

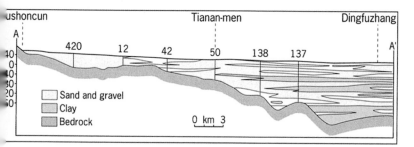

Figure 7.13 Quaternary aquifers in the Beijing area
(*Source*: Volker and Henry, 1988)

3 Study Figure 7.12. In which parts of the city would wells:
a dry up first?
b last longest?
Give reasons in each case.

4 In Figure 7.13 which beds would be the aquifers and which the aquitards? Give your reasons.

Demands on Beijing's groundwater store have been increasing (Table 7.2). By the early 1980s, over 2 700 million cubic metres of water a year were being abstracted (drawn out) from 40 000 wells spread across the city. Annual abstraction was exceeding recharge by more than 300 million cubic metres a year and, consequently, water table levels were falling across an area of at least 1000 km² (Figs 7.14 and 7.15). Between 1961 and 1981, the fall in groundwater levels in some places exceeded 40 m. This is an excellent example of output (demand) exceeding input (supply), and so depleting the store (reserve).

Apart from two unusually wet years in the 1950s, the annual rainfall input for Beijing has remained at between 400 mm. and 800 mm (Fig. 7.16). Yet, when we examine Table 7.3, we can see that the **water budget** of the aquifers has become increasingly negative over time.

Table 7.2 Beijing: increase in groundwater use, 1961–81
(*Source*: Volker and Henry, 1988)

| Year | Increase in groundwater use (million cubic metres per year) | | | |
	Domestic	Industry	Agriculture	Total
1961	157	161	106	424
1971	191	343	747	1281
1981	388	650	1671	2709

Table 7.3 Beijing: input and output relationships of the groundwater store (*Source*: Volker and Henry, 1988)

Number of years when:	1951–60	1961–70	1971–80
R>W	6	3	1
R=W	2	3	1
R<W	2	4	8

Note: R = the rainfall input
W = the water abstracted

Water management

During the 1980s, the population of Beijing grew by a further one million. In response, the city authorities were forced to control the drilling of new wells and the **abstraction** rates from the existing network. By 1994 two methods were being used to create an additional water supply:

• Dams built in the mountains to enlarge the surface reservoir supply.

• Water transferred from the mountains and pumped into the aquifers to recharge the groundwater store. This has the additional benefit of reducing ground subsidence, caused by the fall in groundwater levels.

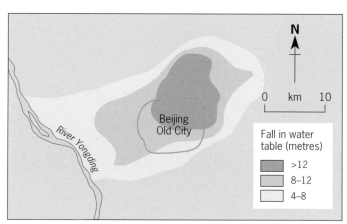

Figure 7.14 Beijing: drop in groundwater levels, 1970–80
(*After*: Volker and Henry, 1988)

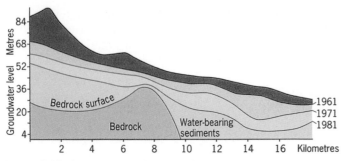

Figure 7.15 Cross-section showing fall in groundwater levels beneath Beijing City (*After*: Volker and Henry, 1988)

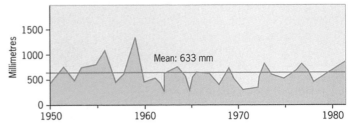

Figure 7.16 Beijing: annual rainfall totals, 1950–80 (*After*: Volker and Henry, 1988)

5 Explain why a falling water table increases the likelihood of surface subsidence.

6 Using Table 7.3 and Figure 7.16:
a Describe the changing relationships between the rainfall input (R) and the water abstracted (W).

b Test the hypothesis that the changing R–W relationship is caused by increased output, i.e. demand from wells, and not by a change in recharge, i.e. the rainfall input.

7 Define the terms 'live' and 'fossil' groundwater.

8 Explain to what extent live groundwater may be defined as a renewable resource. For example, at what level of usage would such live water become non-renewable? (Think of a system with inputs, stores and outputs.)

Live and fossil aquifers

Essential information which we need to have for any sustainable water management policy is whether a groundwater store is 'live' or 'fossil'. Where the store is being replenished regularly by water inputs from the recharge surface area, the groundwater is said to be 'live' (Fig. 7.17). Many present-day arid regions enjoyed moister climates in the past, e.g. the northern Sahara of Africa, during which times groundwater stores were filled. Today, however, the recharge surfaces no longer receive much rainfall and the groundwater stores are not being replenished. The groundwater stores are therefore said to be 'fossil' - a relic of former times (Fig. 7.18).

Figure 7.17 This region of the Atherton tablelands in north-east Queensland, Australia, receives more than 2000 mm of rain a year. The sedimentary formations beneath this rainforest dip westwards under the increasingly dry interior plains, and are the sole source of the water supply. This is a live groundwater store as it is being constantly recharged from the recharge surface

Figure 7.18 In late Pleistocene times rainfall in Arizona, USA, was heavy and the aquifers of the sedimentary basins were filled. Today, however, Arizona is an arid state. Groundwater stores are no longer being replenished – it is fossil water. Increased pumping of this fossil water for irrigated agriculture has caused serious drawdown of the water table.

9 In hot, arid environments, the transfer of water from the basin to surface reservoirs is a common technique. A key problem, however, is high water loss by evaporation.
a Suggest how aquifers might be used to manage the water resource more efficiently.
b Would your suggested strategy work for both live and fossil groundwater stores? Explain your answer using annotated sketches and systems diagrams.

10 Explain why water would have to be pumped to the surface from Wells W_2 and W_3 on Figure 7.19, but would flow freely to the surface from Well W_1.

11a Which of the three wells on Figure 7.19 are artesian wells? Justify your choice.
b Describe what will happen to the potentiometric surface of an artesian well as more water is abstracted.
c Under what circumstances would pumping become necessary at Well W_1?

12 Suggest why a well sunk into a perched aquifer might be relatively cheap to drill, but have a limited water supply potential.

Fossil groundwater is a non-renewable resource and, consequently, water levels in wells which tap fossil aquifers fall rapidly. In the basins of Arizona, 25 per cent of irrigated farmland has gone out of production since 1980 because wells have dried up. This is why the Central Arizona Project, which moves water from the Colorado River through a system of surface transfers, is so vital for the state's economy.

Lower limits
The lower limit of groundwater occurs at a depth where the pore spaces are so few and so small that further downward transmission and storage of water virtually stops. In dense rocks, such as granites, this may be at a shallow depth. However, porous sandstones may permit a deep groundwater store (Fig. 7.20). At depths of more than 10 km, we can say that all rocks are impermeable.

Confined and unconfined aquifers
We subdivide aquifers into three main types according to their position within the surrounding geology and their hydraulic characteristics. There are **unconfined aquifers**, **confined aquifers** and **perched aquifers** (Fig. 7.19). Each type behaves differently when wells are drilled into them, and each has a different water-yielding potential. For example, on Figure 7.19, engineers have drilled three wells (W_1, W_2 and W_3) and the water level in each is different.

The water level in wells sunk into an unconfined aquifer is controlled by the position of the water table, as shown by Well W_3 on Figure 7.19 which has been drilled into the unconfined aquifer A. The upper limit of the saturation zone is the water table (T_1), and it is therefore under atmospheric pressure.

On the other hand, the water level in a well bored through to a confined aquifer depends upon the **hydrostatic pressure** in the aquifer. For example, Well W_2, on Figure 7.19, has been sunk into the confined aquifer B. The upper limit of the saturation zone (T_2) is maintained under pressure by the overlying impermeable strata (aquitards), perhaps thick clays. Thus, the water level in Well W_2 will rise to the level allowed by this hydrostatic pressure. This is determined by the shape and the elevation of the aquifer's recharge area.

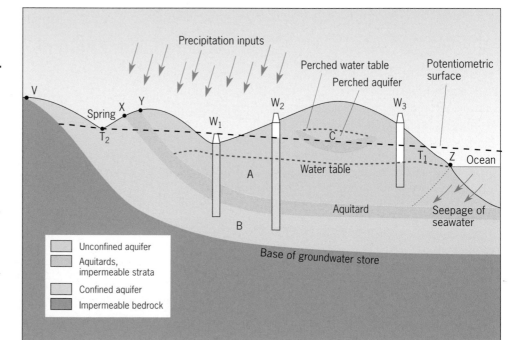

Figure 7.19 Unconfined (A) and confined (B) aquifers are distinguished by whether or not they have an overlying, i.e. confining, impermeable aquitard. Perched aquifers (C) are generally smaller and are created above an isolated impermeable layer

Figure 7.20 Canyon de Chelly National Park, Arizona. These thick-bedded and well-jointed sandstones are excellent aquifers

This is the area of land surface through which rainwater **infiltrates** to refill, i.e. to recharge the aquifer (surface area V–X on Figure 7.19). The level to which the hydrostatic pressure allows the water to rise is known as the **potentiometric surface** (T_2 on Figure 7.19). (Some older books use the term piezometric surface.) The potentiometric surface is the equivalent of the water table for an unconfined aquifer. The recharge area for the unconfined aquifer B on Figure 7.19 extends between Y and Z.

It is important to understand that the draw-down (lowering) of the water table is irregular and likely to be greatest around a well or a cluster of wells (Fig. 7.21). It is rather like the hollow around the straw as you drink a thick milkshake! These **cones of depression** are a common feature of exploited aquifers, and gradually refill when water abstraction stops.

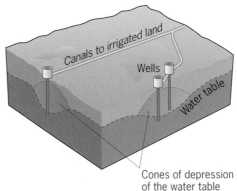

Figure 7.21 Water table draw-down by well abstraction

?

13 Suggest what factors will influence:
a the development of a cone of depression
b the infilling of a cone of depression after water abstraction.

Artesian basins

Basins containing confined aquifers which are fed from recharge areas in mountains, perhaps hundreds of kilometres away, are known as **artesian basins**. The wells sustained by the associated hydrostatic pressure are known as **artesian wells**. Over time, as more water is abstracted from the confined aquifers, the hydrostatic pressure tends to decrease (London Basin case study).

The London basin, England

The London basin (Fig. 7.22) is the most intensively used artesian basin in the UK. This gently curved bowl is made of an alternating sequence of sedimentary formations which vary in permeability and which are exposed around the rim (Fig. 7.23). More than 10 million people live within this basin. It is therefore not surprising that the aquifers have been overdrawn and that there have been concerns for water quality as well as quantity.

Supply – the aquifers

The principal aquifer is the Cretaceous chalk, with substantial amounts of water also stored in the Lower London Tertiary Series (Fig. 7.23). The chalk behaves as an unconfined aquifer in those areas where the series outcrops (see Fig. 7.19). Here, the water table rises and falls seasonally with natural recharge from

Figure 7.22 The London basin, England: Hampton Reservoirs, Middlesex, from the south-west

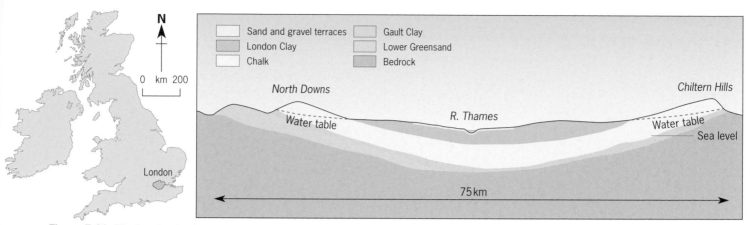

Figure 7.23 The London basin as a groundwater store

precipitation, and generally reflects the surface topography. In the confined zone of the aquifer – in the centre of the basin where the chalk is overlain by sands, clays and silts – the fluctuation in the water table under natural conditions is not great and is mainly caused by well abstractions.

The average annual precipitation over the exposed chalk catchment across the Chiltern Hills, Berkshire Downs and North Downs is 720 mm. Approximately half of this total infiltrates, while the rest is lost by evaporation or transferred by surface runoff. Most of the water which infiltrates moves laterally and emerges eventually as springs and as river discharge. Only perhaps 25 per cent of the subsurface water percolates deeply enough to become part of the 'reservoir' below London. Before people tapped this reservoir, the slowly migrating groundwater eventually discharged into the River Thames.

14 Make a copy of Figure 7.23.
a Colour and name the two main aquifers.
b In a second colour, mark and name the main aquitards.
c Use a heavy line to mark the recharge surfaces of the main aquifers.
d The cross-section runs in a north–south line. Mark north and south at the correct end points of your section.

15 Describe briefly how the London basin illustrates the definitions of:
a an artesian basin
b a confined aquifer.

Demand history

Under natural conditions the London basin has a shallow potentiometric (piezometric) head. Thus, the water level in any wells should be near the surface. However, the number of wells tapping the aquifer expanded rapidly after 1820 and, consequently, the water table fell (Fig. 7.24). During the second half of the nineteenth century, the water table was falling at an average rate of 0.7 m/y.

As the built-up area of London spread, an increasing proportion of the water was removed as direct surface runoff from the urban surfaces into the River Thames and its tributaries. This contributed to the lowering of the water table. Between 1850 and 1965, the water table had fallen by at least 50 m across an area of 200 km² (Figs 7.25–7.28), causing a range of impacts (Table 7.4).

Management responses

By 1945, water engineers had fully understood the problems of falling water levels. A new national Water Act was passed in that year and further exploitation of the London basin aquifer virtually stopped. Since the early 1950s, few new wells have been sunk. Water abstraction continued at about 75 per cent of the pre-1945 level.

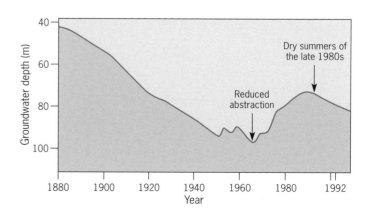

Figure 7.24 Changes in the water table under central London (*Source*: Institute of Hydrology, 1990 and 1994)

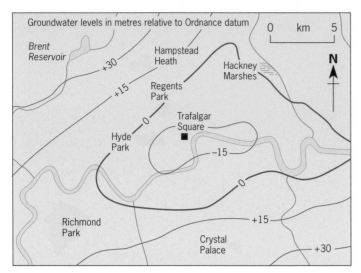

Figure 7.25 Groundwater levels below London, 1850
(*Source*: **Marsh and Davies, 1983**)

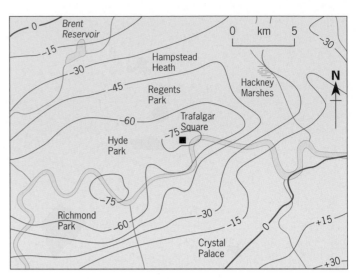

Figure 7.26 Groundwater levels below London, 1950
(*Source*: **Marsh and Davies, 1983**)

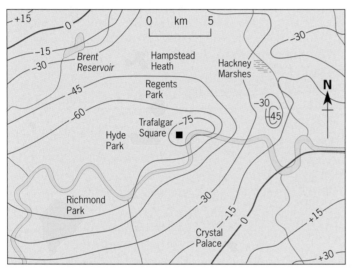

Figure 7.27 Groundwater levels below London, 1965
(*Source*: **Marsh and Davies, 1983**)

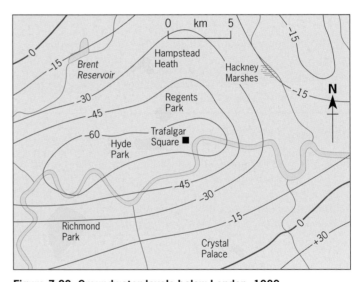

Figure 7.28 Groundwater levels below London, 1980
(*Source*: **Marsh and Davies, 1983**)

Figures 7.25–7.28 The increasing extent and scale of the impact. The figures on the isolines are heights above or below Ordnance datum (OD), i.e. sea level

An increasing proportion of the water supply came from the Thames and Lea surface reservoirs. The result was that by 1980 there were signs of water table recovery (Fig. 7.24). Recovery was also helped by a halving of the water abstraction from the central basin between 1965 and 1980, and by seepage from London's ageing water supply network (Fig. 7.29).

Today, most of London's public water supply is met from surface sources and, since 1992, rises in the water table in some areas have been so rapid that hydrologists and engineers are now concerned about ground deformation and structural problems. Although the above conservation policies allowed water levels to

recover despite three significant drought years in the 1970s, water managers are still concerned. Recovery, i.e. recharge of the groundwater store, remains fragile, as the 1988–92 UK drought revealed. Furthermore, abstraction rates across the outer basin in both the confined and unconfined zones continued to increase through the 1980s. This was triggered by the housing and industrial boom in Hertfordshire and Berkshire. Extraction from the chalk outcrop areas increased by more than 40 per cent between 1950 and 1990. Consequently, catchments such as the Darent, Ver and Misbourne have shown significant reductions in their groundwater levels.

Increased abstraction from the surface recharge areas is worrying, because it reduces the water available for slow lateral percolation to the confined aquifers. One method of maintaining water levels, which water managers are introducing, is by flow and groundwater augmentation. Water is added to rivers, which sustains the flow and maintains some groundwater recharge via the stream bed and banks.

Land subsidence associated with lowering of the water table may be accentuated by prolonged dry spells. Following the 1988–92 drought and the hot, dry summers of 1995 and 1996, there has been increased evidence of stuctural stresses in a number of older buildings in central London.

Technological solutions

Many water supply systems are old and still rely on relatively primitive methods and equipment. Today, however, technological advance enables the installation of storage and delivery systems which are more efficient mechanically, economically and environmentally. Yet critical factors in putting in these new technologies are their huge costs, the engineering problems in built-up areas and the long time-scale involved. None the less, London, where such factors are at their most acute, has succeeded, with the opening in 1994 of the Thames Water Ring Main system (Fig. 7.30a, b).

Table 7.4 The effects of the depletion of the groundwater store beneath London

Effect

1 Boreholes give a reduced yield as water pressures drop. They eventually fail as the water table sinks.

2 Drilling of boreholes becomes more expensive and less economic.

3 The deeper, lower Chalk series is less well fissured than the upper beds. Therefore, yields from the deeper, more costly wells are poorer. (Water transmission through chalk is largely via the fissure and joint system.)

4 Salt water penetrates the aquifers by induced recharge from the lower Thames where it flows over exposed chalk, e.g. by 1965 a zone of saline intrusion up to 8 km wide extended as far west as Lambeth.

5 Land subsidence occurs as artesian pressures decline. This is accentuated by the ever-increasing weight of buildings, roads, etc. Most importantly, this settling up to 1 m in places is uneven, causing structural problems.

6 A reduction of river flows, an increasing failure of springs and a falling water table reduce the inflow into headwaters, e.g. in 1965 the River Colne was estimated to be losing 45 000 m³ per day.

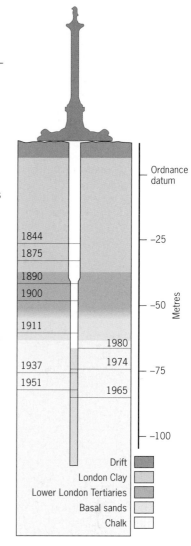

Figure 7.29 Trends below Trafalgar Square (*Source*: Marsh, 1983)

16 Using the London basin as an example:
a Illustrate the idea that a groundwater basin works as an open system.
b Explain how the abstraction capacity of a confined aquifer is determined by the nature and use of the surface recharge area of the aquifer. (Use an annotated diagram in your answer.)

17 Outline the methods being used today to balance the water budget of the confined chalk aquifer beneath the central London Basin.

18 Explain briefly how the Ring Main storage and supply system works.

19 Why is the Ring Main regarded as so necessary and important?

20 List any economic and environmental advantages and disadvantages of the scheme, indicated in the extract.

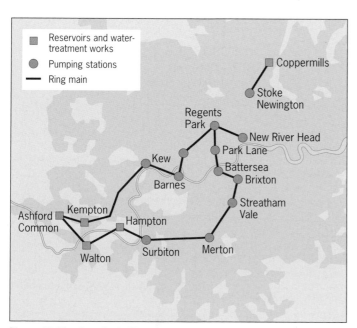

Figure 7.30a London's Ring Main system

Reservoirs are situated at either side of the ring main and extraction shafts puncture the tunnel throughout its length to feed London's arterial water mains, some of which date back as far as 1838. As water is pumped out of the extraction shafts, a siphon effect is created — gravity forces water from the input reservoirs along the ring main towards the shafts from which the water is being extracted.

There were, according to Bensted, several key reasons why the ring was necessary.

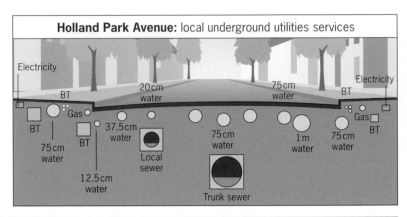

Holland Park Avenue: local underground utilities services

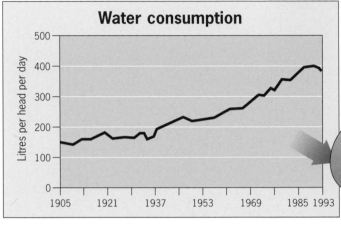

Water consumption

3 Water from the extraction shaft feeds into local water network. Pressure in the older long distance pipes beneath London's roads is thus reduced, cutting down on burst pipes. This avoids flooding and traffic congestion as well as disruption to telephone, electricity and gas supplies.

2 As water is pumped out, gravity from the input reservoirs pushes along the ring main to wherever it is being extracted. This means no electric pumping is required until water is extracted into the local network, significantly reducing costs.

1 Pumping station
Twelve pumping stations (or extraction shafts) take water out of the ring main into London's localities

Demand

Water consumption per capita has risen from 120 litres a day in 1905 to nearly 400 litres now. Consumption is expected to rise 13% between now and 2011 as living standards improve and people bathe more often, own more dishwashers and washing machines, and have more time to wash cars and water gardens. The ring main will carry the bulk of London's water supply — about 1,300m litres a day, or enough to fill the Albert Hall eight times.

Pressure

Many existing mains water supplies, typically built a metre below the surface of London's roads, date back to the 19th century. To cope with greater demand, water pressures have had to be increased dramatically and many of the older mains pipes were being run at beyond their maximum pressure. This has led to frequent burst pipes, interrupting water supplies, disrupting road traffic and often electricity and gas supplies too. The ring means these pressures can be substantially reduced, avoiding the problems and prolonging the life of the existing infrastructure. Reducing pressure also reduces leakage which, before the ring began operations, accounted for as much as 20% of all the water passing through the system.

Cost

More than 100 jobs have been cut as 15 control stations have been reduced to three. Staff numbers at treatment works have also been cut. Only three people operate the ring-main control centre at Hampton, southwest London, and more than £1m was saved in pumping costs last year as the first phase came into operation.

Environment

As the ring main enables transfers of large amounts of water between rivers it raises ground water levels so that rivers such as the Darent, in Kent, which dried up in 1990 and 1991, should never dry up again.

Figure 7.30b (*Opposite*) **How the Ring Main system works**

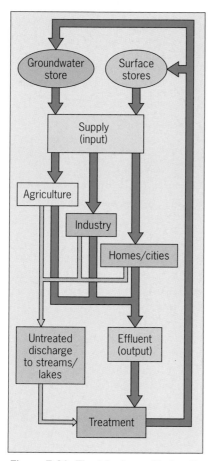

Figure 7.31 The 'single quality level' system

21 Outline the difficulties likely to arise if a water company decides to change from a single quality to a variable water quality recycling policy.

22a The systems diagram of Figure 7.31 summarises the water supply system in a 'single quality level' policy. Construct a similar diagram for a 'variable quality level' policy.
b In what ways do the recycling and variable quality approaches assist the development of water conservation policies?

7.4 Considering the conservation and recycling option

Water management policies in most countries are today organised as integrated systems. The modern systems are based upon a balanced use of both surface and groundwater stores. This is especially true in densely populated and industrialised countries which have experienced the consequences of relying on either one or the other. The Beijing case study (p. 138) shows how an uncontrolled development of groundwater resources led to extensive land subsidence, without being able to satisfy demand. In the USA, the enormous investments in surface storage projects in the Colorado River basin and the Mississippi River basin have caused severe environmental impacts, and again, these projects have been unable to keep pace with expanding demand. A policy which integrates both surface and subsurface stores is likely to be more economic, more sustainable and more environmentally friendly (see California case study, p. 148).

Yet all countries must face the inevitable: first, water resource capacity is finite – there are limits; second, ensuring reliable and sustainable water supplies is expensive; third, supply becomes increasingly costly as demand continues to grow. These realities are focusing the attention of governments and water managers on water conservation. Two key understandings which underpin conservation strategies are first, that water can be used more than once, i.e. it can be recycled, and second, that different uses need different water qualities.

There are three main categories of water users:
• human populations
• agriculture
• industry.

Water used in our homes needs to be potable (of drinkable quality). Once it leaves our homes it requires expensive treatment before it can be released into streams and water bodies and made available for human use once more (Fig. 7.31).

Agriculture and industry, however, are able to use water of lower quality. Even in our homes, water used for flushing toilets need not be of the same quality as that which flows from our taps. This understanding leads to the idea that water can be recycled for certain uses by minimal treatment. this treatment can be carried out at reduced cost. The potential of the recycling and variable quality options is being considered and taken up in a number of countries. For example, in England, Thames Water plc, the company that supplies London, claims that about 10 per cent of its effluent water is reused. Water used upstream of London is treated and released back into the River Thames where it may be reused downstream.

In Japan, for instance, the demand for water has trebled since 1965. At first, the response was to increase pumped abstractions from groundwater stores. This led to serious land subsidence in several cities. Government strategy had to be altered to reduce the water abstractions, and thus, the subsidence. A massive dam-building programme was initiated and since the mid-1980s the surface reservoirs have been the main water source.

However, the severe drought of 1994 caused widespread shortages, causing another shift of strategy. This time the major investments have been in water treatment plants, in order to increase the use of recycled water and introduce systems for use of different levels of water quality. For example, Sumida ward, in Tokyo, is vulnerable to flooding. The ward has had underground storage tanks built for rainwater runoff, and uses the natural and regulated water for flushing toilets and watering parks.

California: an example of a conjunctive operation strategy

The State Water Plan

The issue facing California's water resource managers is straightforward but immense. Seventy-five per cent of the population live in those regions with only 25 per cent of the rainfall (Fig. 7.32). The combination of Californian lifestyle (Fig. 7.33) and intensive irrigated agriculture produces very thirsty consumers. Water managers have integrated surface and groundwater stores in their State Water Plan. The Plan is based upon

Figure 7.33 The Californian life-style: typical water consumption

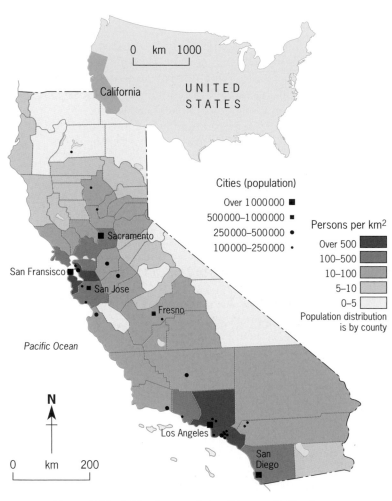

Figure 7.32 California: population (*Source*: Collins-Longman Atlas, 1989)

23 Using Figure 7.32, construct a systems diagram of the conjunctive operation technique. Label the inputs, stores, throughputs and output.

massive inter-basin surface water transfers (Fig. 7.34), and maximum use of the groundwater capacity. It is an example of a **conjunctive operation strategy**.

Groundwater stores

California's groundwater potential looks impressive. Forty per cent of the area consists of basins containing water-bearing strata. There are 450 water basins which give a total store of 1.6 million cubic hectometres (hm^3) (one hectometre = one hectare covered by a one-metre depth of water). However, only 11 per cent of this water is classified as 'usable'. The rest is either inaccessible or too saline.

About 40 per cent of California's water supply comes from the groundwater sources and, consequently, many of the usable water basins are being overdrawn. It is crucial to understand that only 34 per cent of the usage is being replenished by natural and deliberate recharge. A further 50 per cent is made up by **percolation** losses from canals and infiltration of excess irrigation water. (You should note that this 'wasted' water is therefore not actually lost, but re-enters the groundwater store.) In consequence, during the 1980s, overdraft of the groundwater stores was providing 16 per cent of the water supply.

Deliberate recharge

California is making increasing use of the deliberate recharge technique (Fig 7.35). This is a good example of the conjunctive operation strategy at work and emphasises that hydrology functions as an integrated system. Surface water is transferred to spare capacity in the groundwater store. Approximately 65 000 hm^3 are available in California's water basins. By 1990, more than 20 such replenishment schemes were in operation.

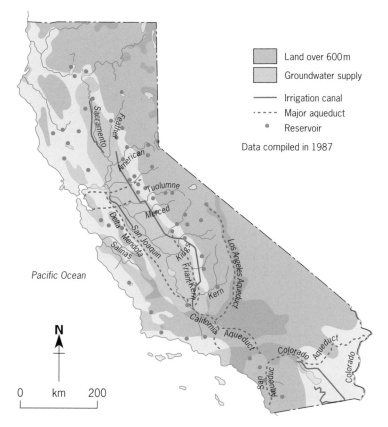

Land over 600 m

Groundwater supply

——— Irrigation canal

- - - - Major aqueduct

• Reservoir

Data compiled in 1987

Pacific Ocean

N

0   km   200

Figure 7.34 California: water supply (*Source*: Collins-Longman Atlas, 1989)

There are advantages of using groundwater storage space:

• There is less impact on the environment and the costs of surface **dams** and reservoirs are reduced.

• **Evaporation** losses are reduced.

• Pollution risks are reduced.

• Water is maintained at low and constant temperatures.

Alternatively, we could keep the groundwater stores as emergency stores for use during periods of drought. They would be recharged in unusually wet years.

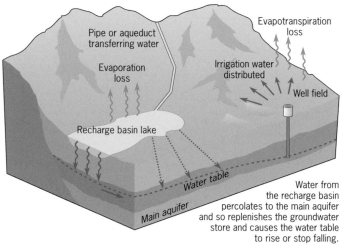

Figure 7.35 The recharge basin technique

Summary

• Groundwater makes up at least 90 per cent of the world's accessible reserve of freshwater.

• Each soil and rock type has a distinctive capacity to store and transmit water down to a certain depth.

• The groundwater store functions as an open system, and has a measurable water budget which determines its capacity for exploitation.

• Water-bearing strata are known as aquifers. There are three main types: confined, unconfined and perched. They may be 'live' or 'fossil' depending on whether they are currently being replenished.

• Water resource managers organise supply by drawing on surface water stores and subsurface stores. Attempts to maintain supply often result in a variety of water management schemes.

• As water demands continue to rise, managers are increasingly turning to the examination of policies for recycling and two-level-quality supplies.

8 Seeking sustainability for UK water resources

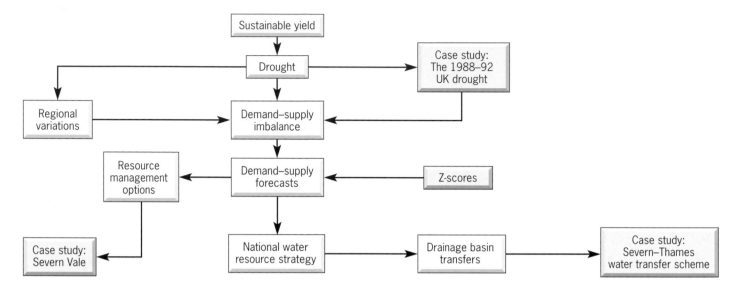

8.1 The concept of sustainable yield

A basic goal for water resource managers is to 'balance the budget' of surface and groundwater stores. As Figure 8.1 shows, water abstractions (outputs) from rivers, reservoirs and aquifers follow five routes. These outputs must be matched by water inputs to the stores (A, B, C on Fig. 8.1). Only when demand made upon the stores is balanced by supply to the stores can a policy of sustainable yield be achieved.

The difficulties UK regional water companies face in achieving sustainable yield arise from three key factors:
- geographical mismatch between water resources and population distribution
- fluctuations in precipitation inputs from year to year (see case study: The 1988-1992 UK drought)
- continuing increase in overall water demand.

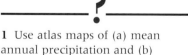

1 Use atlas maps of (a) mean annual precipitation and (b) population distribution to discuss the claim that there is a geographical mismatch between water resources (potential supply) and population distribution (demand) in the UK

Figure 8.1 The five routes water takes to your tap, each including water treatment. The balance between the routes depends upon where we live, and the status of the reservoirs, river channels and the aquifer groundwater store

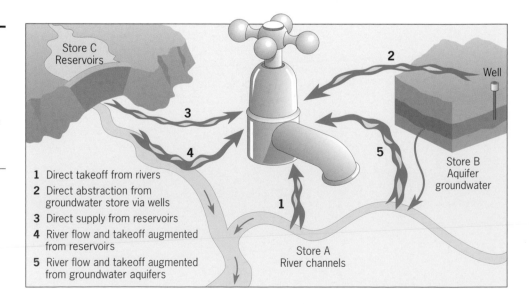

1 Direct takeoff from rivers
2 Direct abstraction from groundwater store via wells
3 Direct supply from reservoirs
4 River flow and takeoff augmented from reservoirs
5 River flow and takeoff augmented from groundwater aquifers

Store C Reservoirs

Well

Store B Aquifer groundwater

Store A River channels

The 1988–92 UK drought

The fragile margin between supply and shortage was harshly demonstrated by the 'Great Drought' of 1988–92. Over extensive areas of the British Isles, these were four of the driest years of the past century (Table 8.1, Fig. 8.3). By 1992, serious deficiencies in precipitation inputs had accumulated, causing the most severe drought in those regions where demand was greatest and supply reserves smallest (Fig. 8.2).

Drought conditions were intensified because 1988–92 was also the warmest five-year sequence in England in more than 300 years. The effectiveness of rainfall was thus reduced, because unusually high proportions of the moisture input were **evaporated**, rather than remaining to recharge streams and aquifers.

Streamflow

By late summer 1992, monthly flows in some eastern rivers had remained below average for nearly four years (Fig. 8.4). Despite rainfall totals only 20 per cent below average, the high evaporation rates and low soil moisture levels meant that runoff was reduced by 50 per cent in many areas (Fig. 8.6).

Table 8.1 Rainfall, August 1988 to May 1992, as a percentage of the 1941–70 average (*Source*: Institute of Hydrology, 1994)

Region	Total rainfall over whole period (mm)	Percentage of average
Great Britain	4280	102
Scotland	6340	115
England and Wales	3080	95
Anglian region	1890	80

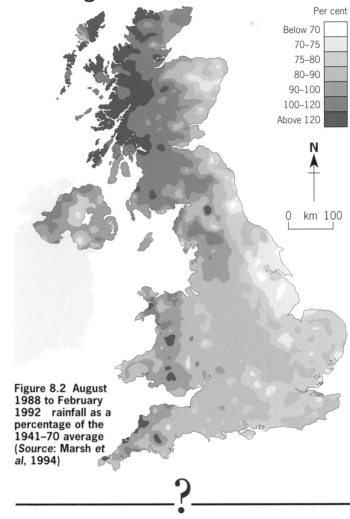

Figure 8.2 August 1988 to February 1992   rainfall as a percentage of the 1941–70 average (*Source*: Marsh et al, 1994)

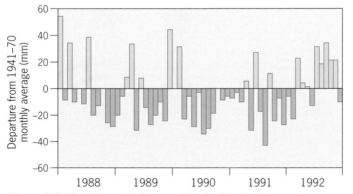

Figure 8.3 Monthly rainfall anomalies for the Anglian region, 1988–92 (*Source*: Marsh et al, 1994)

?

2a From Figure 8.2, across which parts of England were the precipitation deficiencies greatest?
b Which areas received at least average precipitation?
c Summarise the difficulties such patterns may have caused England's water managers.

3 Using Figure 8.6:
a Construct a line graph to plot the percentage of rainfall which appeared in the river each year, from 1960 to 1992.
b Describe the changing relationship between rainfall and runoff in the Ver catchment.
c In which years was the runoff percentage at its lowest?
d Suggest reasons why the rainfall-runoff relationship has changed and, in particular, why the gap is growing wider.

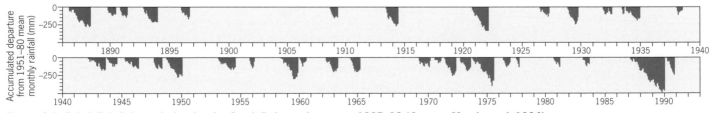

Figure 8.4 Rainfall deficiency index for the South Dalton rain gauge, 1885–92 (*Source*: Marsh et al, 1994)

Figure 8.5 The River Ver in Hertfordshire had dried up completely by May 1992

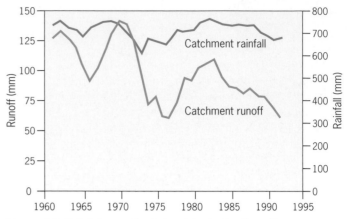

Figure 8.6 Rainfall–runoff relationships in the River Ver catchment, at Hansteads (*Source*: National Water Archive, Institute of Hydrology, 1994)

Stream networks contracted as falling **water tables** caused **base flow**, fed by groundwater, to fail. The combination of drought and heavy water demands caused stretches of UK rivers to dry up for the first time this century (Fig. 8.5).

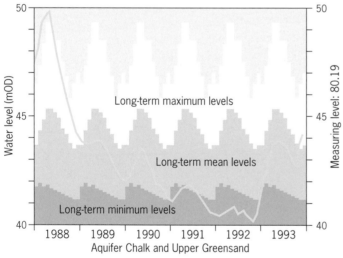

Figure 8.7 The water level in a well at Washpit Farm, Norfolk, 1988–93 (*Source*: Marsh *et al*, 1994)

Groundwater stores

The normal rhythm of groundwater stores across England is a draw-down, i.e. a fall of the water table, during the summer, followed by a recharge, i.e. rise, during the winter months. After several wet years during the mid-1980s, aquifers were well stocked by early 1988. Figure 8.7 records the impact of the drought on the water table over the next four years which fell to record levels. A report from the Institute of Hydrology concludes that 'in the summer of 1992, overall groundwater resources for England and Wales were at their lowest since at least the turn of the century' (Marsh et al, 1994).

4 From Figure 8.7:
a Support the claim that groundwater levels follow a seasonal rhythm.
b Describe what happened to the water table between 1988 and 1992.
c What evidence is there that the 1988–92 drought caused the water table to fall more than ever before recorded?
d During what period was the water table at Washpit Farm at a record low level?

5 Using Table 8.2:
a Express the rainfall–runoff relationship in graphical form and summarise what your graph reveals. (Spearman rank correlation may also be useful.)
b To what extent does the data support the idea that the water supply problem varies according to where you live? Suggest reasons for this variation.

8.2 The dilemma for eastern and southern England

The problems of achieving sustainable yield are especially intense in eastern and southern England, the most densely populated yet driest regions of the UK (Table 8.2). The **groundwater** resource is already being used to its capacity. Thus, further increases in demand and/or a fall in precipitation inputs will result in increased dependence on surface water resources. However, existing rivers and reservoirs have little spare capacity, and in some cases are suffering from over-abstraction, especially in dry years (Fig. 8.8). Therefore, despite **conjunctive operation strategies** (see Section 7.4), the water companies of eastern and southern England face a dilemma. Either they find ways of increasing the yield of surface and groundwater stores within the region, or look to other parts of Britain and construct expensive water transfer schemes.

6a Which region in England and Wales has the most urgent water supply problem?
b Suggest why it might be particularly difficult to solve this water problem by using the region's resources alone.

7 Read Figure 8.8.
a What reason is given for the increased use of groundwater by water companies?
b What impacts is this trend having on river flows?
c What evidence is there that the current policy is non-sustainable in terms of yield and environmental quality?
d Outline the options for restoring river flows and suggest the key issues raised by each of these options.

The urgency of the dilemma was highlighted by the prolonged 1988–92 drought and the hot, dry summers of 1995 and 1996. It is not surprising that there is a growing acceptance of the need to plan at the national scale.

Table 8.2 Water resources by NRA regions (*Source*: Institute of Hydrology, 1994)

Region	Mean annual rainfall (mm)	Mean annual runoff (mm)	Public water supply (1987–8) as percentage of runoff
Thames	704	240	47
Anglian	610	170	14
Southern	794	320	14
Severn–Trent	773	330	12
Yorkshire	833	420	9.1
Wessex	869	370	8.9
Northumbria	879	490	8.3
North West	1217	810	7.8
Welsh	1334	850	2.4
South West	1194	740	2.2

How likely are droughts?

It is important for water resource managers to assess the probability of an occurrence of a stated rainfall amount. One popular technique is to use the z-score formula. Z scores allow us to assess the probability of an occurrence of a stated rainfall amount using the formula:

$$z = \frac{x - \bar{x}}{\sigma}$$

Where:
x = stated value
$\bar{x}$ = mean
σ = standard deviation.

The mean rainfall and standard deviation for the years 1980–9 have been calculated for the R. Lambourn (Table 8.3). This allows us to compare the 1990 data with the previous ten years (although we should remember that the UK drought started in 1988). The annual rainfall total for 1990 was 563 mm and the z score indicates that there is only a one per cent chance of this rainfall occurring, i.e. the total rainfall for 1990 has a probability of occurring only once in a hundred years.

More detailed analysis of this data allows us to discover something of the complexity of the UK drought. For example, the February rainfall in 1990 was an extremely rare event in that it was very heavy.

Table 8.3 Monthly rainfall (mm) for the River Lambourn at Shaw

Date	Jan	Feb	Mar	Apr	May	Jun	Jul	Aug	Sep	Oct	Nov	Dec	Total
1980	46	53	89	19	31	86	58	87	62	94	55	52	732
1981	34	29	161	47	102	35	63	34	124	85	47	108	869
1982	49	38	97	34	33	78	18	55	61	126	103	81	773
1983	78	27	49	95	88	20	50	14	75	66	51	67	680
1984	136	42	60	3	91	30	18	28	105	58	127	79	777
1985	56	39	46	38	75	149	59	81	29	42	48	127	789
1986	93	12	63	61	83	24	38	111	40	73	108	95	801
1987	13	50	65	61	44	96	59	31	47	137	65	38	706
1988	133	49	65	22	38	55	100	67	49	78	34	14	704
1989	38	78	71	69	20	34	34	46	20	66	44	151	671
Mean 1980s	67.6	41.7	76.6	44.9	60.5	60.7	49.7	55.4	61.2	82.5	68.2	81.2	750.2
Standard deviation	39.55	16.88	31.86	25.94	28.58	39.16	23.11	29.13	30.96	28.10	30.57	39.14	59.21
1990 rainfall (mm)	103	126	17	34	8	44	19	35	26	50	27	74	563
Z scores	0.89	4.99	–1.87	–0.42	–1.84	–0.426	–1.33	–0.70	–1.14	–1.16	–1.35	–0.18	–3.16
% probability of 1990 figures	18.4	0	?	34.5	3.6	?	9.7	24.2	?	13.6	9.7	?	1.0

Diminishing return

Jim Manson on the rivers that are water starved

ONE OF THE EFFECTS of soaring water treatment costs has been the increasing reliance by the water industry on groundwater, as distinct from reservoir and river sources, which requires minimal, if any, treatment. By chance, the areas which have traditionally relied on groundwater abstraction are those like Buckinghamshire, where the demand for water is increasing fastest. The problem is that as more and more boreholes are sunk, the rate of abstraction threatens to exceed the rate of replenishment, causing the underground springs and rivers to run dry.

The National Rivers Authority (NRA) says it is adopting a 'softly, softly' approach to the issue. A spokesman insisted that 'there is nothing that can be done to increase river flows in the short term,' adding that the reviewing of abstraction licences was 'a long-term measure and one that is unlikely to alter significantly overall abstraction levels.' Five rivers were named in 1989 by the CPRE: the Pang, the Misbourne, the Ver, the Darent, the Wey and Letcombe Brook. Each has been affected differently according to the

environment of the surrounding area. For example, the perennial heads of the rivers Pang, Ver and Misbourne have all shifted — the Misbourne by 5 km — while chalk-bedded rivers like the Darent in Kent have insufficient flow because of the combined effect of over- abstraction and leakage through the river bed.

In 1986 Thames Water commissioned Sir William Halcrow & Partners to examine the environmental problems arising from over-abstraction of these rivers and to recommend methods of alleviating them by re-establishing 'adequate flows' — everyone seems to rule out the prospect that the rivers will be restored to their proper natural flows.

In its report, Halcrow noted that abstraction has had a severe effect on the rivers. They often dry up in summer, river channels are no longer managed for land drainage purposes, the general appearance of the rivers has deteriorated and trout have almost disappeared.

In setting new flow targets Halcrow had to 'balance the requirements of water supply and the protection of the environment'. In other

words, on cost grounds, the company was to rule out the possibility of reducing abstraction. Here then, as the Government's policies on water come into direct conflict with pressure on the water companies to keep operating costs down, the politically sensitive nature of the abstraction issue becomes clear. But Halcrow also rejected a controversial water industry proposal, to increase flows through the use of sewage effluents, due to water quality problems.

The favoured approach was to put in the new boreholes to abstract water from the aquifers and then to pump water into the rivers at certain times of the year at selected points. Existing boreholes are close to springs and rivers, in valley bottoms. Consequently, abstraction tends to dry up the river sources. Halcrow proposes that new boreholes be sunk at around 3km distance from the river to draw water which has collected underground during winter and pump it through pipelines during the summer. The company also recommends that lining work be carried out to prevent leakage and to create narrower river beds to help maintain flows.

Figure 8.8 Water-starved rivers (*Source: The Guardian*, 20 July 1990)

?

8a Calculate the z scores and probabilities for the River Lambourn (using Appendix A3 and Table 8.3) for March, June, September and December.
b Plot the percentage probability scores on a reverse bar chart for 1990. Indicate which months were above and below the mean by using the z scores. A positive value indicates a wet month and a negative value indicates a relatively dry month.
c Comment on the nature of the UK drought in 1990, using Table 8.3 and your graph.
d Describe the likely groundwater levels between the beginning and the end of 1990.

9 Use the data of Table 8.3 to discuss this claim: Short-term climatic variability is a major obstacle to the effectiveness of a policy of sustainable water supply in the UK.

8.3 Responding to drought

Responding to drought in England and Wales
Over England and Wales as a whole, groundwater accounts for about one-third of the public water supply. However, in eastern and southern England more than half of the supply is drawn from the Chalk and upper Greensand aquifers. Each year approximately 25 per cent of the natural recharge to aquifers is abstracted for water supply and to sustain river flows. It is clear, therefore, that the reduced recharge of the aquifers from 1988 to 1992, over extensive areas less than 50 per cent of normal, affected water supplies significantly.

Private consumers, such as farmers, with their own shallow wells drilled mostly into chalk, are the first to suffer at times of drought. Water companies maintain river flows and water supplies by making increasing demands upon the surface reservoir stores. As inputs from runoff are reduced by drought, extra demand results in serious draw-down (Fig. 8.9).

During the 1988–92 drought, there was no surplus water for deliberate recharge of aquifers. By August 1990, 12.5 million customers were under a hosepipe ban, and 18 million had restricted water use. Yet the supply network held up remarkably well. None the less, the drought raised a number of issues for future management.

Environmental quality
Water managers have responsibilities for maintaining environmental quality. Thus, at periods of very low flow, they conserve wetland and aquatic habitats by using water from reservoirs and groundwater stores to increase stream **discharge**. As drought progresses this becomes increasingly difficult. For instance, if too much water is drawn from reservoirs, **algal blooms** can spread

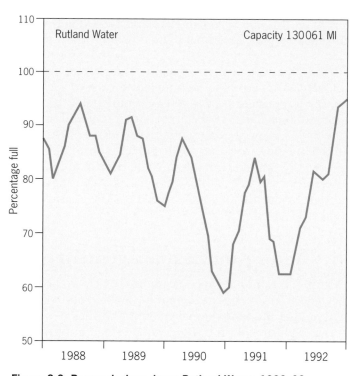

Figure 8.9 Reservoir draw-down: Rutland Water, 1988–92

Figure 8.10 Algal blooms: Rutland Water

?

10 Outline the reasons why it is valuable to increase stream discharge during periods of very low flow.

11 Use the information of Figure 8.11.
a What problem is Thames Water facing and how does it propose to solve the problem?
b Outline the technique used to estimate the 'value' of the R. Kennet.
c Create a table to show the results produced by the EA and the DETR.
d Estimates of 'value' using cost–benefit techniques, include economic, social and environmental factors. Give an example of each of these factors in the R. Kennet example.
e Use the R. Kennet example to demonstrate the difficulties faced by water resource managers in attempting to achieve a policy of sustainable yield. (Remember – 'yield' may include economic, social and environmental dimensions.)

Stream of abuse

HOW MUCH is the River Kennet worth? Last week, following a long public enquiry in autumn 1996, the Department of the Environment put a value on the river's environmental quality. And it is using it to uphold Thames Water's licence to pump more than 13 million litres of water from the Kennet a day, no matter how low it flows.

The Kennet, a chalk stream running west into the Thames from the Marlborough Downs, is one of England's finest trout streams. It is also of high ecological value, and has been designated a Site of Special Scientific Interest. However, low flows are contributing to the siltation of its gravel beds and the prolific growth of blanket weed.

The Environment Agency wanted to restrict Thames Water's licence to pump water from aquifers under the river to increase flows downstream of the Axford pumping station, near Marlborough, estimating that the river would be 'worth' an additional £13.6 million as a result. The sum was based on an extra 'use value' from recreation and angling of £400,000, and an extra 'non-use' value of £13.2 million.

But the head of the DETR's Water Supply and Regulation Division, Richard Vincent, determined otherwise. While accepting the EA's use-value estimate, he reduced non-use value to £300,000, producing a total benefit worth £700,000.

He then compared the figure with the £6.2 million cost to Thames Water of developing new infrastructure to compensate for the reduced pumping. Accordingly, he struck out the EA's attempt to reduce pumping to 3 million litres a day at times of low flow, ruling that Thames Water could continue to pump 13.1 million litres a day for the indefinite future.

But is it right to compare the value of a river to the cost of an infrastructure invest-ment? The latter is easily calculated, but the value of the environment is not so readily tied down – as the £12.9 million 'gulf' between the EA's and DETR's estimates in the case of the Kennet demonstrates.

The EA's non-use value was founded on the assertion that the 3 million households in Thames Water's area would be willing to pay 32p a year for the environmental benefits of reduced pumping. Taken over 30 years at the 6 per cent Treasury discount rate, that produces a capital value of £13.2 million. Vincent reduced the number of people to 100 000, each judged willing to pay 25p per year, producing a value of £300 000.

In fact, neither figure is satisfactory: both are based on arbitrary figures unsupported by credible research. And neither even begins to reflect the intrinsic value of the river, its wildlife and its landscape.

At the Kennet inquiry, Thames Water argued that the same benefits that would arise from reduced pumping would also result from redesigning the river channel and weirs to increase water velocity and create pools and riffles, and from from reducing soil erosion and agrochemical use in the Kennet catchment – all at far lower cost. The way is now open for the warring parties and others (including local farmers and the Ministry of Agriculture) to come together and agree on the catchment-wide plan for the Kennet's restoration.

Figure 8.11 Assessing the 'value' of a river (*Source*: *The Guardian*, 4 March 1998)

in warm weather, as occurred on Rutland Water in 1992 and 1995 (Fig.8.10). In consequence, managers may apply for a 'Drought Order' from the EA and the DETR.

If the Order is approved, this allows the water company to abstract more than the agreed volume of water from rivers to help replenish reservoir levels. This may result in dangerously low stream flows and environmental degradation of the aquatic ecosystem. That is, sustaining environmental quality of a reservoir may threaten environmental quality of a river. It is not surprising therefore, that cost–benefit techniques are being applied to attempt to assess the 'value' of a stream or reservoir. Such techniques include environmental, social and economic variables in efforts to quantify the impacts of alternative strategies. So far, the results are imprecise and controversial, as the example of the R.Kennet illustrates (Fig. 8.11).

> **The Environment Agency**
> **Vision**: A better environment in England and Wales for present and future generations
> **Primary aim**: To protect and improve the environment and contribute towards sustainable development through the integrated management of air, land and water. Responsibilities include water resources, pollution prevention and control, flood defence and conservation.

8.4 National policy and resource management

In 1989 the government set up the National Rivers Authority (NRA) to be responsible for water policy and resources management in England and Wales. This occurred at the same time that the ten regional water authorities which supplied UK water were privatised. In 1995 the NRA was absorbed into the new Environment Agency (EA) that lies within the DETR.

In 1994 the NRA, in response to issues raised by the 1988-92 UK drought, published a Development Strategy for the period 1995-2021. The full title of the report, 'Water: Nature's precious resource. An environmentally sustainable water resources development strategy for England and Wales', summed up the NRA approach, i.e. water is 'precious' – scarce, finite – and management is to be based on sustainability and concern for the environment. The hot, dry summers of 1995 and 1996 emphasised the urgency of the problem, and in 1997, the EA produced its National Water Resources Strategy, based on the 1994 NRA proposals. The strategy is based on analysis of four key questions:
• What is the existing supply–demand relationship?
• What is likely to be the future demand for public water supply, industry and agriculture?
• How can river flows be protected from the effects of excessive abstraction?
• What are the options for balancing demands and supply?

Table 8.4 Objectives and principles of the 1997 National Water Resources Strategy

Objectives

• Securing a sustainable balance between water use and environmental requirements (quantity)
• Achieving a progressive enhancement of the water environment (quality)

Principles		Example
Sustainable development	There should be no long-term systematic environmental deterioration due to water resource development and water use. Long term groundwater abstraction ahould be less than average recharge.	The water table in the Chalk and Upper Greensand aquifer must be maintained at agreed levels over time. Allowing for normal seasonal variation, these levels must be high enough to supply springs and allow recharge to streams in order to sustain healthy aquatic communities.
Precautionary principle	Where significant environmental damage may occur, but knowledge on the matter is incomplete decisions made and measures implemented should err on the side of caution.	If there is any uncertainty about the environmental impacts of the building of a dam and reservoir complex the development should not go ahead until this uncertainty is removed.
Demand management	Management measures to control waste and consumption.	Installation of water meters in homes and charging by the litre for water used. This encourages families to use water more carefully.

?

11 Essay: Study Table 8.5. To what extent is it true to say that, by the year 2021, the largest shortfall in water supply will be in those regions with the most rapid growth in demand if no new resources are made available? Use appropriate graphical and statistical techniques to support your answer. Justify your choice of techniques.

12a Analyse the intended national strategy for water resource management in terms of the definition of sustainable yield (p. 150).
b Think carefully about the interests and priorities of the key players (gatekeepers) and suggest problems that may arise in the implementation of this strategy

From this analysis the EA has identified two objectives and three principles for the strategy (Table 8.4). It is important to bear in mind that the 'strategy' is not a formal plan: preferred options and implications are set out, using several demand level forecasts. Implementation will involve agreements between the main stakeholders (see box below).

The strategy includes a ten-point Action Plan which sets a series of targets to be achieved by cooperation between the key gatekeepers, e.g. the requirement for Water Companies to reduce leakage from supply systems. Thus Severn Trent Water reduced their leakage level from 21 per cent in 1995 to 13 per cent in 1999. Future development options are based on NRA and EA data which forecast that 'currently there is a surplus in water supply resources. However, in 30 years' time … a supply deficit could occur in most areas' (NRA, 1994) as Table 8.5 indicates.

The main conclusions are therefore:
• total supply must be increased
• regions in the north and west with potential surplus resources must increasingly be the source for shortage regions in the south and east.

Existing surface and groundwater stores in eastern and southern regions are already exploited to capacity. As early steps in the implementation of the strategy, each Water Company is required to produce a Water Resources Plan. In parallel, the EA is producing a series of Local Plans, based on drainage basins. Each Local Plan will provide and information base and guidelines to assist in decision-making (see Severn Vale case study, p.158).

Table 8.5 Demand–supply relationships in 2021 for a medium-growth scenario (*Source*: NRA, 1994)

NRA region	Demand increase (% of 1991 demand)	Supply shortfall if no new supplies are made available (million litres per day)
Northumbria	10	0
Yorkshire	8	29
North West	0	0
Severn–Trent	12	182
Anglian	27	100
Southern	15	57
Thames	7	270
Wessex	15	58
South West	27	40
Welsh	5	38

Key players in water resource management

Environment Agency [EA]   Works within the requirements of the Water Resources Act, 1991; Environment Act, 1995; is 'responsible for ensuring that water resources are managed effectively and for the benefit of everyone and the environment.'

Water Companies   Work within the requirements of the Water Industries Act, 1991; are 'required to supply water to meet all existing and new domestic demands (regardless of the availability of water resources) if requested by landowners, occupiers or the local planning authority' and 'plan effectively to provide water supplies in their areas in the future and to protect and enhance the natural environment.'

Holders of Abstraction Licences   Are 'responsible for compliance with conditions imposed on the licence', e.g. no abstraction permitted when discharge falls below a 'prescribed flow'.

Water resource management in the Severn Vale

In August 1999 the EA published its Local Environmental Plan for the Severn Vale. This covers the lower section of the R. Severn basin below the junction with the R. Teme south of Worcester (Fig. 8.13). As it enters the Severn Vale, the R. Severn has a mean flow of 8980 megalitres/day (Ml/d), although there are wide fluctuations from year to year (Fig. 8.12). Because of the natural flow fluctuations and increased upstream water abstractions in the middle and upper basin above Worcester, the EA requires a management strategy that maintains a minimum flow of 850 Ml/d. This is achieved by inputs from surface and groundwater stores.

Flow support sources

Within the Severn Vale there are three significant aquifers that act as groundwater stores (A, B, C on Fig. 8.13):

A Jurassic Limestone and Cotteswold Sands of the Cotswold escarpment
B Carboniferous Limestones of the Forest of Dean
C Triassic Sandstones around Newent.

When these aquifers fail to sustain the required minimum flow, water managers can call upon two sources from the middle and upper Severn basin.

The Llyn Clywedog reservoir

The Clywedog dam and reservoir scheme was completed in 1968. It lies across a Severn headstream in mid-Wales (See Fig 8.19). The main purpose of the scheme is for urban water supply, and the maximum permitted release for river flow regulation is 500 Ml/d (1 per cent of the reservoir storage capacity). The first release was in 1976, and during the dry summers of the 1990s, releases have become more frequent.

The Shropshire Groundwater Scheme

The Clywedog permitted releases are inadequate to ensure the required minimum flows along the lower Severn. In consequence, since 1984, a system of boreholes and wells has been developed to draw water from aquifers in Shropshire, along the middle section of the Severn basin. The maximum permitted abstraction for river regulation is 235 Ml/d.

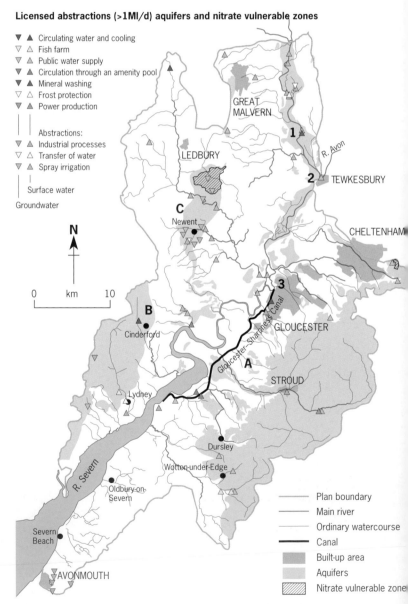

Figure 8.12 Mean monthly flows of R. Severn at Bewdley, 1961–98

Figure 8.13 Licensed abstractions from the Severn Valley

Water resource uses

The map shows that, as in many UK drainage basins, a variety of users abstract water from the lower Severn (Fig. 8.13). The total licensed abstractions are 568 Ml/d. The dominant use is for public water supply (Fig. 8.14), with three major abstraction points (1, 2, 3, on Fig. 8.13), each for a different user (Table 8.6).

These existing permitted abstractions (568 Ml/d) already approach the required minimum flow (850 Ml/d), although we must remember that much of the water eventually returns to the river. However, demand within the Severn Vale continues to grow and water use restrictions occur during hot, dry spells, e.g. the summers of 1995 and 1996.

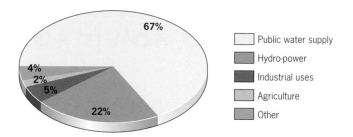

Figure 8.14 Licensed abstraction uses of surface and groundwater, % of total

13a Describe briefly how the lower Severn basin works as an open system, with inputs, stores, throughputs and outputs
b In the Severn Vale region, water resource demands are approaching the current supply capacity. Suggest the options managers have for increasing future supplies and assess the benefits and problems of each option.

Table 8.6 Public water supply

Ripple, near Upton-on-Severn	Accounts for 60% of the water abstraction for public water supply and is transferred to Coventry; much returns to the lower Severn via the R. Avon, following treatment.
Tewkesbury	Supplies much of Gloucestershire; accounts for 25% of the total abstraction.
Gloucester	Supplies the Gloucester–Sharpness canal, from which some water is abstracted to augment the Bristol area supply; 15% of the total abstraction.

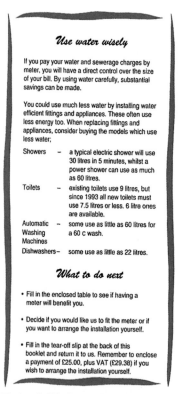

Figure 8.15 Promoting the benefits of water meters (*Source*: Thames Water Utilities, 1994)

8.5 Development options

The NRA/EA strategy has three basic components:
• surface storage schemes (reservoirs) in the north and west, including Wales, to be upgraded and enlarged
• inter-basin water transfers to deliver additional water to rivers, reservoirs and aquifers in the east and south (Fig. 8.16)
• the introduction of strengthened demand control measures, such as metering and pricing, to encourage consumers to use water more efficiently (Fig. 8.15).

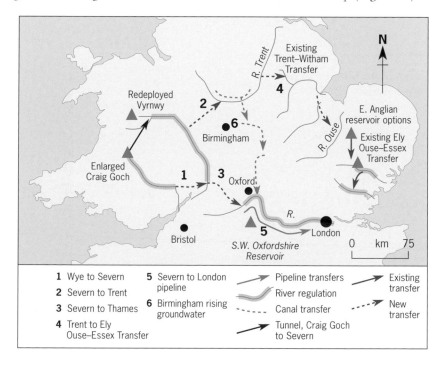

Figure 8.16 Proposed inter-basin water transfers in the south-east of the UK (*Source*: NRA, 1994)

Canals to solve south's water shortage

CANALS ARE TO BE USED to move drinking water to the parched south-east of England.

Pumping trials transporting groundwater from Birmingham to London have proved successful, and by this time next year the first contract to supply water from the north-west and Wales to the south-east is expected to be running.

British Waterways is using its 3,000 miles of canals, as well as its 93 reservoirs across the country as 'holding tanks' for the scheme. It is one of a number of ideas the public-owned company is using to generate funds to modernise and repair the network.

Money from selling drinking water will go towards the £237m backlog in repairs and maintenance, and help to return the canal network to pristine condition.

The recovery and reopening of the Stroud Cotswold canal between the Severn and the Thames was possible, because the route could be used for navigation and for pumping water from west to east to supply London.

Although a national water grid has long been talked of as a way of solving the south-east's shortages, it has been seen as too costly. But the canals have been used to sell drinking water to Bristol since the nineteenth century, and in the Midlands industries use the network for their supplies.

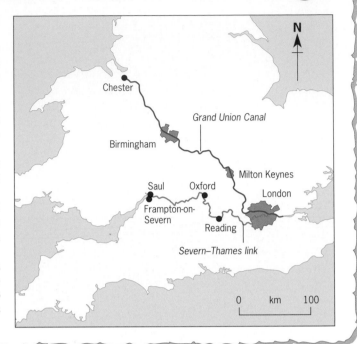

Figure 8.17 A water transfer option (*Source: The Guardian*, 28 June 2000)

During the 1990s, average domestic water bills doubled. A number of storage and transfer schemes were proposed and evaluated, primarily in terms of cost. For example, the existing Kielder Water reservoir in Northumberland will continue to have a surplus capacity of up to 500 million litres a day for the needs of north-east England. Transfer schemes running south are technically feasible but are rejected for the present as being too costly. In contrast, the eastward transfer of water to the upper Thames basin from upgraded Welsh storage schemes is likely to be less expensive and is supported by the EA (see case study, p. 161). The use of canals as transfer routes is favoured by the DETR to control costs and use existing infrastructure (Fig. 8.17).

14 Water transferred into a drainage basin can be used in four ways:
a directly by consumers
b to enlarge river discharge
c to increase existing reservoirs and supply new reservoirs
d to recharge aquifers.
Discuss how the external inputs affect the delivery system summarised in Figure 8.1 (p. 150).

15 Consider the EA development options. Assess the impact of each option by constructing a matrix to show the advantages and disadvantages for (a) the EA, (b) the water companies, (c) the consumer.

Figure 8.18 Haweswater, Lake District National Park. This reservoir flooded a farming valley and settlement in the 1920s, resulting in a significant change of environmental character

Environmental considerations

Maintaining and enhancing water quality, aquatic habitats and concern for the impact of development schemes are important elements in the EA's policy. For example, they feel that impacts from existing water storage and transfer schemes in the Lake District and Peak District National Parks have already reached acceptable limits (Fig. 8.18). Therefore they do not propose increasing supplies from these sources. Despite growing demand in eastern, southern and south-western England, several proposals to construct reservoirs have been rejected. This is mainly due to the environmental impact of structures and water surfaces in lowland countryside, often on high quality agricultural land.

River Severn – River Thames water transfer, England

The basic scheme

The basic Severn–Thames water transfer scheme involves abstracting water from the lower River Severn near Deerhurst and discharging it into the upper River Thames at Buscot (Fig. 8.19). This would resurrect a similar proposal made over a century ago. The Thames would then convey water downstream for final transfer into existing reservoirs near London. To avoid the potential environmental problems of mixing 'foreign' water with the Thames water, a possible option would be a 90 km pipeline from Deerhurst direct to the London reservoirs. This would cost at least £117 million.

Some storage space would be required at Deerhurst to allow for sediment to settle. At the Thames end, further storage would be needed for blending and control functions, but disused gravel pits in the Thames Valley are likely to be available. The Thames–Severn Canal, if refurbished, could also be incorporated.

In this basic scheme 'abstractions could be made at times of higher flows in the River Severn.... This option provides only limited additional resources, but could be a relatively low-cost solution to slowly increasing demand. The reliable yield could be up to 146 million litres per day and the capital cost would be £5.7 million' (NRA, 1994).

Enhanced scheme

Enlarging the Craig Goch reservoir

The Craig Goch reservoir is one of several in the Elan Valley, part of the River Wye catchment. There are two suggestions for its enlargement:

1 The present dam could be raised by 49 m. Then, if a tunnel were cut northwards to the upper Severn at Llanidloes, the extra water stored could be used to regulate the low flows. The reliable yield would be 775 million litres per day. The scheme would cost £105 million.

2 A tunnel could be cut to the upper Wye at Nannerth near Rhayader. The increased Wye flow would then provide for an abstraction near Ross-on-Wye, from

which a pipeline would cross the Severn at Deerhurst and follow the line to the River Thames described above. This scheme would cost £72 million.

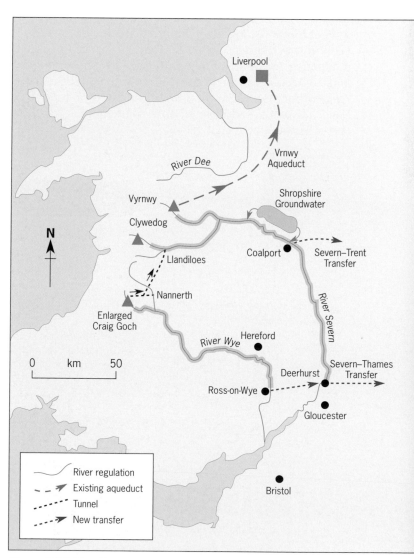

Figure 8.19 The Severn-Wye water regulation options (*Source*: NRA, 1994)

Changing the use of the Vyrnwy Reservoir

This reservoir in the upper Severn catchment currently supplies water directly by gravity to Liverpool along the Vyrnwy Aqueduct. While maintaining a minimum flow along this aqueduct of 60 million litres per day, up to 147 million litres per day could be made available for regulation and supply along the River Severn. Costs would be £42 million, spent on upgrading outlet facilities at Vyrnwy and replacing the supplies lost to the Liverpool area, e.g. by abstracting and treating water from the River Dee.

Environmental issues

1 Water quality and biological impacts of transferring water from the lower Severn into the upper Thames – the **hydrochemistry** and therefore the aquatic ecosystems are different.

2 The effects on salmon migration along the Severn and Wye rivers. Ecologists believe a minimum prescribed flow (PF), with artificial pulses of higher flows to trigger salmon runs, must be maintained in the River Severn if the salmon migration is to be safeguarded. Fishing is an important recreational and economic activity along both rivers.

3 Pipeline routes must take into account conservation and archaeological sites. These are also possibilities for enhancements, e.g. restoration of the Thames and Severn canal would have environmental and recreational benefits.

4 Impacts of dam enlargement. Developments at Craig Goch would result in impacts upon the Eleynydd Site of Special Scientific Interest (SSSI) and other areas of conservation value. Such impacts would be 'of particular concern for the Countryside Council for Wales' (NRA, 1994). If the option to use the Wye as the regulator is taken, this would raise 'a number of concerns since the whole river, including the riparian (bank) habitats, has been classified as an SSSI and as such is of national value' (NRA, 1994). Furthermore, the Wye is an important salmon river and flow levels are crucial.

5 The Vyrnwy options would affect the flora and fauna along the River Vyrnwy, again including salmon stocks. Water quality and temperature impacts, resulting from drawing off water from deeper in the reservoir, could be reduced by modifying levels of outlets from the dam.

16a List the costs and benefits of the Severn-Thames water transfer scheme.
b Evaluate the scheme according to your lists.
c State whether you agree with the scheme, giving your reasons.

Summary

- The goal of water resource management is sustainable yield.

- Increasing efforts are being made to include social and environmental factors as well as economic factors in the measurement of sustainability.

- The Environment Agency (EA) is the government body responsible for water resource management in England and Wales. The EA is not itself a supplier, this being the duty of private water companies.

- The 1988-92 drought and the hot, dry summers of 1995, 1996 highlighted the pressure on current water resource supply capacities, especially in eastern and southern England, i.e. demands exceed sustainable yield.

- Approximately one-third of UK water supplies are abstracted from groundwater stores (aquifers). In eastern and southern regions this source exceeds 50 per cent and abstraction rates from several major aquifers are non-sustainable.

- In 1997 the government published a national strategy for water resources for the period to 2021. The plan is based on sustainable yield, the precautionary principle and demand management. It involves both quantitative and qualitative targets.

- The preferred strategy is for large-scale water transfers from the west and north where there is surplus capacity, to the east and south where untapped reserves are minimal.

9 Water quality and pollution

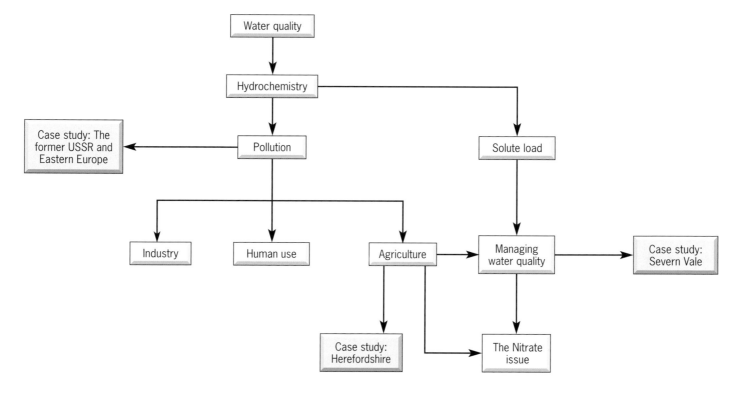

9.1 Introduction

Water consumption (quantity) and access to safe water (quality) are key indicators of quality of life, and figures highlight the unacceptable contrasts across the world (Table 9.1). Globally, the volume of waste water in the consumptive use of water has risen as demands have risen (Fig. 9.1).

Water quality has become a global environmental issue, as important as water quantity and distribution (Fig. 9.2). For instance, the Rwandan refugee tragedy of 1994 was intensified by the spread of water-borne diseases such as cholera, when the only sources of water for more than one million people were severely polluted. However, the water quality issue is not restricted to the

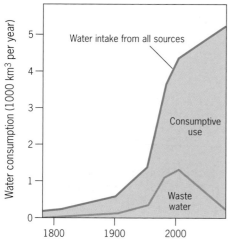

Figure 9.1 Rise in consumptive and waste water usage

Table 9.1 Contrasts in water quantity and quality, 1996 (*Source*: Newson, 1998)

Top five	Domestic consumption (m³/person)	Access to safe water (% of population)
1 Australia	606	98
2 Kuwait	338	100
3 Canada	288	99
4 New Zealand	270	97
5 USA	246	98
Bottom five		
129 Burkina Faso	5	67
130 Mali	3	49
131 Guinea-Bissau	3	26
132 The Gambia	2	56
133 Haiti	2	41

The annual World Development Report groups 133 countries into 3 income classes. The figures in this table are the top five 'high income' countries and the bottom five 'low income' countries, using the domestic water consumption indicator.

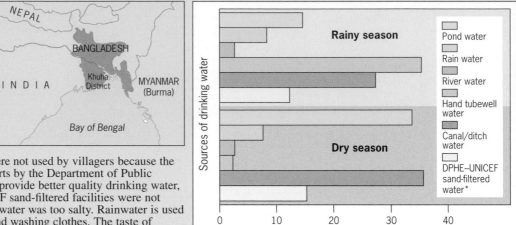

A 1992 survey of 36 households in 12 villages in the Khuha district of south-west Bangladesh reveals the problems and resourcefulness of the villagers in providing drinking water. As the district lies near to the ocean, surface and groundwater sources are often saline.

The area has 53 tubewells, but only 27 were in working order at the time of the survey. Eleven of these were not used by villagers because the water was too salty. Despite efforts by the Department of Public Health (DPHE) and UNICEF to provide better quality drinking water, nearly half of the DPHE-UNICEF sand-filtered facilities were not used. This is because the groundwater was too salty. Rainwater is used for drinking, cooking, bathing and washing clothes. The taste of rainwater was preferred for cooking and making tea.

Figure 9.2 Khuha District: sources of drinking water during the wet and dry seasons

?

1a Draw an annotated systems diagram to summarise the pollution issue described in Figure 9.3.
b List the 'interested parties' and their positions in the issue.
c In what ways does this example illustrate the complexity of water pollution issues and why they are so often very difficult to deal with?

Figure 9.3 River Dart, Devon – cancer clusters cause health scare (*Source:* The *Observer,* 21 August 1994)

economically developing countries. For example, in 1996, more than 200 water abstraction sources in England and Wales exceeded the European Union's (EU) nitrate directive limit of 50 milligrams per litre (mg/1) of nitrate (NO_3) for drinking water (Fig. 9.3).

9.2 Water quality

Water quality sounds straightforward, but in reality it is complex. 'Pure' water is made up of hydrogen and oxygen (H_2O), but all water in the environment contains other constituents. Measures of water quality are based upon these chemicals, that is, the **hydrochemistry** of the water. Water quality, therefore, refers to the properties of the water. However, 'quality' is assessed with reference to the job water is doing or the way in which it is to be used. For example, the water quality, in terms of its hydrochemistry, required to support a vigorous aquatic ecosystem in a river is quite different from that delivered to our taps for us to drink. Water abstracted from rivers or **aquifers** for drinking purposes undergoes considerable treatment before its quality is tested. In this chapter we explore the idea that 'quality' is a relative or comparative concept.

Cancer linked to river pollution

Polly Ghazi
Environment Correspondent

UNTIL recently, the picturesque village of Buckfastleigh in south Devon was renowned only for its ancient abbey, in an idyllic setting on the banks of the River Dart.

But in the past few weeks it has become the focus of a major health scare as officials investigate possible links between cancer clusters in nearby Torbay and chemicals pumped into the Dart's shallow waters.

One of England's best salmon and trout rivers, with its pristine source in the remote wilds of Dartmoor, the Dart is an unlikely possible culprit for a pollution blackspot. But Buckfastleigh's main employers, two wool processing factories, one owned by the Axminster Carpet Company, have pumped

hundreds of thousands of tonnes of industrial waste, via sewage works, into the river for the past two decades.

Public health officials believe that industrial detergents discharged after being used to clean sheep fleeces may be partly to blame for the high number of women dying from breast cancer in south Devon.

Tap water supplied from the Dart to Torquay, Brixham and Paignton, the popular coastal resorts of Torbay, is being tested for traces of the suspect chemicals.

The investigation, launched by three district councils, represents a national test case into the public health risk from old-fashioned 'non-ionic' detergents pumped into rivers via sewage works. The detergents are known to be toxic to river life and are being phased out by many users.

There are no national standards setting safe levels of factory discharges of non-ionic industrial detergents, 18 000 tons of which are used in Britain every year. But a spokesman for the National Rivers Authority said spot checks in the Dart had found only 'very low traces' of nonylphenols, the main breakdown product under suspicion.

Only one of the companies discharging trade waste into the Dart, Devonia Products, still uses non-ionic detergents and a spokesman said alternatives were being urgently discussed.

A South-West Water spokesman said tests at its Torbay drinking water treatment plant over the past fortnight had found no traces of the suspect chemicals. 'Torbay's drinking water is safe and meets all the UK and European standards,' he said.

Water quality management

Water quality management is complex because the water abstracted from a stream or a **groundwater store** is the output from several processes operating through the **drainage basin** (Fig. 2.6). Remember that much water has arrived in the river channel not from **quickflow** runoff, but via **slowflow** routes through the soil and groundwater stores (see Chapters 2 and 7). This journey may have taken several decades. Thus, geology, climate, vegetation and land use all interact to influence the properties of stream water, groundwater and consequently tap water (Fig. 9.4). In general, the more intensive and varied the human activities in a drainage basin, the more difficult is water quality management.

Figure 9.4 Nitrate concentrations at boreholes under a limestone aquifer and a sandstone aquifer (*Source*: MAFF, 1993 and 1996)

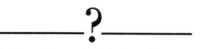

2 From Figure 9.4, during the 1980–93 period, what were the maximum and minimum nitrate concentrations in the groundwater of the:
a limestone
b sandstone aquifer?

3 Groundwater will eventually enter into streams. Describe the seasonal patterns of nitrate concentration in a stream whose basin is underlain by:
a limestone
b sandstone.

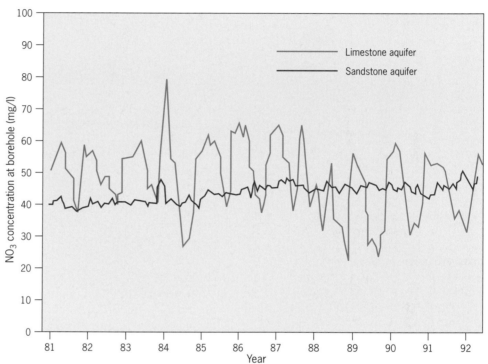

9.3 The pollution of rivers, lakes and seas

In this section we shall focus mainly on river water **pollution**, but similar factors affect groundwater, and we must remember that there is a close two-way relationship between stream water and groundwater.

Definitions

Rivers have their own in-built 'purification power', i.e. processes which work to absorb and control the effects of the introduced materials. This is called the **assimilation capacity** of the river and is an example of **negative feedback**. Each river has its own unique assimilation capacity, and within a river there will be variations over time. Some researchers claim that 'it is upon the in-stream processes of purification that we depend across the world when using rivers as conveyor belts for the waste products of housing, farming and industry' (Newson, 1992). Deltas play an important role in this purification process (Fig. 9.6).

None the less, waters do become polluted, so what do we mean by 'water pollution'? A simple definition is 'the introduction of damaging loads or concentrations of material or compounds' (Newson, 1992). Notice the word 'damaging'. This refers to the impacts on living organisms in the river (the biotic community) and to effects on users of water abstracted from the river. This is distinct from **contamination,** which is a general term used to refer to

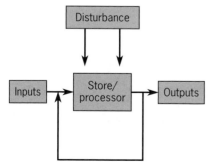

Figure 9.5 Pollution disturbs the instream purification process

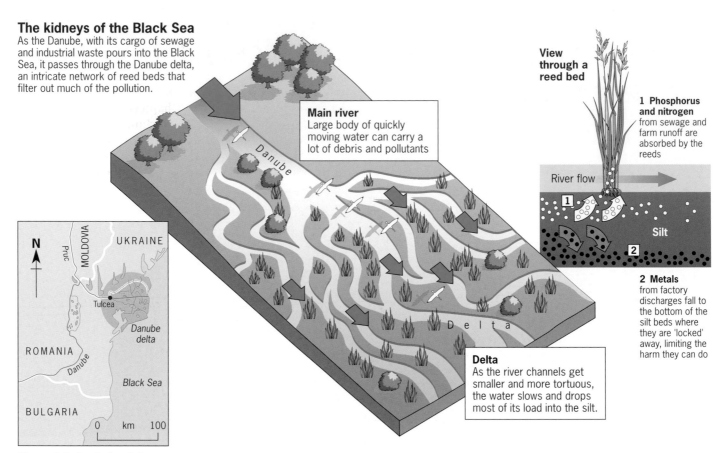

The kidneys of the Black Sea
As the Danube, with its cargo of sewage and industrial waste pours into the Black Sea, it passes through the Danube delta, an intricate network of reed beds that filter out much of the pollution.

Main river
Large body of quickly moving water can carry a lot of debris and pollutants

View through a reed bed

1 Phosphorus and nitrogen from sewage and farm runoff are absorbed by the reeds

River flow

Silt

2 Metals from factory discharges fall to the bottom of the silt beds where they are 'locked' away, limiting the harm they can do

Delta
As the river channels get smaller and more tortuous, the water slows and drops most of its load into the silt.

Figure 9.6 A role for deltas

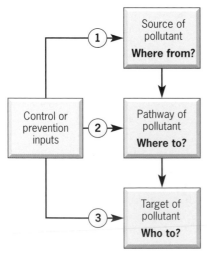

Figure 9.7 The pollution process

'the introduction of new material and compounds to the system' (Newson, 1992), i.e. not necessarily at damaging levels. Pollution disturbs the water system, causing a change in hydrochemistry and in water quality (Fig. 9.5). We can summarise the pollution process in terms of *sources, pathways* and *targets* (Fig. 9.7). Control and prevention may focus on any of these components, but most essentially on the sources of pollution.

Inputs of contaminants and pollutants come from two types of source:
• **Point sources**: discharges into a river at a specific location, e.g. sewage effluent from a pipe; irrigation ditch return flow.
• **Diffuse sources**: inputs are from an area rather than a point and often arrive in the channel via bed and banks after soil water and groundwater **percolation**, e.g. nitrate and phosphate excesses from agricultural fertiliser; acid rain.

Clearly, diffuse sources of pollution are more difficult than point sources to identify, monitor and control in both rivers and aquifers.

Water pollution of rivers and lakes is a global problem reflecting three main causal factors: changes in agricultural techniques; growth of urban populations and their wastes; the advance of industrial technology. Even where the sources and causes are known, and when action has been taken, pollution is proving very difficult to control (Fig. 9.8). In densely populated, industrialised regions, such as the Great Lakes of North America, or the UK, the difficulties are perhaps not surprising. In the UK alone, there are more than 12 000 licensed discharge points along our rivers and lakes (Fig. 9.3).

Across extensive areas of the economically developing world, people take drinking water directly from rivers and shallow wells without further treatment (Fig. 9.2). Also, there are widespread inputs of untreated sewage and industrial effluents into these same streams and aquifers. This situation clearly produces a pollution hazard, although populations exposed regularly to such conditions develop a degree of resistance.

Polluted Great Lakes linked to health crisis

Claire Trevena in Toronto

POLLUTION in the Great Lakes is being linked to a spread in cancer, damage to human reproductive systems, and developmental problems in children.

A report yesterday by the International Joint Commission, the water quality watchdog for the five lakes, called on the US and Canadian governments and industry to halt the discharge of chemical waste into the lakes because it was ending up in the food chain.

Efforts to control the discharge of toxic compounds had failed and substances which were supposed to be banned were being released into the environment.

Canada and the US signed a water quality agreement in 1972 to try to improve the quality of the Great Lakes. But the commission said governments and industry did not realise how great the problem still was.

Among the commission's recommendations was that the chemical industry find a way to halt the use of chlorine in manufacturing.

But it has wider goals, and called on the Canadian and US governments to find out what pollutants were being released, and establish a timetable for them to be banned.

The commission admitted that these recommendations had been around since the agency was formed 22 years ago; now the evidence of a threat to human health was greater.

While the report was welcomed by environmental groups, the chemical industry said there was still not enough evidence to support a ban on certain compounds.

Figure 9.8 Water quality issues for Canada and the USA in the Great Lakes (Source: The Guardian, 18 February 1994)

?

4 Study Figure 9.8.
a What are the pollutants and where do they come from? You may find it useful to base your answer on a systems diagram.
b What effects do these pollutants have?
c What evidence is given which suggests that pollution is difficult to control?
d Why do you think this pollution is proving so difficult to control?

Industrial pollution sources

In Europe, as in North America, water pollution control is a complex and slow process, partly because it is often an international problem and because the range and source of pollutants are so varied (Table 9.2).

As long ago as 1974, the countries surrounding the North Sea, including the UK, signed an agreement known as the Paris Convention. The aim was to reduce industrial discharges of heavy metals into rivers. (Seas and oceans are the sinks into which rivers dump their pollutant loads.) In 1990, in response to growing public concern, another agreement was signed. This aimed to reduce discharges of 38 poisonous substances by 50 per cent by 1995.

Within the UK, industrial pollution of rivers affects both river life and water supplies (Fig. 9.9). For instance, for several days in April 1994 approximately 100 000 people in the Worcester area of the Severn Valley were unable to use their tap water. The river which supplied their water was polluted by a point source chemical discharge from a factory further upstream at Wem, in Shropshire. Not all such problems arise from present-day industry, as earlier industries can leave problems behind. Uncontrolled metal mining in the headwater catchment of the R. Tyne ceased a century ago. Yet today there is continuing pollution via toxic sediments deposited in the floodplain downstream. Who is responsible, who should pay and how control can be achieved, have become important issues as mining declines extensively across the UK (Fig. 9.10).

Unfortunately too, priorities, standards and powers to regulate vary from country to country. For example, some Communist regimes, e.g. China; the former USSR, have been criticised for neglecting pollution impacts of industrialisation (see Former USSR case study, p. 169).

Urban sources of pollution

Despite the high profile some incidents achieve, industry is not the major source of river pollution in the UK (Figs 9.11 and 9.12). Sewage, largely from urban areas, is the main source, and is more than one-quarter of all pollution.

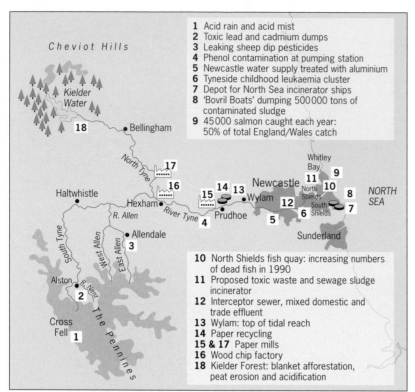

1 Acid rain and acid mist
2 Toxic lead and cadmium dumps
3 Leaking sheep dip pesticides
4 Phenol contamination at pumping station
5 Newcastle water supply treated with aluminium
6 Tyneside childhood leukaemia cluster
7 Depot for North Sea incinerator ships
8 'Bovril Boats' dumping 500000 tons of contaminated sludge
9 45000 salmon caught each year: 50% of total England/Wales catch

10 North Shields fish quay: increasing numbers of dead fish in 1990
11 Proposed toxic waste and sewage sludge incinerator
12 Interceptor sewer, mixed domestic and trade effluent
13 Wylam: top of tidal reach
14 Paper recycling
15 & 17 Paper mills
16 Wood chip factory
18 Kielder Forest: blanket afforestation, peat erosion and acidification

Figure 9.9 The River Tyne: an ecological disaster zone? (*Source: Environment Guardian*, 16 March 1990)

Figure 9.10 Water pollution from old mines (*Source: The Guardian*, 15 April 1994)

5 Study Figure 9.10.
a What has caused the pollution?
b What are the effects?
c What are issues involved in solving the problem?
d What do you think should be done, who should pay and who should be responsible? Give reasons for your answer.

6 From Figures 9.11 and 9.12, compare and contrast the character of water pollution in England and Wales with that of Scotland. Suggest possible reasons for any differences you identify.

Table 9.2 Sources of water pollution (*Source*: Newson, 1992)

Type	Factors influencing
Domestic sewage	BOD; suspended solids; ammonia; nitrate; phosphate
Chemical industry	BOD; ammonia; phenols; non-biodegradable organics; heat
Iron and steel manufacturers	Cyanide; phenols; pH; ammonia; sulphides
Coal mining	Suspended solids; iron; pH; dissolved solids
Metal finishing	Cyanide; copper; cadmium; nickel; pH
Dairy products	BOD; pH
Oil refineries	Heat; ammonia; phenols; oil; sulphide
Power generation	Heat

Note: BOD = the biological oxygen demand, a common measure of organic pollution. It represents the amount of biochemically degradable substances in the water or effluent sample. A test sample is stored in darkness for five days at 20ºC and the amount of oxygen taken up by the micro-organisms present is measured in grams per cubic metre. A clean mountain stream will have a value in the region of 0.05 mg/l.

Acid water in old mine shafts 'damages the balance of life'

WHERE coalfields have been closed, as in County Durham, contamination of rivers and drinking water becomes a serious risk as mines, once kept dry by pumping, fill and overflow.

Northumbria Water, which extracts large quantities of drinking water from the River Wear, has expressed serious concern about the overflow. The acid water from mine shafts would damage the balance of life in the river and, according to the National Rivers Authority, kill most of the fish.

Some water tables in mining areas have been controlled for centuries by pumping from old shafts. Otherwise acid water percolates through, picking up heavy metals and other pollutants before overflowing into rivers. British Coal is keeping some pumps going in the Durham coalfield to prevent ecological damage, but maintaining them will cost several million pounds a year. The Government has yet to decide who will pay after BC is privatised.

Any proposal to turn pumps off has to be backed up by a detailed justification

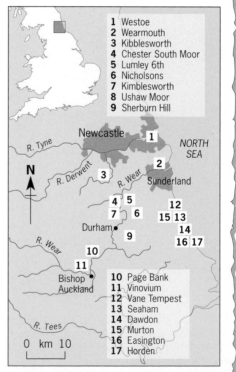

1 Westoe
2 Wearmouth
3 Kibblesworth
4 Chester South Moor
5 Lumley 6th
6 Nicholsons
7 Kimblesworth
8 Ushaw Moor
9 Sherburn Hill

10 Page Bank
11 Vinovium
12 Vane Tempest
13 Seaham
14 Dawdon
15 Murton
16 Easington
17 Horden

by BC. There is no proposal at present to do so in the sensitive southwest area of the Durham coalfield at Vinovium, Page Bank and Ushaw Moor.

At Westoe, near Wearmouth, pumps have been turned off, but pumping will restart from new submersible pumps in three to six months.

This is despite huge expenditure on treatment plants and strict regulations, such as the 1993 EU Urban Waste Water Treatment Directive. Treatment plants remove about 95 per cent of the polluting load of sewage before the water is discharged into inland rivers. The water service companies responsible for sewage treatment and disposal in England and Wales (in Scotland and Northern Ireland there are Regional Councils) must obtain formal consents from the EA to discharge treated sewage. Consent conditions vary according to the assimilative capacity of the receiving waters, but this does not account for the wide regional variations in standards recorded (Fig. 9.13). Yet incident levels are falling. In 1997, 8 per cent of sewage treatment works were below the required standard, compared with 23 per cent in 1986.

Figure 9.11 England and Wales: water pollution incidents reported by source of pollution, 1991 (*Source*: Institute of Hydrology, 1993)

Figure 9.12 Scotland: water pollution incidents reported by source of pollution, 1991 (*Source*: Institute of Hydrology, 1993)

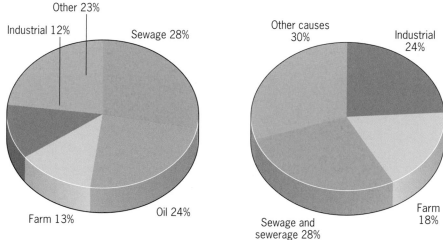

Figure 9.13 England and Wales: river and canal quality, 1980, 1985 and 1990 (*Source*: Institute of Hydrology, 1993)

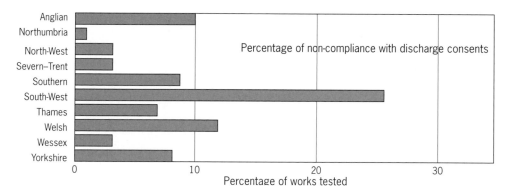

Water pollution in the former USSR and Eastern Europe

Water pollution is a problem not only in capitalist systems. Since the communist regimes of Eastern Europe and the USSR collapsed at the end of the 1980s, the environmental impacts of their centralised command economies and the consequences of more than four decades of over-investment in heavy and heavily pollutant industry have been revealed. Across the vast expanses of the former USSR, all major rivers are polluted (Fig. 9.14). Throughout Eastern Europe, water pollution is a major problem: from the Baltic to the Black Sea and along the main arteries of the rivers Vistula, Oder and Danube we see closed beaches, decimated fish stocks and hazardous drinking water (Fig. 9.15). In trying to achieve rapid industrial growth, environmental controls were often neglected.

By 1994 in the former USSR, waste from Moscow included 15 tonnes of metals daily to four massive sewage plants. At least three tonnes of this passes into the Moscow River and on to the Volga. Further east, environmentalists have become increasingly concerned over Lake Baikal. It is the world's deepest lake, and one of the purest, but by the late 1980s, parts were classified as 'severely polluted'. The main sources of the pollution are the huge Baikalsk pulp and paper mills near Irkutsk on the lake's southern shore. Yet, as the figures of Table 9.3 show, by 1990 the Russians had responded to the ecological threat by improving the treatment of wastes. Indeed, in 1992, the Russian government promised to close the mills, but by 1994 they were still open.

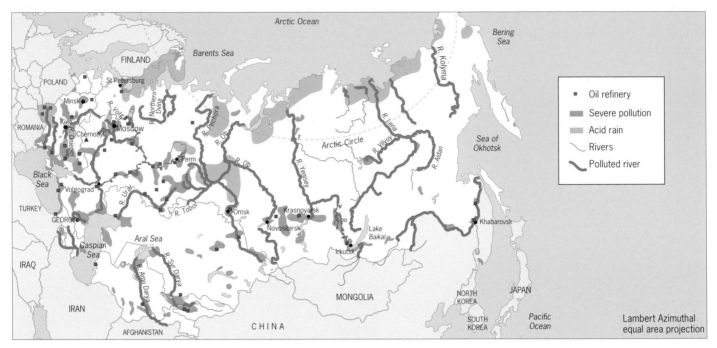

Figure 9.14 A universe of pollution (*Source*: Institute of Geography, Russian Academy of Sciences; Natural Resources Defense Council, Washington DC)

Czech Republic
70% of rivers are polluted by mining wastes, nitrates, liquid manure and oil. 40% of all sewage is untreated. 50% of all drinking water is contaminated.

River Danube
Because the Danube serves as a border between countries, it is used as a convenient dumping place. It has attracted a wide variety of polluting industries from its source in Germany to its mouth in Romania, including chemicals, iron and steel, paper and petroleum.

Hungary
Adequate sewerage systems exist for only 46% of the population. Almost 800 towns and villages use water thought to be unfit for consumption. Over 100 000 tonnes of nitrogen seeps into groundwater supplies annually.

Former East Germany
66% of rivers and 23% of standing water bodies need cleaning. Noxious emissions from power stations are uncontrolled. Organic waste is responsible for 80% of the pollution and metals for 3%.

Baltic Sea
Greenpeace has labelled the Gulf of Gdańsk 'an ecological disaster zone'.

Poland
50% (6 billion m³) of industrial and municipal effluent is dumped into Poland's rivers every year. The Vistula, from Warsaw to the sea at Gdańsk, is too polluted to be used even in industry. 95% of the river water is unfit for drinking.

Romania
85% of Romania's main rivers contain water unfit for drinking. Pollution of the River Tisza, which flows into Hungary, is causing concern to the Hungarian government.

Bulgaria
Experts forecast that by the year 2000 the Black Sea will be dead if pollution rates continue.

Figure 9.15 Water problems in Eastern Europe

Table 9.3 Quality of treated water released by Balkaisk Mills (*Source*: George, 1994)

Year	Prime pulp (tonnes/ year)	Fresh water flow (m³/y)	Sewage water flow (m³/y)	pH	BOD (mg/l)	Suspended substances (mg/l)	Mineral substances (mg/l)	Oxygen (mg/l)	Sulphur organics (mg/l)	Phenols (mg/l)	Chlorides (mg/l)	Sulphates (mg/l)
1985	215.005	116.688	674	6.4	4.5	9.3	618	7.1	0.13	0.011	93	307
1986	224.000	110.160	629	6.4	2.5	6.4	606	7.3	0.17	0.011	105	301
1987	219.000	106.910	599	6.4	1.7	3.2	568	7.8	0.15	0.011	101	250
1988	217.790	89.805	587	6.4	1.4	2.3	521	7.7	0.16	0.009	97.3	234
1989	213.869	83.285	587	6.4	1.8	2.7	485	—	0.16	0.009	93.8	230.4
1990	191.141	81.376	575	6.3	1.3	3.0	448	7.5	0.16	0.008	91	211

We must remember too that pollutants, once they enter the drainage basin stores, may be released slowly and delivered to streams and lakes many years later. For example, during the 1950s and 1960s, a nuclear military complex 80 km north of Chelyabinsk, in the Ural Mountains, poured wastes into the R. Techa. A reporter writing in 1994 claimed, 'river banks and **sediment** still tingle with long-lived caesium and strontium' (Edwards, 1994). The fallout from the Chernobyl nuclear disaster of 1987 continues to pollute groundwater and rivers. Pollution from oil spills may be stored in soils and streams for long periods, especially in the fragile tundra **ecosystems** of the Arctic northlands.

Figure 9.16 Burning oil lake following the oil spill, Usinsk

> This disaster was waiting to happen. The pipeline is 20 years old and it's been leaking, on and off, since 1988. We're worried that the hot oil will enter the permafrost and remain there for generations. We shall be sending experts to advise on the spill.

US government official

> This is not an ecological disaster. Nothing or no one has suffered. About 14 000 tonnes of boiling oil has escaped, but the spill has been contained. Most of the oil has been cleaned up, but the temperature has now dropped to -10°C and further work will have to wait until spring. I doubt that the oil will have a dangerous effect on the tundra.

Komineft oil company executive

> We realise that we originally underestimated the size of the spill. This is a dangerous ecological situation and we will continue to work through the winter to clear the oil. Freezing temperatures will turn the oil into a slow-moving sludge which will be easier to clean.

Spokesperson for the Russian government

> I haven't read that much about the spill. It hasn't really been in the news. Perhaps it's because few people live in that part of the country. Anyway, the oil will end up in the Arctic, not Moscow.

Architect in Moscow

> Our river water is contaminated with oil and the snow on the river banks is a grey sludge. The fish smell of oil and are inedible.

Villager living 300 km downstream of the Pechora River

> This is the largest spill since the 1989 Exxon Valdez disaster in Alaska. About 60 000 tonnes of oil have been spilt.
> We fear that the oil will flow down the Pechora River and into the Barents Sea. Precious tundra wildlife such as Arctic foxes, lemmings, snowy owls and reindeer will be affected. Thousands of migratory birds, some rare, such as the Bewick swan, will arrive in spring. The Pechora is also Europe's richest salmon river, where thousands of salmon come to spawn in spring. If oil has been slowly leaking over time, effects are already likely to have accumulated in other fish.
> During the warmer summer months the oil will become vaporous and spread more widely through the tundra region.

Environmentalist

Figure 9.17 The ecological impact of the oil spill (*After*: *The Guardian*, 26 October 1994 and *The Sunday Times*, 30 October 1994)

8 Draw an annotated systems diagram (inputs–stores–throughputs–outputs) to explain why stream pollution may continue long after the initial input of oil has stopped.

9 Read Figure 9.17.
a Outline what happened in the Usinsk oil spill.
b In what ways do the long cold winter and the frozen environment influence the impact of the pollutants?
c Why do you think the various interested parties have such contrasting understandings and opinions of the event and its consequences?

Oil spill in the Arctic

In August 1994 an oil pipeline burst near the town of Usinsk, in the Pechora drainage basin (Fig. 9.18). An earthen dam built to contain the spill then burst in September after heavy rain. An area of more than 67 km² was covered by a slick 10 cm deep (Fig. 9.16).

Close to the Arctic Circle, this region has a fragile tundra ecosystem underlain by a deep zone of permafrost. During the summer and autumn of 1994 there was much secrecy and uncertainty about the oil spill. As late as November figures varying from 14 000 tonnes to 60 000 tonnes of oil spillage were still being claimed. Yet three things were indisputable:
• Large quantites of heavy crude oil had spread on to the tundra and into rivers.
• The pollution had moved down the Pechora River into the Barents Sea.
• Clean-up efforts were inadequate (Fig. 9.17).

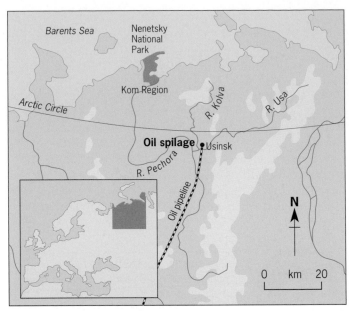

Figure 9.18 The Arctic oil spill (*Source: The Sunday Times*, 30 October 1994) Times Newspapers Ltd 1994

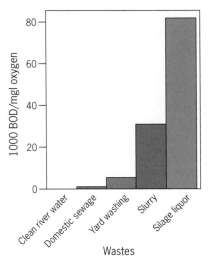

Figure 9.19 Silage liquid as a powerful pollutant (*Source*: Newson, 1998)

Agricultural sources of pollution

In addition to artificial fertiliser residues, farms generate several forms of effluent which can cause pollution. First, the rigorous cleansing process on dairy farms produces large volumes of water which contain impurities. Secondly, there is slurry or animal waste. This is commonly spread thinly and irregularly across fields and, once there, causes few problems unless flushed into rivers by heavy rain. However, if it is left in high concentrations in farmyards or on fields near streams, it can be dangerous – undiluted slurry is 100 times more polluting than domestic sewage. Thirdly, there is silage. This is cut grass which is allowed to ferment in the absence of air to produce an animal feed rich in sugars. Unlike hay, the grass for silage does not need drying and, because it is easy to store and handle with modern equipment, silage production in England and Wales trebled between 1976 and 1986. Unfortunately, the silage process produces a liquid effluent with a polluting power higher than animal waste (Fig. 9.19). It is very acidic (has a low pH) and has a very high **biological oxygen demand** (BOD). Consequently, once it reaches streams, it has a disastrous effect upon aquatic life.

Where slurry and silage effluent are allowed to leak from the farm storage areas, impacts can be rapid and severe. Pollution occurs because bacteria use oxygen in the water to break down the high organic content. This results in deoxygenation of the water, which quickly kills fish and other aquatic life.

Waste and silage effluent leakage make up a large proportion of all farm incidents in England and Wales (Fig. 9.20), and their number more than doubled during the 1980s to over 3500. The reasons for this are mixed (Fig. 9.21; see Herefordshire case study, p. 173).

In the early 1990s there were signs that the increases in UK river pollution had been stopped. Less intensive agriculture, the introduction of stricter building, storage and handling regulations from 1991 and firmer prosecutions all helped. The Government, too, has introduced positive schemes to encourage farmers to improve river water quality. For instance, in May 1994 a 'water fringe habitat scheme' was launched in six pilot areas (Fig. 9.22). The aim is to encourage farmers to stop applying fertiliser or pesticide across a 20 m wide fringe either side of a stream. This will protect the water from pollution, allow the growth of plants as a buffer zone from agriculture, and improve the

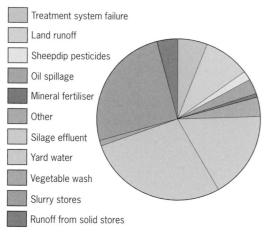

Treatment system failure
Land runoff
Sheepdip pesticides
Oil spillage
Mineral fertiliser
Other
Silage effluent
Yard water
Vegetable wash
Slurry stores
Runoff from solid stores

Figure 9.20 England and Wales: total farm pollution incidents by cause, 1986 (*Source*: Water Authorities Association, 1987)

'The main cause or [river] deterioration are sewage effluents and agricuultural practices with a few localised problems... of particular concern is the impac of repeated pollution incidents in rural areas. Silage liquors and animal wastes are so polluting that even small qantities can be sufficient to affect water quality'.

Figure 9.21 Reasons for waste and sewage leakage (*Source*: HMSO, 1986)

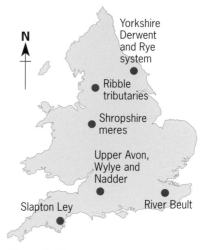

Figure 9.22 Pilot water fringe areas, 1994 (*Source*: *The Guardian*, 16 May 1994)

stream's in-built 'purification power'. The fringes will also act as wildlife habitats and corridors for movement and colonisation. In 1997 the grants payable to farmers joining this scheme were £250–400 per ha.

A Herefordshire farming incident, England

A change in farming practice

Land on a farm in North Herefordshire slopes gently northwards towards a stream which flows into the River Teme (Fig. 9.23). In 1984 the farmer decided to intensify his animal-rearing enterprise. In order to keep more cattle, he built a new shed (at A) to house 80 animals through the winter. To increase the feed supply, he changed his feeding regime from mainly hay to silage and so dug a long silage pit (at B). During the winter, when the ground is generally too wet to allow animal waste to be spread on the fields, the waste was cleared from the shed and piled outside (at C).

The consequences

In the wet spring of 1988, water pollution was recorded 4 km downstream in the River Teme. The source of the pollution was traced back to the farm. Slurry from the shed and manure piles, and silage from the pit had reached the field ditches by surface runoff and ground seepage. This had then been transported by the local stream to the River Teme.

The solution

The farmer taken to court and fined. He was given advice on the storage and handling of the wastes and silage, and was required to upgrade his buildings and change the farm layout. He received a grant to help with the cost of these changes. First, he relocated his silage pit (at D) further from the field ditches. Next, he laid a leakage-free waste yard (at E) outside his animal shed and reorganised the drainage from the shed to lead into this yard. Since completion in 1991, there has been no further evidence of water pollution.

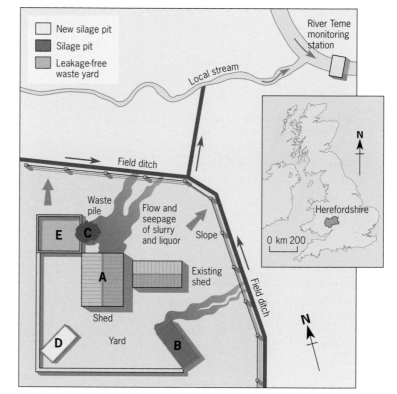

Figure 9.23 Managing a farm pollution source

10 Explain the role played by changing farming practice in causing pollution.

11 Explain why the changes made since the court case have reduced the risk of stream pollution.

9.4 The solute load of rivers

Most of the pollutants we have discussed are found in water in their dissolved state. They become part of the **solute load** of a river. However, we must not forget that all rivers have a hydrochemistry. In the environment there is no stream which consists of 'pure' H_2O. It is normal for streams to carry and transfer a solute load. In this section we explore what we mean by 'normal'. By focusing on the nitrate content of our water, we shall examine how these 'normal' conditions are altered.

From Table 9.4 we can see the major properties of water in the River Stour (Fig. 9.24). The table shows the main constituents of the solute load of this river and summarises the river's hydrochemistry. The details are complicated, but we can pick out three basic understandings:

- There is a wide variety of dissolved materials in the river.
- The solute load shows year-to-year variation.
- There is a range of values for all constituents of the solute load within a particular year.

Table 9.4 River Stour at Langham, Essex: water quality

	Year 1989			Year 1992			Years 1974–91
	Mean	**Max**	**Min**	**Mean**	**Max**	**Min**	**Average**
Temperature (°C)	11.7	21.5	2.0	12.1	23.5	3.0	11.3
pH	8.3	9.0	7.8	8.4	9.1	8.0	8.2
Conductivity (yS/cm)	871	1011	716	942	1280	799	914
BOD (mg/l O)	2.6	7.8	0.7	3.0	10.4	1.0	3.2
Nitrate (mg/l N)	6.33	15.10	0.50	7.49	19.96	1.30	7.80
Chloride (mg/l Cl)	72.0	293.0	35.5	78.4	180.0	48.5	68.9
Total alkalinity (mg/l CaCO$_3$)	253.0	285.0	295.0	242.7	280.0	219.0	246.2
Silica (mg/l SiO$_2$)	10.57	46.10	3.70	8.53	13.83	0.32	7.72
Sulphate (mg/l SO$_4$)	90.7	119.0	71.6	194.4	191.3	69.9	104.1
Calcium (mg/1 Ca)	128.8	145.0	108.0	137.8	171.0	108.0	134.4
Magnesium (mg/l Mg)	8.3	11.8	6.2	7.41	10.70	5.70	8.80
Potassium (mg/l K)	8.6	12.7	5.6	7.43	9.60	4.60	7.60
Sodium (mg/l Na)	47.5	67.0	31.0	40.3	56.0	24.1	43.9
Suspended solids (mg/l)	11.6	122.0	0.5	22.6	166.0	2.5	16.1

Table 9.5 Mean solute load concentrations in the world's rivers (*Source*: Newson, 1992)

Solute	Average load (mg/l)
Calcium (Ca^{2+})	13.5
Magnesium (Mg^{2+})	3.6
Sodium (Na$^+$)	7.4
Potassium (K$^+$)	1.35
Chlorine (Cl$^-$)	9.6
Sulphate (SO$_4{}^{2-}$)	8.7
Hydrogen carbonate (HCO^{3-})	52.0
Silicon oxide (SiO$_2$)	10.4
Total all solutes	106.6

?

12 Study Tables 9.4 and 9.5. Compare the River Stour's hydrochemistry with the world averages.

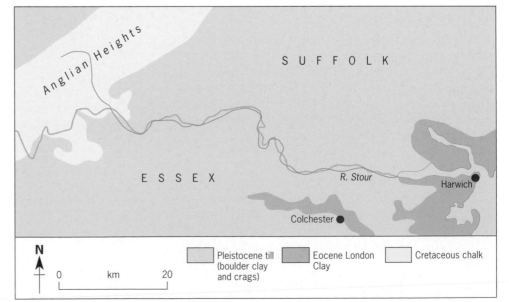

Figure 9.24 The River Stour drainage basin is a mainly rural, intensively farmed catchment of 578 km². The headwater catchment is underlain by chalk, with the middle and lower course crossing less pervious glacial tills and clays

The R. Stour is affected by human activities. **Streamflow** is increased by intermittent pumping from an Ely–Ouse water transfer scheme and occasional borehole pumping. It is also influenced by groundwater abstraction and recharge. Water is abstracted for industrial, agricultural and public use. However, the R. Stour's solute composition is not unusual, nor is it an especially polluted river. In the 1990 National River Quality Survey (see Fig. 9.29), it is listed in Class 2, which indicates a 'fair' water quality.

All rivers, therefore, carry varied solute loads (Table 9.5). This load, that is the stream's **hydrochemistry,** is influenced by **discharge**, water temperatures and the pathways that water takes to reach the channel (Fig. 9.25). For example, in the Peak District of the southern Pennines, streams with headwaters on Carboniferous Limestones have a different chemical make-up from streams which originate on Millstone Grits. So, we talk of 'hard' or 'soft' water from our taps. Streams from acid peat moorlands differ from streams within deciduous woodlands, and so on. The mean pH of stream water is approximately 4.6, but commonly ranges from 4.0 to 5.0.

Figure 9.25 Sources of solutes to streams (*Source*: Newson, 1992).

13 From Figure 9.25, suggest three of the effects that increased human activities could have upon the other solute sources to streams.

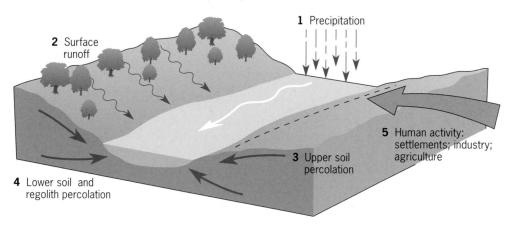

1 Precipitation
2 Surface runoff
3 Upper soil percolation
4 Lower soil and regolith percolation
5 Human activity: settlements; industry; agriculture

Relationships between discharge and solute load

We can measure the quantity of the solute load, i.e. how much there is, or its concentration, i.e. how much there is per unit volume. Hydrologists usually use concentration levels, e.g. milligrams of solute per litre of water. Thus, if discharge doubles while the amount of a particular mineral remains constant, then the concentration will be halved.

Figure 9.26(a) *Below left*
River Leach: seasonal changes in the nitrate concentration of the channel and nearby spring (*Source*: Burt and Haycock,1992)

Figure 9.26(b) *Below right*
River Leach: stream discharge hydrograph (*Source*: Burt and Haycock, 1992)

Dilution and pumping effects

The relationship between river flow and its solute concentration is complex. In some situations, concentration decreases as flow increases. This is known as the **dilution effect**. In other cases, concentration may increase as flow increases. This is known as the **pumping effect**. We can illustrate both effects by studying nitrate concentrations. In a mainly rural catchment, such as the R. Leach in the Cotswolds (Fig. 9.26), nitrate levels in streams may rise as flow increases after a rainstorm, shown by the storm hydrograph peaks, A, B and C.

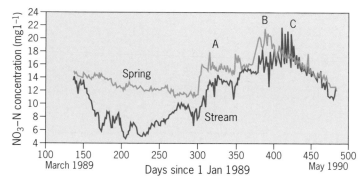

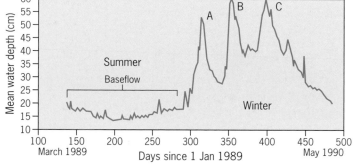

14 From Figure 9.26:
a Summarise the nitrate concentration regime of the channel and spring flows.
b Suggest reasons for the differences between the two regimes.
c Explain why nitrate concentration in the stream channel is more closely correlated with the discharge hydrograph than are the spring concentration levels.

This is caused by surface runoff and soil water flow 'flushing' nitrates from the fields, i.e. a pumping effect. In a mainly urban catchment, on the other hand, sewage effluent may constitute a high proportion of the low flow. At high flows the nitrate may become diluted, so that nitrate concentration decreases as flow increases, i.e. the dilution effect.

In densely occupied countries such as the UK, most river basins include both urban and rural land uses. As a result, their hydrochemistry exhibits what is called mixed mechanism responses to fluctuations in discharge.

Variations in solute load character

We should also understand that each of the water input sources shown in Figure 9.25 will have a distinctive hydrochemistry. Thus, when discharge consists entirely of the **baseflow component**, the regolith and groundwater stores are the main sources of water, and the solute composition will depend heavily upon the nature of the bedrocks. Following a storm, surface runoff and soil water from the upper horizons increase, flushing solutes from organic sources and, in farming areas, chemicals such as nitrates. Thus, hydrologists need to distinguish between base flows and storm flows, and to be able to assess the contribution of each to the total solute load carried by a stream.

A measure of the base flow/storm or runoff flow is the **base flow index (BFI)**. This is 'the fraction of streamflow over a given period which is base flow' (Institute of Hydrology, 1992). In 1985, for the Kirkton Burn hydrograph at Balquhidder the BFI was 0.35, i.e. 35 per cent of the total flow in that year was base flow (Fig. 9.27).

It is important for water quality managers to distinguish between solutes with a natural origin and those resulting from human activities (anthropogenic). The outcome of the complex ways in which these variables interact is that it is very difficult to measure, explain and therefore forecast the solute load of rivers. Even after a five-year national study of UK rivers, the Institute of Hydrology has concluded, 'The detailed nature of the links and interactions between natural hydrochemical processes, anthropogenic processes and the dynamics of stream chemistry is not yet fully understood' (Littlewood, 1992).

9.5 Managing water quality in UK rivers

The Environment Agency (EA) is the government body with primary responsibility for maintaining and improving water quality and for pollution control in England and Wales. However, the EA must negotiate with and

Figure 9.27b Kirkton Burn above Balquhidder at base flow during a prolonged dry spell

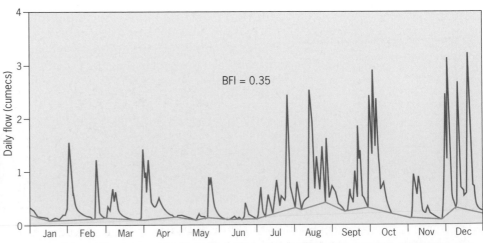

Figure 9.27a Kirkton Burn at Balquhidder: hydrograph with separated flow, 1985 (*Source*: Littlewood, 1992)

co-ordinate the work of several other bodies (Fig. 9.28). There are similar structures in Scotland and Northern Ireland. All work within the framework of UK laws and EU Directives on water standards.

Effective management requires a consistent and reliable information base. Before the setting up of the EA in 1995, national water quality surveys grouped rivers into four classes (Fig. 9.29). By the mid-1990s, the surveys showed that over 90 per cent of the total length of rivers in England and Wales fell into Class 1, 'good' or Class 2, 'fair' quality. This compared with 99 per cent in Scotland (including lochs) and 95 per cent in Northern Ireland. The figures for 1980 were 90 per cent, 94 per cent and 93 per cent, respectively. Alongside the surveys, a national data base, called the Harmonised Monitoring Scheme (HMS), has been set up. More than 220 monitoring stations send regular water sample records to be input to this data base. The EA has adopted a new six-class system, known as the General Quality Assessment (GQA). The GQA for a river identifies and measures four aspects of quality: chemical, biological, nutrients, aesthetic (see Water Quality case study, Severn Vale, p. 178).

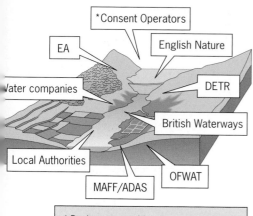

Figure 9.28 Key players in water quality control

?

15 Make a list of factors which might influence the quality of river water. Identify 'natural' and 'human' factors separately.

16 From Figure 9.29, select two rivers in different regions which show significant stretches of 'poor' (Class 3) and 'bad' (Class 4) water quality. Use atlases and other reference material to suggest reasons for this poor quality.

17 Of the ten water regions of England and Wales, Northumbria shows the lowest proportion of polluted rivers. Less than three per cent are 'poor' or 'bad'. The highest pollution proportions are recorded for the North-West and South-West, both with 19 per cent classed as 'poor' or 'bad'. Suggest reasons for these characteristics.

18 Use the Severn Vale case study material to illustrate the complexity of water quality control in intensively developed drainage basins.

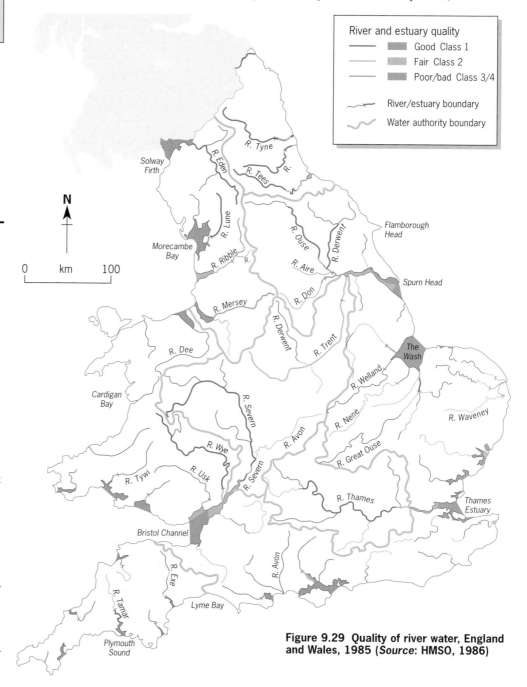

Figure 9.29 Quality of river water, England and Wales, 1985 (*Source*: HMSO, 1986)

Water quality in the Severn Vale

The Severn Vale management unit covers the middle and lower R. Severn drainage basin and has a population of 545 000. (see also Chapter 8, p. 158) There is a comprehensive system of sewage treatment works (STW) capable of returning 100 m3 of treated water to rivers and estuaries each day (Fig. 9.31). These surface water discharges are from domestic and industrial users. There are more than 100 industrial companies with effluent discharge consents, including large businesses such as Birds Eye Walls, Rank Xerox, Du Pont. Because of population growth and industrial expansion, in 1997 the EA identified 28 STWs as requiring upgrading.

We must remember too, that most pollution does not come from STWs (Fig. 9.30). Fortunately, at present, serious pollution incidents are rare. It is not surprising therefore, that the rivers in the Severn Vale vary in water quality (Table 9.6), with significant stretches classed D (poor to bad) in terms of chemical contents (Fig. 9.32).

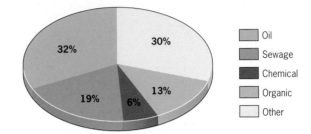

Figure 9.30 Pollution incidents in Severn Vale, 1998

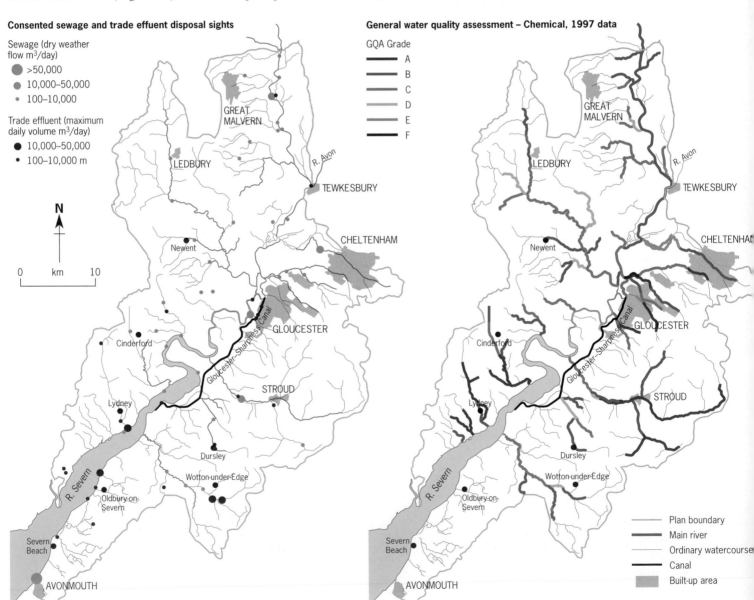

Figure 9.31 Sewage and trade effluent disposal, Severn Vale

Figure 9.32 Water quality; chemical criteria, Severn Vale

Table 9.6 Water pollution incidents, Severn Vale, 1997–8		
Class of incident	1997	1998
Class 1	1	0
Class 2	26	14
Class 3	439	363
Total	466	377

Class 1 Incident at Gloucester–Sharpness Canal
The class one incident in 1997 is an example of where a major response was required to prevent a serious accident from occurring. On 14 January 1997, fish were reported to be in distress on the Gloucester-Sharpness Canal at Slimbridge due to high ammonia concentrations in the water. The source of the problem was traced to a sewage treatment works which, due to very cold weather conditions was not functioning properly. A surface water intake supplying the north of Bristol is located approximately 4 km downstream at Purton. To avoid problems with treatment, water was diverted from the River Frome to the River Severn. The quantity of water abstracted from the River Severn at Gloucester was also increased to maintain levels in the canal.

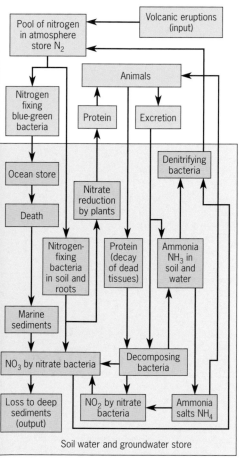

Figure 9.33 The nitrogen cycle

9.6 Water quality and the nitrate issue

Natural processes ensure that all streams contain nitrogen (N), most commonly in nitrate form (as NO_3). For example, decomposition of organic matter in the surface litter layer and the soil horizons releases nitrogen as soluble nitrate. Nitrogen is an essential element in all living matter, and is recycled through the nitrogen cycle (Fig. 9.33). During photosynthesis, plants such as cereal crops use about 30 kg of nitrogen to form one hectare of green plant surface. Yet concern is growing that human activities – urban and rural – are causing nitrogen and nitrate levels to rise dangerously in many rivers and aquifers. For example, nitrate levels in the river water of several regions exceed the EU prescribed limit of 50 mg/l (Figs 9.34 and 9.35).

Excess nitrate can become a health hazard and, when in conjunction with phosphate, can lead to eutrophication of surface waters. Thus it has become a high-profile environmental issue.

Eutrophication

Pollution can be caused by the presence of too little or too much of specific solutes. Eutrophication means 'excessive enrichment', that is, too much, in this case of nitrogen and phosphorus. The normally low concentrations of nitrogen and phosphorus in water bodies control the growth of organisms, including phytoplankton and algae. However, if concentrations increase, these elements can become pollutants by making water unfit for human consumption or by encouraging **algal blooms**. Excess nitrates, mainly from inefficient application of artificial fertiliser on farmland, lead to the growth of green algae. The main sources of excess phosphates are farm wastes and treated urban sewage effluents. These generate blue-green algae.

Algal blooms, seen as surface blankets across the water, are most common on lakes, reservoirs and ponds, especially during warm, dry spells. At such times water flow and movement is minimal. The growth of such blooms is a steady process whereby oxygen availability gradually decreases (Fig. 9.36). Eventually everything in the food chain is affected. During the 1988–92 UK drought, algal

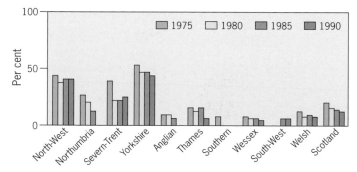

Figure 9.34 Mean percentage of sampling points where ammoniacal nitrogen exceeded 0.5 mg/l N, 1975–90

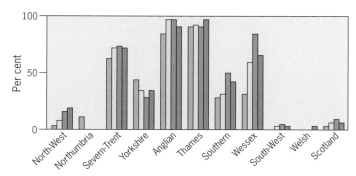

Figure 9.35 Mean percentage of sampling points where nitrate exceeded 5 mg/l N, 1975–90

19 Use the data of Figures 9.34 and 9.35 to assess the accuracy of the statement that nitrate levels in rivers have been rising over the past 20 years.

blooms became particularly widespread (see Chapter 8) as water bodies shrank and **throughflow** was reduced. Water supplies from some reservoirs were threatened and water-based recreational activities suspended. For example, the large Rutland Water reservoir in the East Midlands was seriously affected and closed for water sports over several periods during the 1990–2 summers. Similar problems recurred during the hot, dry summers of 1995 and 1996.

The issue
In the UK, agriculture is most frequently blamed for high nitrate concentrations in river water. However, the relationship between agricultural practices and nitrate levels is not simple, and so the solution will not be easy. Two scientists wrote in 1992: 'The popular misconception is that the nitrate problem is caused by farmers applying too much fertiliser to crops so that the surplus left after harvest is leached away in the following winter; this is too simplistic' (Burt and Haycock, 1992).

Nitrates in the farm system
There are six sources of nitrate in the farm system (Table 9.7). Three aspects of farming practices influence how much of these nitrate inputs are 'lost', i.e. leached, to streams and aquifers:
• the amount of organic and inorganic fertilisers applied
• the timing of the applications
• the crop and animal feeding patterns adopted.
  In this system (Fig. 9.37) the aim of the farmer and the hydrologist is to match the nitrate input to crop needs and so maximise the proportion which is output as products rather than lost to streams and aquifers. The efficiency of

Table 9.7 Sources of nitrate in the farm system

Input	Nitrogen (kg/ha/y)
1 Mineralisation of soil organic matter	50–100
2 Effects of cultivation, released by ploughing of a 3-year ley (rotation grass)	100–200
3 Mineralisation of organic nitrogen from crop residues	Variable according to crop patterns
4 Fertiliser residues	5–50 (cereals low, potatoes high)
5 Organic manures	Very variable according to animal densities
6 Atmospheric inputs (dissolved in rain)	40–50

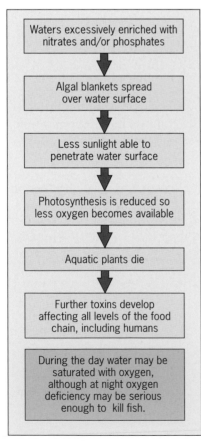

Figure 9.36 The development of algal blooms

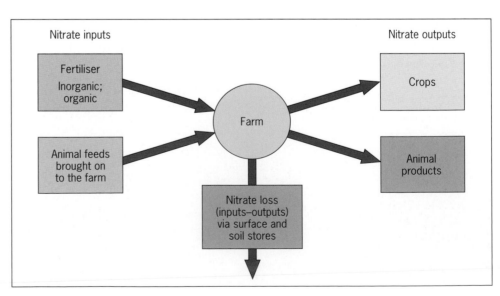

Figure 9.37 Nitrates in the farm system

?

20 Use Figure 9.37 to explain the development and impact of 'eutrophication'.

21 Explain why eutrophication is more common on standing water bodies than in streams.

22 Suggest ways of reducing eutrophication.

23 Study Figure 9.38.
a In which month is the soil nitrogen contrast greatest between early- and late-sown fields?
b Why might the timing of this maximum contrast have a particularly strong impact upon stream hydrochemistry?
c Suggest reasons why soil nitrogen concentration in fields with late sowing falls so rapidly during March.

the system will be affected by three variables: the crop yield per hectare; how much nitrate is already stored in the soil; and the loss of available nitrogen before the crop takes it up.

These decisions interact with climatic rhythms and hydrological processes (Fig. 9.26a, b). For example, in the UK stream and groundwater flows are lowest during the summer months. In this season, too, nitrogen take-up by plants is greatest. Consequently, from late spring through summer, leaching of nitrates is at a minimum. During the late autumn and winter months, heavier rainfall inputs, lower water take-up by plants, and reduced **evapotranspiration** cause soil and groundwater stores to become **saturated**. Runoff, **infiltration**, deep percolation and stream recharge combine to increase **leaching**.

Influence of farming practices

Farming practices can accelerate or slow down the leaching process. For instance, autumn ploughing triggers a surge of nitrate release and an increase in leaching. This can be particularly severe where the land is left bare until spring planting. For this reason the MAFF strongly advises farmers to plant as early in the autumn as possible. This gives ground cover and allows the young plants to take up nitrogen, and so reduces winter leaching (Fig. 9.38). It is worth noting that conservationists are concerned about this trend to autumn planting. These crops, e.g. winter wheat and barley, may be harvested too early in the following summer for many ground-nesting birds and other field animals to complete their nesting and rearing cycles. This early harvest, and the increased early mowing of meadows for silage, are significant factors in the reduction in numbers of many species of farmland birds.

Government responses

Because of the impact of nitrate levels on aquatic ecosystems and upon public water supplies, the UK government introduced in 1990 the Pilot Nitrate Scheme to run for five years. Its aim was to reduce nitrate inputs to the groundwater store from farmland. The main strategy was to designate ten Nitrate Sensitive Areas (NSAs), within which 'voluntary but substantial agricultural restrictions' were introduced (Fig. 9.39). In return for joining the scheme, farmers were compensated for loss of profits resulting from the changes in farming practice. (In 1993, compensation could be as high as £380 per ha.)

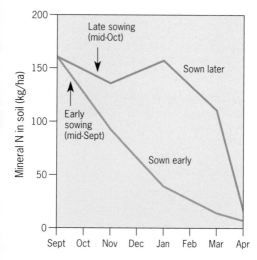

Figure 9.38 The effect on nitrate leaching of sowing winter wheat early or late (*Source*: MAFF, 1993)

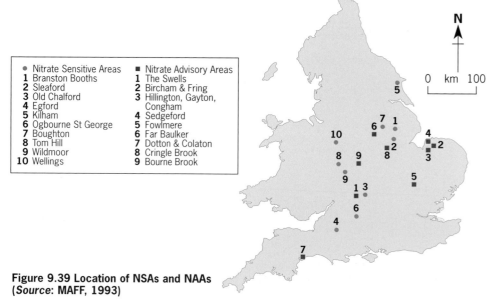

Figure 9.39 Location of NSAs and NAAs (*Source*: MAFF, 1993)

Integrated river basin management

Understanding the movement of water within our environment is essential for managing river catchments in an integrated and sustainable way. This is not just an issue of water quality, but also water quantity, to ensure water is in the right place at the right time.

The challenge for the Agency is to minimise activities that adversely affect surface and groundwaters, and to maximise the benefits that can be derived from a well-managed river basin system. Principally through Local Environment Agency Plans (LEAPs), we reconcile the various and often conflicting demands placed on natural waters when exercising our duties relating to: water quality, flood prevention, fisheries, navigation, recreation, conservation, disposal of waste waters and water abstraction.

Plan targets and actions

Our key performance targets for integrated river basin management are to:
• ensure that all waters are of suitable quality for their different uses, deliver class upgrades in water quality to 800 km of rivers, increase bathing water compliance from 89 per cent to 93 per cent by 2000, and bring about a 5 per cent year-on-year reduction in the number of unsubstantiated pollution incidents
• construct and improve flood defences to protect around 300 000 additional housing equivalents each year, and in locations served by a flood warning system ensure that 80 per cent of properties flooded receive a prior warning by 2001
• reduce nutrient levels at 20 SSSIs affected by nutrient enrichment by 2001.

Figure 9.40 Water quality and the 1999–2000 Corporate Plan of the Environment Agency (*Source*: Environment Agency, 1999)

The scheme had four main requirements for the farmer:

1 application of the correct (economic optimum) amount of nitrogen fertiliser to each field, with reductions in fertiliser input for winter cereals and oilseed rape
2 a limit of 170 kg N/ha/y as livestock manure
3 a ban on the autumn application of slurry or poultry manure
4 use of cover crops where land would otherwise be bare during autumn and winter.

The farmer is also advised against grassland ploughing, especially in autumn.

In addition nine Nitrate Advisory Areas (NAAs) were designated where advisory campaigns were run to encourage farmers to adopt good practice (Fig. 9.39). Seven of the nine NAAs were mainly groundwater catchments.

Since 1995 these schemes have been integrated into a national code of 'Good Practice'. For example, where a stream or groundwater is identified as 'polluted' by nitrates, its catchment is designated as a Nitrate Vulnerable Zone (NVZ). Farmers must then follow a code of practice for timing and level of application of fertiliser and manure. In 1999 there were 68 NVZs in the UK. These schemes form important elements of the broader aims and policies of the EU and the EA (Fig. 9.40).

Summary

- All rivers and water bodies contain solute loads – the water's hydrochemistry. This is determined by a range of environmental variables. It is most commonly measured in terms of the concentration, i.e. the amount of a constituent per unit volume.

- The hydrochemistry of a river changes over time, especially in relation to discharge.

- Streams contain their own in-built 'purification power'. An important strategy for water managers is to sustain this power.

- People can alter the hydrochemistry and quality of river water, intentionally and accidentally.

- Water managers need to be able to distinguish between natural and anthropogenic components of the river's hydrochemistry.

- Water quality management involves two key dimensions: the maintenance of healthy biotic communities and the provision of potable (drinkable) water supplies.

- Water pollution results from the introduction of material and compounds at damaging levels of concentration.

- Point and diffuse pollution from human activities are caused by: agriculture, e.g. nitrates, farm wastes; cities, e.g. domestic wastes; industry, e.g. process effluents.

- Bodies such as the EA in the UK and agencies of the EU are setting increasingly rigorous water control standards. However, consistent water quality maintenance is proving very difficult to achieve.

Appendices

A1 Spearman's rank correlation coefficient

The Spearman rank correlation coefficient uses data measured on an ordinal or rank scale. It is particularly useful in surveys of attitudes or decision-making, where respondents are often asked to rank their preferences.

n = number of pairs
d = difference in rank of each pair of values

Spearman rank correlation coefficient $(r_s) = 1 - \left[\dfrac{6\Sigma d^2}{n^3 - n} \right]$

When you have calculated r_s, you need to find its statistical significance. This enables you to discover whether or not r_s is the result of a chance association. To do this you need to consult a significance table.

The critical values of r_s, for $n = 4$ to $n = 30$ are at the 0.05 and 0.01 levels of significance. The larger the value of r_s, the more significant the result. For numbers of pairs greater than $n = 30$, the value of r_s, changes very little.

Significance level (one-tailed test) (*Source*: Siege (1956) after Olds, 1938 and 1949)

n	0.05	0.01
4	1.000	
5	0.900	1.000
6	0.829	0.943
7	0.714	0.893
8	0.643	0.833
9	0.600	0.783
10	0.564	0.746
12	0.506	0.712
14	0.456	0.645
16	0.425	0.601
18	0.399	0.564
20	0.377	0.534
22	0.359	0.508
24	0.343	0.485
26	0.329	0.465
28	0.317	0.448
30	0.306	0.432

A2 The National Water Archive

Both the scientific understanding of hydrological processes and the assessment and management of water resources depends, to a considerable degree, on the ready availability of relevant hydrological data. The increasing number of people at risk from floods and drought around the world, and the recent evidence of the continuing vulnerability of the UK to the impact of unusual climatic conditions, underline the need for appropriate data on all elements of the hydrological cycle to strengthen the foundations upon which improved water management procedures are based.

A significant proportion of the UK data presented in this book derives from the National Water Archive (NWA) maintained by the Institute of Hydrology (IH) at Wallingford. The NWA is one of the Natural Environment Research Council's six Designated Data Centres, the purpose of which is to fully exploit – and improve accessibility to – the enormous volumes of environmental data currently being collected.

The Institute of Hydrology has been a natural focus for the acquisition and exploitation of major hydrological databases for many years: long-running experimental catchments in central Wales and in Scotland have furnished a wealth of data on hydrological processes, and since 1982 management of the National River Flow and National Groundwater Level Archives has been undertaken by IH and the British Geological Survey (BGS), respectively (BGS is also part of NERC and shares the Wallingford site with IH). These databases form the kernel of the National Water Archive, but a broad range of hydrological and related data sets have been absorbed into the co-ordinated management that it provides. Data holdings range from the catchment scale to national and, in the case of the Worlds Flood Archive, global scales. The value of the basic data is increased by the availability of interrelated spatial information: for example, detailed computerised representations of the UK river network and UK soil maps.

To make the archived data available to a large number of users a comprehensive suite of retrievals has been developed. Examples appear throughout this volume and descriptions of the retrieval services appear in the Hydrological Data UK publications, a series of yearbooks and reports dealing with nationally archived data and significant hydrological events. The yearbooks bring together the principal data sets relating to catchment rainfall, river flow and groundwater levels for the UK; water quality data are also featured for a representative network of monitoring sites.

Access arrangements vary between data sets held under the NWA umbrella, but for busy river flow and groundwater level data a modest handling charge is made; there is a 50 per cent reduction for educational usage, and charges may be waived for bona fide research investigations. Charging policies are under review.

Individuals or organisations wishing to use the National Water Archive retrieval services, or to enquire about the range of data sets available, should contact:

The National Water Archive Office
Institute of Hydrology
Maclean Building
Wallingford   Tel: 01491 838800
Oxfordshire OX10 8BB   Facsimile: 01491 692424

A3 Table of z scores

z	Column A p	Column B p_1	Column C p_2
0.0	0.000	0.500	1.000
0.1	0.040	0.460	0.920
0.2	0.079	0.421	0.841
0.3	0.118	0.382	0.764
0.4	0.155	0.345	0.689
0.5	0.191	0.309	0.617
0.6	0.226	0.274	0.549
0.7	0.258	0.242	0.484
0.8	0.288	0.212	0.424
0.9	0.316	0.184	0.368
1.0	0.341	0.159	0.317
1.1	0.364	0.136	0.271
1.2	0.385	0.115	0.230
1.3	0.403	0.097	0.193
1.4	0.419	0.081	0.162
1.5	0.433	0.067	0.134
1.6	0.445	0.055	0.110
1.7	0.455	0.045	0.089
1.8	0.464	0.036	0.072
1.9	0.471	0.029	0.057
*1.96	0.475	0.025	0.050
2.0	0.477	0.023	0.046
2.1	0.482	0.018	0.036
2.2	0.486	0.014	0.028
2.3	0.489	0.011	0.021
2.4	0.492	0.008	0.016
2.5	0.494	0.006	0.012
*2.28	0.495	0.005	0.010
2.6	0.495	0.005	0.009
2.7	0.496	0.004	0.007
2.8	0.497	0.003	0.005
2.9	0.498	0.002	0.004
3.0	0.499	0.001	0.003
3.1	0.499	0.001	0.002
3.2	0.499	0.001	0.001
3.3	0.499	0.001	0.001
3.4	0.500	0.000	0.001
3.5	0.500	0.000	0.000

Note:

Col A: p = the probability of a value lying between the mean and the corresponding value of z.

Col B: p_1 = the probability of a value exceeding the given value of z (a one-tailed probability).

Col C: p_2 = the probability of a value exceeding either +z or −z (a two-tailed probability).

*Critical care values of z corresponding to the 0.05 and 0.01 levels (two-tailed) have been given to two decimal places.

After Lindley and Miller (1953).

A4 MAFF guidelines for choosing a flood defence strategy

A Preliminary thinking
- Are people and/or built or natural assets at risk?
- How urgent is it?
- What options are available?
- What are the likely environmental consequences?

B Developing and appraising the options
There are four flood defence options:

1 **Do nothing**.

2 **Reduce** – maintain flood defences at a lower standard of protection in the future if maintenance of existing levels is difficult to justify.

3 **Sustain** – present standards of flood defence are sustained by maintenance work.

4 **Improve** – the standards of flood defences are improved beyond the current design level or by new projects.

C Choose the preferred option
This choice is made from the short list of alternatives which are environmentally, technically and economically acceptable. Options are ranked by cost–benefit ratio and by an Environmental Impact Assessment if environmental impacts have not been given monetary values and included in the cost–benefit analysis.

D Design of the preferred option in detail

E Operational phase, i.e. construction and maintenance

F Post-project appraisal
This is an important step, since it allows evaluation of the project's effectiveness in environmental and engineering terms. This information can then be used in deciding upon future flood management strategies.

Flood defence schemes are subject to the normal planning procedures in England and Wales, and local councils and other organisations are involved in the process. Some schemes are discussed by public inquiry. New flood defence works generally require planning permission.

A5 Environmental Impact Assessment

Environmental Impact Assessments (EIAs) were introduced in the 1988 Town and Country Planning Regulations. The aim of an EIA is to discover the likely environmental impacts of a planning proposal such as a flood alleviation scheme. The environmental impacts and issues raised by an EIA form an environmental statement which then becomes part of the decision-making and planning process, along with economic and technical factors.

At Ashby Folville, the NRA was involved in consultations with several agencies as part of the EIA, such as the County Council and the Director of Museums. The issues highlighted were: 1) The village is a conservation area; 2) The area is one of archaeological importance; 3) The stream channel was of ecological significance; 4) Public rights of way were involved.

Schemes such as the flood alleviation proposal of Ashby Folville (see the example below) always require planning permission from the Local Authority and, despite the EIA, there is no guarantee that there will be no environmental damage.

FLOOD DEFENCE CAPITAL WORKS – ENVIRONMENTAL IMPACT ASSESSMENT FORM

Watercourse _Twyford Brook_   LTS/LTN ....   Location _Ashby Folville_

From NGR ....   To NGR ....   FDC Prog. no ....

Start date ....   Completion date ....

Under Section 16 of the Water Resources Act 1991 it is a legal requirement to ensure that all operational activities are assessed for their impact on the environment.

Environmental aspects	Yes/No
Visual amenity	*Yes*
National Parks/Area of Outstanding Natural Beauty	*No*
Conservation area	*Yes*
High visual amenity area	–
Requires enhancement	–

Historic	
Scheduled ancient monuments	*No*
Area of archaeological importance (County Site)	*Yes*
Listed buildings and structures	*?*
Registered historic gardens	–
Other interesting features	–

Natural history	
SSSI/NNIR	*No*
Geological SSSI	*No*
Local nature reserve	*No*
County sites/prime sites	*No*
County Trust Reserve	*No*
TPO	*?*
Fisheries	*Yes*

Recreation	
Public footpath/bridleway	*Yes*
Angling	*No*
Watersport/recreation	*No*
Other bankside recreation	*No*

Other

References

Barrow, C (1987) *Water resources and agricultural development in the Tropics*, Longman Scientific and Technical.

Barry, R G and Chorley, R J (1982), *Atmosphere, weather and climate*, Methuen and Coltel.

Beven, K and Carling, P (1992) in Carling and Petts (eds), *Lowland floodplain rivers*, Wiley.

Boon, PJ et al. (1992), *River conservation and management*, Wiley.

Bramner, H (1990), 'Floods in Bangladesh. Geographical background to the 1987–8 floods', *The Geographical Journal*, 156, 1, Royal Geographical Society.

Briggs, D and Smithson, P (1989), *Fundamentals of physical geography*, Routledge.

Brookes, A (1985a), 'River channelisation in progress', *Progress in physical geography*, 9.

Brookes, A (1985b), 'Downstream morphological consequences of river channelisation in England and Wales', *Geographical Journal*, 151, 1, Royal Geographical Society.

Brown, A (1992), *The UK environment*, Department of the Environment, HMSO.

Burt, T (1987), 'Measuring infiltration capacity', *Geography Review*, 1, 2, Philip Allan Publishers.

Burt, T H and Haycock, N E (1992), 'Catchment planning and the nitrate issue: a UK perspective', *Progress in Physical Geography*, 16, 4.

Carling, P A and Petts, G E (eds) (1992), *Lowland floodplain rivers: geomorphological perspectives*, Wiley.

Centre for the Study of Regulated Industries (1994-5), *The UK water industry*, CIPFA.

Clowes, A and Comfort, P (1987), 'Process and landform, conceptual frameworks', *Geography*, Oliver and Boyd.

Cobb, C E (1993), 'Bangladesh: when the water comes', *National Geographic*, 183, 6.

Cooke, R U and Doornkamp, J C (1990), *Geomorphology in environmental management*, Oxford University Press.

Department of the Environment, Environmental Protection Statistics Division, Room Al 05, Romney House, 43 Marsham Street, London SW1P 3PY.

Dister (1985), in Carling, P A and Petts, G E (eds) (1992) *Lowland floodplain rivers: geomorphological perspectives*, Wiley.

Ericksen, N J (1986), 'Creating flood disasters', *Water and soil*, NWASCA, New Zealand.

Falkenmark, M (1977), 'Water and mankind – a complex system of mutual interaction', AMBIO, 6, 1.

George, R (1994), 'Lake Baikal, Siberia', *Wideworld*, September.

Goudie, A (1 990a), *The human impact on the natural environment*, Blackwell.

Goudie, A (1 990b), *The Landforms of England and Wales*, Blackwell.

Gregory, K J and Walling, D E (1973), *Drainage basin form and process: a geomorphological approach*, Edward Arnold.

Hanwell, J D and Newson, M D (1973), *Techniques in physical geography*, Macmillan Education.

Harris, G L (1992), 'Influence of farm management and drainage on leaching of nitrate from former floodlands in a lowland clay catchment', in Carling and Petts, *Lowland floodplain rivers*.

Haque, C E and Zaman, M Q (1993), 'Human responses to riverine hazards in Bangladesh: a proposal for sustainable floodplain development', *World Development*, 2 1, 1, Pergamon Press.

Hilton, K (1979), *Process and pattern in physical geography*, Collins Educational.

Hilton, K (1985), *Patterns in physical geography*, Bell and Hyman.

Hollis, G E (1977), 'Canon's Brook catchment', *Hydrological Sciences Bulletin*, XXII.

Hollis, G E (1988), 'Rain, roads, roofs and runoff: hydrology in cities', *Geography*, 73, 1, The Geographical Association.

Howell, P P and Allen, J A (eds), 1990 *The Nile: resource evaluation, resource management, hydropolitics and legal issues, conference proceedings*, Royal Geographical Society and School of Oriental and African Studies, London.

HMSO (1986), Department of the Environment, *River quality in England and Wales*, 1985.

Hussain, M D and Ziauddin, A T M, (1992), 'Rainwater harvesting and storage techniques from Bangladesh', *Waterlines*, 10, 3.

Kern, K (1992), 'Restoration of lowland rivers: the German experience', in Carling and Petts, *Lowland floodplain rivers*.

Kesel, R H et al. (1992), 'An approximation of the sediment budget of the Lower Mississippi River prior to major human modification', *Earth Surface Processes and Landforms*, 17, 7.

Knapp, B and Child, S (1979), 'Updating geomorphology: hydrological effects of man's activities', *Teaching Geography*, 5, 2, The Geographical Association.

Knapp, B et al. (1989), *The challenge of the natural environment*, Longman.

Kwebenah Acheampong, P(1988). 'Water balance analysis for Ghana', *Geography*, 73, 2, The Geographical Association.

Lajczak, A and Jansson, M B (1993), 'Suspended sediment yield in the Baltic drainage basin', *Nordic Hydrology*, 24.

Lewis, G and Williams, G (1984), *Rivers and wildlife handbook*, RSPB/RSNC.

Lvovitch, M 1 (1973), *Transactions of American Geophysical Union*, 54, p.34, Fig 1. C) 1973 American Geophysical Union.

Marsh, T J et al, (1994), *The 1988–92 UK drought*, Institute of Hydrology.

Marsh, T J and Davies, P A (198 3), 'The decline and partial recovery of groundwater levels below London', *Proceedings of the Institute of Civil Engineers*, 74, 1.

Marsh, T J and MacRuairi, R E (1993), '1988–92: a demonstration of the United Kingdom's vulnerability to drought', *BHS Fourth National Hydrology Symposium*, Cardiff.

McDonald, A T and Kay, D (1988), *Water resources: issues and strategies*, Longman Scientific and Technical.

Ministry of Agriculture, Fisheries and Food (1993), *Solving the nitrate problem*, HMSO.

Ministry of Agriculture, Fisheries and Food (1994), *Flood and coastal defence: project appraisal guidance notes*, HMSO.

National Rivers Authority (1994), *Water: nature's precious resource*, HMSO.

Newson, M (1979), 'Up and down and seldom average: streamflow variability with time', *Teaching Geography*, 4, 3, Longman.

Newson, M (1992), *Land, water and development*, Routledge.

Oliver, H R and Oliver, S A (1988), *Geography Review*, 1, 3, Philip Allan Publishers.

Park, C (1983), *Environmental hazards*, 'Aspects of Geography' series, Macmillan Education.

Pearce, F (1993), *New Scientist*, 18 September.

Pearce, F (1994), *New Scientist*, 20 August.

Penning-Rowsell, E C and Handmer, J W (1988), 'Flood management in Britain: a changing scene', *Geographical Journal*, 154, 2, Royal Geographical Society.

Raabe (1968), *Deutscher Rat fur Landespflege*, Bonn.

Roberts, C R (1989), 'Flood frequency and urban-induced channel change: some British examples', in Beven, K and Carlos, P (eds) *Floods: hydrological, sedimentological and geomorphological implications*, Wiley.

Ross, S M et al. (1990), 'Soil hydrology, nutrient and erosional response to the clearance of terra firma forest, Maraca Island, Roraima, northern Brazil', *Geographical Journal*, 156, 3, Royal Geographical Society.

Severn–Trent Water Authority (1978), *River Soar basin report*, Corporate Planning Department.

Smith, K (1993), 'Riverine flood hazard', *Geography*, 78, 2, The Geographical Association.

Sutcliffe and Lazenby (1990), in Howell and Allen, *The Nile*.

Tivy, J and O'llare, G (198 1), *Human impact on the ecosystem*, Oliver and Boyd.

Thames Water Utilities Ltd (1994) 'Optional metering scheme: Will I benefit from paying by meter?', Thames Water plc.

Thoms, M C and Walker, K F (1992), 'Channel changes related to low-level weirs on the River Murray, South Australia', in Carling and Petts, *Lowland floodplain rivers*.

Thornes, C R (1992), *River meanders: nature's answer to the straight line*, inaugural lecture, University of Nottingham.

Thornes, C R et al. (1993), *Natural and engineered channels*, University of Nottingham.

UNEP (1993), *Environmental data report*, 1991–92, UNEP/Blackwell.

Volker, A and Henry, J C (1988), *Side effects of water resources management*, IAHS.

Walker, K F et al. (1992), 'Effects of weirs on the littoral environment of the River Murray, S. Australia', in Boon et al, *River conservation and management*.

Ward, R C (198 1) in Ward, R C and Robinson, M (1990), *Principles of hydrology*, McGraw-Hill International (UK).

Water Authorities Association (1987), in *Data support for education – water pollution*, Nature Conservancy Council (1988).

Weyman, D and Wilson, C (1975), 'Hydrology for schools', *Teaching Geography*, Occasional Paper, 5, 25, The Geographical Association.

Wheeler, D A (1988), 'Water resource problems in Catalonia', *Geography*, 73, 1, The Geographical Association.

White, I D et al. (1986), *Environmental systems*, Allen and Unwin.

Witherick, M and Carr, M (1993), *The changing face of Japan*, Hodder and Stoughton.

Glossary

Abstraction Removal of water from rivers, lakes, etc. or from groundwater for human use.

Actual evapotranspiration (**AET**) See **Evapotranspiration**.

Aggradation The building up of the land surface or river bed by deposition of sediment.

Algal bloom A huge growth of algae in a water body due to overfeeding by water pollutants (see **Eutrophication**).

Alluvial fan A cone-shaped depositional landform, formed by water in semi-arid or arid seas.

Alluvial morphology The shape of landforms produced by alluvium (a sedimentary deposit made by a river).

Aquifer A permeable rock, such as limestone, which is capable of holding and transmitting groundwater. In a **confined aquifer** the upper boundary of the water body is formed by an overlying aquitard (less permeable bed). In an **unconfined aquifer** groundwater is not confined by an aquitard and the top surface is the water table where porewater pressure is equal to atmospheric pressure. In a **perched aquifer** the underlying impermeable bed is not continuous over a large area but is sufficient to support an unconfined aquifer above the main groundwater body.

Aquitard A less permeable rock in a sequence of permeable rocks which may be able to transmit water, but not in economic quantities.

Artesian basin A basin structure containing water under hydrostatic pressure in an aquifer.

Artesian well Well dug into water existing under hydrostatic pressure.

Assimilation capacity The ability of natural processes in the river ecosystem to absorb and control the effects of introduced materials such as pollutants.

Bankfull discharge The state of a river's flow, at which the channel is completely filled from the top of one bank into another. Beyond this point, overbank flow occurs.

Base flow The flow of water in a river which is produced by subsurface processes, especially groundwater flow.

Base flow Index (**BFI**) The fraction of streamflow over a given period which occurs as baseflow, i.e. fed by slow throughflow and groundwater flow rather than from faster stormflow processes.

Bed armouring The lining of a river bed with coarse debris as a result of the selective removal of fine material. This sediment 'armour' can protect the bed from erosion.

Bifurcation ratio (**Rb**) The ratio of the number of streams of a particular order to the number of streams of the next highest order within a drainage basin. Most values lie between ratios of 2:5 and 3:5.

Biological oxygen demand (**BOD**) Used as a measure of organic pollution in water. It represents the amount of biochemically degradable substances in the water or effluent sample. A test sample is stored in darkness for five days at 20ºC and the amount of oxygen taken up by the micro-organisms present is measured in grams per cubic metre.

Braided channel A river channel which divides and rejoins around piles of larger sediment. Associated with seasonal regimes.

Capacity (**stream**) The total sediment load of a river at a particular time or location.

Capillary action Surface tension and adsorptive forces which allow water to rise or move. The mechanism by which water moves upwards through part of the regolith known as the capillary fringe.

Catchment area The area of land which water drains into a river or stream.

Channelisation Modification of river channels for flood control, navigation, etc.

Char A depositional feature in a river formed when deposits build up above water level. These islands are mobile and temporary.

Clear water erosion Increased erosion downstream of dams which occurs as a result of the rescued sediment load. The river has increased energy to erode its bed.

Competence The size of the largest sediment particle that can be carried by a river at a particular place/time.

Cones of depression The area below and around a well, where the water table has been lowered as a result of water abstraction via the well.

Confined aquifer See **Aquifer**

Conjunctive operation strategy A policy in which several sources of supply are combined.

Contamination Introduction of a foreign substance to an environment, which is capable of causing pollution.

Corrasion Another name for abrasion, i.e. erosion by rock hitting rock, e.g. by sediment in a stream striking the bed and banks as it is transported.

Cost–benefit ratio The ratio of the costs and benefits of a proposed scheme, such as a flood control measure. For the scheme to be economically viable, the benefits must be higher than the costs, i.e. greater than 1:1.

Critical erosion velocity The stream velocity which is able to entrain sediment.

Culvert A subsurface pipe inserted to transfer water, e.g. beneath a road.

Dam A barrier built across a river to create a body of water.

Delta The deposition of sediment at the mouth of a river.

Depression storage Storage of water in hollows and holes in the ground surface.

Diffuse source See **Pollution**.

Dilution effect The process by which concentration of a solute decreases as discharge increases.

Discharge Water flowing past a gauging station within a given period. Usually expressed in cumecs: cubic metres per second.

Drainage basin The area of land drained by a river and its tributaries. Bordered by higher land or watershed.

Dual regime See **Regime**.

Dynamic equilibrium A state of balance which is constantly adjusting to changing conditions.

Ecosystem A self-regulating biological community in which living things interact with the environment. Ecosystems can be small or large, e.g. a tree, a tropical rainforest, depending on the interests of the person who defines the ecosystem.

Ephemeral channel Channel which only contains water after intermittent downpours of rain, separated by longer periods when the channel is dry.

Eutrophication The process by which excess nutrients are added to streams and standing water bodies, causing rapid expansion of aquatic plants and animal life, which in turn reduces oxygen supply in the water.

Evaporation The process by which water is changed to water vapour (gas) by molecular transfer.

Evapotranspiration The loss of moisture to the atmosphere by the combined processes of evaporation and transpiration. **Actual evapotranspiration** (**AET**) takes into account atmospheric, soil moisture and plant characteristics. **Potential evapotranspiration** (PET**)** is the amount of evapotranspiration which would occur if enough water was available.

Field capacity The amount of water remaining in a freely drained soil after all gravity water has been removed.

Flashy hydrograph See **Hydrograph**.

Floodplain Land over which a river spreads during seasonal or short-term floods. It is modified by shifts of the river's course.

Floodway A channel designed and located to transfer floodwaters.

Flow duration curve A graph which plots the frequency distribution of mean daily flow of a river at a particular gauging station. It indicates the percentage of time during which particular discharge rates are equalled or exceeded.

Fluvial system The interrelated parts of a river/water system.

Gauging station A site where river flow is measured using continuous readings over time or at a specific point in time. River discharge is most commonly measured.

Graded profile The long profile of a stream where erosion, transport and deposition are in a state of equilibrium. Discharge and available energy are in balance with available load.

Groundwater store The water held below the water table in aquifers. Groundwater flow describes the movement of water below the regolith.

Groyne An artificial construction built out from a shoreline or river bank to collect material and to inhibit erosion.

Horton's law of stream numbers The inverse relationship between the stream order and the number of streams of that order in a drainage basin.

Hydraulic action The force exerted by moving water on the bed and bank materials of a channel.

Hydraulic radius (**HR**) The cross-section of water flowing through a channel divided by the wetted perimeter of the channel. Also known as hydraulic mean depth.

Hydrochemistry The chemical make-up of the solute load of a stream.

Hydrograph Graph of water flow in a river channel over time. The storm hydrograph records the surge of discharge past a stream gauge which is the result of a single rainstorm. A river which responds quickly to a rainfall input, giving a high peak and rapid rise on the graph, is described as giving a **flashy hydrograph**.

Hydrological cycle The movement of water through the set of environment stores and pathways.

Hydropolitics The politics of water management issues which involve interstate or international discussion/agreement.

Hydrostatic pressure The fluid pressure exerted by the underlying column of water in a body of water when at rest.

Infiltration The movement of water, from rainfall or snowmelt, into the soil. **Infiltration capacity** is the maximum rate at which water can enter the soil in a particular case. **Infiltration rate** refers to how much water is passing through in a certain time.

Interception loss The process whereby a proportion of the precipitation input is caught and held by vegetation.

Intermittent stream Stream which flows seasonally.

Knickpoint A break of slope in the long profile of a stream. Often the upper limit along the stream to which downcutting triggered by rejuvenation has reached.

Laminar streamflow See **Streamflow**.

Leaching The removal of dissolved chemicals from the soil as precipitation drains down.

Levee A bank of sediment along the edge of the river channel, deposited naturally with floodwaters. Natural levees are often raised and strengthened artificially to contain floodwaters.

Long profile A longitudinal section of a stream channel drawn from source to mouth along the thalweg. Usually expressed graphically as a curve.

Manning's roughness coefficient A measure of the resistance of the channel to river flow. This depends upon the nature of the bed and bank material, vegetation cover and sinuosity of the channel.

Meander A pronounced bend in a river with a sinuosity ratio greater than 1:5.

Negative feedback The feedback mechanism in a system which keeps the system stable or in dynamic equilibrium. It decreases the amount of change by reducing some of the inputs.

Opportunity cost A measure of the return to be gained by using resources to produce a good or service as opposed to the return to be gained by using the same resources to produce an alternative good or service.

Overland flow The component of the precipitation input which is transferred to a stream channel by movement across the ground surface. **Saturated overland flow** occurs when excess water flows across the ground surface when the subsurface is saturated.

Perched aquifer See **Aquifer**.

Percolation The process by which water moves downwards through rock. Often used for deeper movement below the water table.

Perennial stream Stream with permanent discharge.

Permeability The ability of rock, sediment or soil to permit water to flow through it.

Point bar Sediments laid down on the inside of a meander bend.

Point source See **Pollution**.

Pollution A condition which occurs when environmental features become adverse to the normal existence of living organisms. Pollution from a single entry point, e.g. a sewage outflow pipe, is called **point source** pollution. Pollution which has its source over a wide area, e.g. from agricultural fertilisers applied over several fields, is called **diffuse source** pollution.

Porosity The volume of water which can be held (stored) within a rock or soil.

Positive feedback The feedback mechanism in a system which causes the system to become unstable or break down. It increases the amount of change by raising some of the inputs.

Potential evapotranspiration (PET) See **Evapotranspiration**.

Potentiometric surface The level to which water will rise within an aquifer. Also known as the piezometric surface.

Precipitation The deposition of water in either liquid or solid form. It usually reaches the earth's surface from clouds in the atmosphere and includes rain, sleet, snow, hail, dew and frost.

Pumping effect The process whereby concentration of a solute increases with stream discharge.

Quickflow processes That component of the precipitation input which is delivered to the stream channel by overland flow, or rapid soil transfer.

Recurrence interval The length of time before a flood of a certain scale is likely to occur again. How often a storm and flood of a certain size is likely to occur, e.g. a 100-year flood.

Regime The seasonal discharge rhythm of a stream. A **dual regime** is when there are two seasonal peaks, while a **uniform regime** refers to a stream with a single seasonal peak.

Regolith The layer of broken material overlying bedrock.

Rejuvenation A renewal of available energy in a stream which permits accelerated erosion, entrainment and transportation. The stream has more energy and can do more work.

Revetments Artificial strengthening along a river bank to reduce erosion and control floods.

Runoff Water that moves across the surface of the land into streams rather than being absorbed by the soil.

Salinisation The build-up of salts in water and soils in and and semi-arid areas.

Saturation The state when a parcel of air can hold (store) no additional moisture at that temperature and pressure.

Sediment Particles derived from rock material by weathering and erosion. **Sediment yield** is the amount of sediment output from a store, e.g. a slope, a stream bed, over a given period. **Sedimentary deposits** are areas of sediment which have been laid down by natural processes, e.g. by a river as it floods over its floodplain. Some sedimentary deposits form distinctive landforms.

Sinuosity The degree to which a river channel swings from side to side, usually expressed as a ratio between channel length and valley length.

Slowflow processes The hydrological processes which transmit water slowly to the river channel, e.g. slow throughflow and groundwater flow. These make up the baseflow of the river.

Soil moisture budget The balance between moisture inputs and outputs in a soil over time.

Soil moisture deficiency A condition in which more water is being lost from a soil (output) than is arriving into the soil (input).

Soil moisture recharge An increase in water content stored in a soil.

Soil moisture surplus A condition in which there is more water entering and being stored in a soil (input and store) than is being lost or taken out (output).

Solute load That component of a stream's load which is held and transferred in the dissolved state.

Stemflow The components of precipitation input which, having been intercepted by vegetation, run down plant stems to the ground surface.

Storm hydrograph See **Hydrograph**.

Streamflow The movement of water in a stream channel. There are two main types of streamflow: (1) **Laminar streamflow** is the movement of stream water in a series of layers. Usually low velocity over a smooth surface. (2) **Turbulent streamflow** is the movement of stream water as a collection of swirling eddies. Associated with high velocities over rough surfaces.

Sustainable Which can be continued because it does not use resources faster than natural processes can replenish them.

Thalweg The long profile of a river which follows the line of maximum flow.

Throughfall Water which drips from leaves and stems to reach the ground surface.

Throughflow The downslope movement of water through the regolith.

Transpiration The process by which plants lose moisture as water vapour through their leaf stomata into the atmosphere.

Turbulent streamflow See **Streamflow**.

Unconfined aquifer See **Aquifer**.

Uniform regime See **Regime**.

Water budget/balance The balance between the inputs (precipitation) and outputs (runoff, evapotranspiration, soil and groundwater storage changes) of a drainage basin. We can show the relationship or balance between water inputs and outputs by a water budget graph.

Watershed The water-parting from which headstreams flow to separate drainage basins.

Water table The upper surface of the zone of saturation in a permeable rock. Rainwater percolates to the water table whenever precipitation exceeds evapotranspiration.

Wetted perimeter The line of contact between the water and the river channel.

Collins Educational
77–85 Fulham Palace Road
London W6 8J13
An imprint of HarperCollins *Publishers*

First published 1995
Reprinted 1996
Second edition 2001
10 9 8 7 6 5 4
ISBN-13 978 0 00 711429 0
ISBN-10 0 00 711429 X

Victoria Bishop and Robert Prosser hereby assert their moral right to
be identified as the Authors of this Work.

Edited by Melanie McRae
Designed by Andy Williss
Picture research by Caroline Thompson
Artwork by Contour Publishing, Tom Cross, Joan Corlass,
Jerry Fowler, Jeremy Glover, TTP International
Cover design by Derek Lee
Printed and bound in Hong Kong.

The authors and publishers are grateful to Richard Batchelor, and to
Terry Marsh of the Institute of Hydrology, for their detailed
comments on the typescript. They would also like to acknowledge the
considerable help given by the Institute of Hydrology in providing
data and visual resources for the book.

Acknowledgements

Every effort has been made to contact the holders of copyright
material, but if any have been inadvertently overlooked the
publishers will be pleased to make the necessary arrangements at the
first opportunity.

Photographs
The publishers would like to thank the following for permission to
reproduce photographs.

AFP/Robyn Beck, Fig. 1.7;
Associated Press AP, Figs 6.3, 6.36;
Victoria Bishop, Figs 3.21, 3.22, 3.23, 5.6, 5.7, 5.10. 5.11, 5.12;
The Cheltenham Newspaper Company Ltd, Fig. 6.1;
Altaf Hussain/DRIK Photo Library, Fig. 6.32;
Environmental Images/P Ferraby, Fig. 8.10, Warford, Fig. 9.16;
Firo-Foto, Fig. 4.29;
GettyOne Stone, Fig. 5.43;
Holt Studios International/I Spence, Fig. 8.1;
Institute of Hydrology, Figs 3.3, 5.5, 8.5;
Institute of Hydrology/Scot Rail, Fig. 6.14;
JB Pictures/F Hoffman, Fig. 6.30;
London Aerial Photo Library, Figs 6.27, 7.22;
Magnum Photos/F Mayer, Fig. 4.34;
NASA, Fig. 4.44;
NHPA/D Woodfall, Fig. 5.22, S Dalton, Fig. 6.8;
'PA' Photos, Figs 3.7, 6.23;
Panos Pictures/B Paton, Figs 4.1, 4.2, D Constantine, Fig. 7.3;
Robert Prosser, Figs 2.14, 2.20, 2.21, 3.1, 4.11, 4.12, 4.40, 4.41, 4.55,
5.31, 5.32, 6.17, 7.18, 7.20, 7.33, 8.18, 9.27b;
RGS London, Fig. 3.40;
Science Photo Library, Fig. 2.3;
Still Pictures/M Edwards, Fig. 3.31, D Dancer, Fig. 4.59;
Caroline Thompson, Figs 3.47, 7.17;
Professor D E Walling, Fig. 4.62.

Cover photograph: GettyOne Stone

Maps

Map reproduced from Ordnance Survey Landranger mapping with
the permission of The Controller of Her Majesty's Stationery Office.
© Crown copyright, Licence Number. 100018599
Extract from: Reading, Windsor and surrounding area 1994 1:50000
(Fig. 6.6).

Index